CORNELL STUDIES IN ANTHROPOLOGY

RUSEMBILAN:
A Malay Fishing Village
in Southern Thailand

Cornell Studies in Anthropology

This series of publications is an outgrowth of the program of instruction, training, and research in theoretical and applied anthropology originally established at Cornell University in 1948 with the aid of the Carnegie Corporation of New York. The program seeks particularly to provide in its publications descriptive accounts and interpretations of cultural process and dynamics, including those involved in projects of planned cultural change, among diverse aboriginal and peasant cultures of the world.

Fishermen of Rusembilan launching a *kolek*. The upright tree, on a float of crossed planks, serves later as a marker for one end of the fishing net.

RUSEMBILAN:

A Malay Fishing Village in Southern Thailand

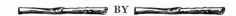 BY

THOMAS M. FRASER, JR.

Cornell University Press

ITHACA, NEW YORK

This work has been brought to publication with the assistance of a grant from the Ford Foundation.

© 1960 by Cornell University

CORNELL UNIVERSITY PRESS

First published 1960

PRINTED IN THE UNITED STATES OF AMERICA

BY THE VAIL-BALLOU PRESS, INC.

JN
750
30J.1593
F7 F842r

Foreword

MALAYAN and Siamese cultural studies are still very meagerly cultivated fields; but the even more specialized study of peoples of Malayan culture who reside within the political borders of modern Thailand is a fallow field indeed. In 1956 Thomas M. Fraser, Jr., who had received graduate training in anthropology at Columbia University, undertook, in company with his wife, to break ground in this difficult area. The present book, based largely on field data gathered by Mr. and Mrs. Fraser while living in a Thai Malay coastal village and traveling in the southern part of the country, is the first study of its kind devoted to this segment of the people of Thailand, to their way of life, to the way in which a Malay community relates to its region, and to the Thai nation as a whole. Indeed, as the author points out, this is the first published account of any Malay community in Thailand or anywhere else which deals with all the major aspects of the cultural behavior of a Moslem Malay peasant group. Mr. Fraser's work thus constitutes a novel addition to Malay studies and a unique contribution to studies of Thailand.

The meagerness of our knowledge of the Malay people of Thailand was forcibly brought home to me during the year before Mr. and Mrs. Fraser settled down to their field work in Rusembilan, the small Malay village near the ancient southern Siamese port city of Pattani, which is described in this study. Several of my colleagues and graduate students in the Cornell University Southeast Asia Program undertook the preparation of a handbook on Thailand, which was issued in 1956 by the Human Relations Area Files. In connection with the work the relevant literature in Thai, Malay, and western European languages was combed for material on the Thai Malays. Nothing of significant value was found. The scanty information on the subject finally included in the Cornell Thailand handbook (and the subsequent revision of it edited by Wendell Blanchard and associates and published in 1958) was provided almost entirely by our fellow workers of the Cornell Research Center in Bangkok as a result of their direct but necessarily cursory inquiries made on the spot in Thailand. The work which the Frasers were then doing in southern Siam would have provided —and now provides—many answers to questions which could hardly be asked and much less answered then.

Little is known of the origins of either the Malay or the Thai peoples, but the story of their contacts, some of which is retold by Mr. Fraser, falls within the period of historical records. Before this period the Malays were to be found in the southwestern extremities of mainland and island Southeast Asia. They were a segment of the large and far-flung Malayo-Polynesian (or Austronesian) linguistic stock whose families had voyaged as far by sea as Madagascar in the west, Easter Island in the east, and Taiwan in the north, while others on the mainland, such as the Cham, extended from the eastern coasts of what is now Vietnam as far west as the northern central plains of Thailand, where they could be found in the sixth or seventh centuries of our era. It was about this time, too, that Thai- (or Tai-) speaking peoples first entered the historical scene in southwestern China. These two linguistic stocks, the Malayo-Polynesian and the Thai, were at that time separated on the Southeast Asian mainland by the ancestors of the Vietnamese (whose origins are also dim) and to the south and west by speakers of Mon-Khmer languages, such as Cambodian. But already peoples speaking Thai languages had begun to move southward from China into the Vietnamese and Mon-Khmer area and toward the block of Malay-speaking peoples in the southern peninsula. In what was to become Thailand in the course of subsequent centuries the Mon-Khmer languages would give way almost entirely to Thai; this may have been simply a cultural phenomenon, however, not necessarily implying any major accompanying biological or demographic shifting or replacement of the peasant populations involved.

It was not until the thirteenth century, well into the historical period, that Thai kingdoms are known to have been established within the boundaries of present-day Thailand. In a remarkably short time thereafter, indeed by the middle of the fourteenth century, expanding Thai power was able to contend with the great Javanese empire of Majapahit in claims of suzerainty over the entire Malay Peninsula and its Malay population. From the petty states of the Peninsula, centering on small but often cosmopolitan and wealthy trading communities, the Thai crown demanded tribute of gold, tin, and other precious goods and the right to carry on increasingly important commercial activities. During the fifteenth century many of these states were organized into a loose hegemony under Malacca, the newly founded entrepôt port which grew in wealth and power with amazing rapidity. The rising importance of Malacca helped spread Islam among the Malay states throughout the entire southern half of the Peninsula, but the Buddhist kingdom of Siam, with its capital now at Ayudhya in the central Thai plain, was still able to maintain its claims over the predominantly Malay and Moslem populations to the south. Just as Siam on the fringe of the Middle Kingdom sent tribute (though irregularly) to Nanking or

Peking, so it claimed tribute from Malacca and such lesser states as Trengganu, Pahang, or Pattani on its own southern fringe. These claims so impressed the Portuguese that Albuquerque, even before the great port of Malacca fell to his besieging forces in August 1511, found it politic to send off an envoy to the court of Siam in Ayudhya. From a Siamese regime confronted by troubles to the west, north, and east the Portuguese were able to obtain rights to share in the trade of a number of the peninsular communities.

In the four and a half centuries that have elapsed since the Portuguese first reached Malacca, Thai power has contracted and expanded and contracted again and again. The early loosely organized hierarchical arrangement of overlapping tiers of tributary states—small umbrellas under the protection of larger and higher umbrellas which in turn were under those still higher and larger—has given place in mainland Southeast Asia to the more recent Western arrangement of theoretically equivalent sovereign states with defined and mutually exclusive national boundaries. Thailand's national border in the south was most recently drawn to include a very substantial number of the northern congeners of the Moslem Malay peoples of the Peninsula, all of whose ancestors at one longer or shorter time or another were subjects of the Thai crown. This Malay block in the four southernmost provinces of modern Thailand constitutes the largest ethnic minority group residing within the boundaries of the Thai state not of its own free will, but by the accidents of political history. They are members of the Thai state, not because they have come like the Chinese to Thailand from overseas and could return, but only because extensive areas inhabited by Malays have been incorporated into the Thai kingdom during its remarkable southward expansion. As recently as 1900 Thai Malays recognized as their own prince the royal Malay Moslem Raja Abdul Kadir of Pattani. Since the forced abdication of this prince, the Malay Moslems of southern Thailand

have not always willingly succumbed to either the power or
the blandishments of the central Thai government. Today they
constitute within the body politic of Thailand a still unassimi-
lated and politically awakening group, to which the Bangkok
government, particularly since the war and the independence
of Malaya, has given increasing attention.

Mr. Fraser's work is concerned with a small community of
these Malays as they are found in southern Thailand today. The
community-study type of research has been one of the chief
employments of cultural anthropology almost from the first
establishment of the discipline. Anthropology, by definition, is
the study of man, but in actual practice it has tended to be the
study of the common or the simple man, if any human being
may be called simple. The anthropologist, whether working in
Nova Scotia or in New Ireland, in the potato fields of the high
Andes or the paddy fields of lowland Southeast Asia, has tried
to understand the whole compass of life which bounds the experience of the ordinary person: his technological and economic life; his social, political, recreational, and religious organization; his systems of ideas, sentiments, and values and the
linguistic and other symbols through which these are expressed,
together with the interrelations of these different aspects of his
cultural behavior and the ways in which they change and resist
change in response to internal and external influences. Even
to begin such a complicated task, the cultural anthropologist
of necessity has had to limit his studies to a circumscribed community of people functioning within the context of a surrounding territory. Although the anthropologist thus works with a
relatively small human group, he works systematically, through
an adequate cycle of time, and above all intimately or closely
with real people whose cultural behavior, if not necessarily typical, is at least representative of an area or type. A series of such
descriptions and interpretations of cultural behavior is, he feels,
a useful contribution to the larger abstractions involved in the

study of whole and complex nations or regions. The anthropologist hopes further that such studies of specific communities may also contribute to an understanding of the real processes involved in changing human behavior in a world which for the past two or three centuries at least, and at an increasingly rapid rate, has begun to experience the first cultural revolution in human history that promises to be global or even extraterrestrial in extent.

Because of our major interest in the problems of describing and interpreting the phenomena of planned and unplanned cultural change, the editors of the Cornell Studies in Anthropology welcome Mr. Fraser's account of cultural processes in a Malay community of modern Thailand as one of the studies in our series. In an age when many scholars pursue costly and elaborate group research, involving the slow collaboration of specialists whose work depends on the completion of the work of others, Mr. and Mrs. Fraser are to be congratulated on four-handedly providing a useful and stimulating contribution to our knowledge of the anthropology of Southeast Asia.

LAURISTON SHARP

Ithaca, New York
September 1959

Acknowledgments

BOTH my wife and I wish to acknowledge the invaluable assistance given us by many individuals, Malay, Thai, and American, in Thailand and particularly those in the Pattani area. Special thanks are due to the villagers of Rusembilan for putting up so good-naturedly with our questions and occasional awkwardness. Among all the people who showed us so much kindness and co-operation, we owe perhaps the most to Mohammed Abdul Kadir, our interpreter, and to Dr. Vichien Suebsaeng, who in our first weeks in Pattani took us into his family and was throughout our stay a close friend.

For constant assistance and encouragement while in the field and during the preparation of the manuscript I am particularly indebted to my wife, Dorothy Durham Fraser. Her role as housewife and friend of the village women added immeasurably to our rapid acceptance by the people of Rusembilan, and without her presence in the village many sources of information would have remained inaccessible to the author.

Grateful acknowledgment is made to George Allen and Unwin, Ltd., for permission to reprint the *fatihah* from *The Meaning of the Glorious Koran* by Mohammed Marmaduke Pickthall.

THOMAS M. FRASER, JR.

Barpali, Orissa, India
June 1959

Contents

Illustrations

Plates will be found following page 12

RUSEMBILAN:

A Malay Fishing Village
in Southern Thailand

CHAPTER I

Introduction

THIS study was made with the purpose of investigating the social and cultural organization of a reasonably typical Malay community in southern Thailand in order to throw light on several problems. Over the past several decades Thailand has been given much attention by Western social scientists, from the economic surveys of Zimmerman and Andrews [1] to the intensive interdisciplinary program of field work being conducted at present by the Cornell University Southeast Asia Program. Economic and political studies predominate, but recently a number of anthropological community studies have been launched by anthropologists working both alone and in teams with other social scientists.[2] Until now, however, all major field work has been

[1] Carle C. Zimmerman, *Siam: Rural Economic Survey, 1930–31*, and James M. Andrews, *Siam: Second Rural Economic Survey, 1934–35.*

[2] Among these recent studies the Cornell University project at Bang Chan is the most important. The following are preliminary reports on various aspects of the project: Lauriston Sharp *et al.*, *Siamese Rice Village: A Preliminary Study of Bang Chan, 1948–1949;* Kamol Janlekha, *A Preliminary Study of the Economic Conditions of Rice Farmers in Bang Chan, Thailand;* Hazel M. Hauck *et al.*, *Aspects of Health, Sanitation, and Nutritional Status in a Siamese Rice Village: Studies in Bang Chan, 1952–1954;* Rose K. Goldsen and Max Ralis, *Factors Related to Ac-*

confined to the areas of Thailand north of the Isthmus of Kra, and even in those surveys that deal with the south as a region, there is little or no differentiation between the Malay population in the southernmost provinces and the predominantly Thai population in the rest of the peninsula. Thus, this study, by dealing with an area of Thailand little known to social scientists and by attempting to understand the position of the Malay population in the framework of the Thai nation, may help to add to the total picture of Thailand that is being drawn by modern social scientists.

In terms of the study of Malay culture and society, there have been many excellent monographs written on specific topics in anthropology and the other social sciences,[3] but there has been no study defined to encompass the total sociocultural organization of a Malay community. The study conducted by Raymond and Rosemary Firth [4] in Kelantan and Trengganu included most of the sociocultural data from the communities studied, but because of the topical orientation of the publications, they cannot be considered as complete community studies.

Aside from studying the sociocultural organization of a whole community, it was the purpose of this study to explore aspects of

---

ceptance of Innovations in Bang Chan, Thailand. Other studies include Howard K. Kaufman, *Bangkhuad: A Community Study in Thailand;* John E. deYoung, *San Pong, A Village in North Thailand;* and G. William Skinner's anthropological analysis of the Chinese community in Bangkok, *A Study of Chinese Community Leadership in Bangkok Together with a Historical Survey of Chinese Society in Thailand,* and *Chinese Society in Thailand.*

[3] Walter W. Skeat, *Malay Magic;* Richard O. Winstedt, *The Malay Magician, Being Shaman, Saiva, and Sufi;* Richard O. Winstedt, *The Malays: A Cultural History;* R. J. Wilkinson, *A Malay-English Dictionary;* articles in the *Journal of the Royal Asiatic Society* (Straits Branch and Malayan Branch) and Federation of Malaya, *Annual Report,* various years; and Norton Ginsburg and Chester F. Roberts, Jr., *Malaya.*

[4] Raymond Firth, *Malay Fishermen: Their Peasant Economy,* and Rosemary Firth, *Housekeeping among Malay Peasants.*

the following problems: In what way and to what extent does the Malay community in southern Thailand form a part of a regional and national whole, and how may it be said to be discontinuous from such a whole? As Steward remarks, "If the community is conceptualized as a sociocultural segment of a larger whole, it follows that many of the latter's problems must be studied in the communities." [5] It was proposed to study just how Rusembilan and other Malay communities were integrated into the natural structure of Thailand and how the social structure and cultural patterns reacted to points of stress in the process of integration.

It was also proposed to investigate the process of change occurring within the community and to determine what differential factors were operative in the process. It was realized that residence of less than a year within the community would not be sufficient to study the complete range of change within the community or to analyze fully any one type of change. It was hoped, however, that sufficient data could be observed to warrant certain valid generalizations and to provide a base line for further research in southern Thailand.

Field Procedure

The field data on which this report is based were gathered during a period of residence in the village of Rusembilan from February through September 1956. For the two months prior to taking up residence in the village and in the month following, the author and his wife traveled in northern Malaya and throughout peninsular Thailand, particularly in the area of Pattani. During their stay in the village, several more trips were made to Malaya, and many of the important Malay communities in the southern Thai provinces were visited.

The choice of a particular village was largely fortuitous. After consultations with government officials and businessmen and with the Cornell Research Center in Bangkok, it was decided

[5] Julian Steward, *Area Research: Theory and Practice*, p. 51.

that the coastal area between Pattani and Narathiwat would provide the most suitable location for this study. From a base in Pattani the coastal Malay villages in the area were surveyed. Rusembilan was finally chosen for several reasons. On the first visit to the community, the villagers were talking of buying motorboats for the coming fishing season when the economically important *kembong* would be netted, and this seemed to be an ideal opportunity to observe the effects of the introduction of a major technological change. Furthermore, the community was located near enough to Pattani so that the villagers had ample opportunity for close contact with a large commercial center and the Thais of Pattani. And the community itself was large enough so that it should exhibit most of the social and cultural elements typifying Malay communities in the area, and yet it was small enough so that it seemed possible to gain a reasonably accurate picture of the community as a whole. The choice was further determined by the easy accessibility to Pattani and by the fact that land would be provided in the village and a Malay house built for the author and his wife in a very short time; in addition the villagers appeared genuinely eager to have such visitors settle among them.

Field work was conducted in a generally informal manner. A considerable amount of time was spent sitting with the men in the coffee shops, listening to them talk, talking with them, and asking them questions. Some data were collected through formal interviews, but the bulk of the information came from informal conversations with men and women in village houses or in that of the author or as the villagers went about their daily work. Invitations were received to all village ceremonies during the early part of the stay in the community, and later attendance was simply expected—someone would even be sent for them if the author and his wife were not there for one reason or another.

Because of the specialized nature of many of the village activities, little attempt was made to participate actively in ordinary village affairs. The author and his wife were viewed as community assets in some ways that were unexpected. The daily trips of the author's wife to market provided "bus service" for up to twenty women and their fish in the seven-passenger Land Rover, and for the same reason, attendance with the villagers at feasts in other communities was often urged. Presence of Americans in the village, plus a certain amount of deference shown to them, as Americans, by some Thais, greatly enhanced the prestige of the whole village. One morning an unknown Malay was found sitting for an unusually long time under a palm tree by the author's house—he had come from a village fifty miles inland for a ride to market in the "white man's car." Last, but not least, the site on which the house of the author was built had previously been thickly inhabited by *hantu* or malicious spirits, and to walk across the darkened lot at night had been a genuinely uncomfortable experience for the villagers before the house with its kerosene pressure lantern was there.

There were perhaps twenty men and women who might be called main informants. These were mostly in the age group between thirty and sixty-five, but they represented a cross section of occupational, income, and religious groups. Casual contacts were had with about two-thirds of the village population, and one house-to-house survey of population, occupational-group, and boat-group affiliation was completed. Except for personal friends of the author and business contacts in Pattani, there were no Thai informants as such. Information was co-operatively given by Thai government officials, including the Rusembilan schoolteacher.

Orthography

The transcription of all Malay words is given in the standardized romanization used in the Federation of Malaya.[6] The

[6] Wilkinson, *op. cit.,* and other dictionaries and handbooks on the Malay language, such as M. B. Lewis, *Teach Yourself Malay.*

Standard Malay form of words is used, whenever possible, in order to minimize the errors in phonetic transcription stemming from not insignificant individual variations in the Pattani dialect and in order to be readily comparable with other works dealing with Malay subjects. The standard romanization used through the text follows.

All vowels have only their "continental" value. The "indeterminate" *e* (as in *oxen*) has not been differentiated from the long *e;* it was felt that this omission would cause no difficulty to most readers of English and that those with a knowledge of Malay would be able to draw the distinction themselves. Consonants are similar to English consonants. The *j, ch,* and *y* are used for their corresponding English sounds rather than to follow the Indonesian orthography. The consonant *ng* is always pronounced as *ng* in *singer; ngg* as *ng* in *finger; ngk* as *nk* in *sinker;* and *ny* as *ny* in *canyon.*

CHAPTER II

The Place and the People

ALTHOUGH situated in Thailand, Rusembilan is culturally, linguistically, and racially a Malay community. In all respects this community and most others in this area of southern Thailand are closely related to the Moslem communities in the Federation of Malaya; they differ markedly in respect to their patterns of social interaction as well as cultural systems from the Buddhist Thai villages scattered sparsely throughout the area. The village of Rusembilan is located in the province of Pattani on the east coast of the Malay Peninsula. (See Figure 1.) Pattani is only one of three southern Thai provinces on this coast, but its name, usually written Patani outside of Thailand, generally refers to the whole area including the provinces of Yala and Narathiwat. The 1947 population of Pattani province was 203,155,[1] of which approximately 75 to 80 per cent are Moslem Malays. Except for the few Thai villages in the inland sections of the province, the non-Malay element of the population is concentrated in the provincial capital, Pattani. Accurate population density figures

[1] Information provided by the Office of the Governor, Changwat Pattani, Pattani, Thailand, from Government of Thailand, *Census BE 2490* (1947).

7

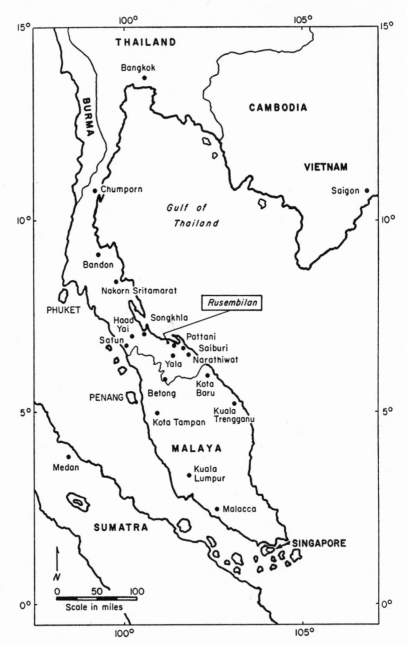

Figure 1. Malay Peninsula.

are extremely difficult to find for any of the southern provinces, but according to Skinner, the density ranges from 55 to 105 persons per square kilometer in the districts away from the capital and is over 105 in the capital district.[2]

Pattani province is chiefly an agricultural region with approximately 172,000 acres devoted to the cultivation of wet rice, 47,-500 acres to rubber growing, and 24,500 acres to other crops, chiefly coconuts and other fruits.[3] Fishing is important along the coast, and there is a considerable export volume of fish to Bangkok and Singapore. Industry in the area is insignificant, and although there are large tin-mining operations in Yala province and some gold in Narathiwat, Pattani lacks both these metals in commercial quantities.

Topographically, Pattani is almost exclusively low alluvial plain, a large part of it included within the delta system of the Pattani and Po Ni Rivers. From the flat coastal strip which may be inundated for distances of a mile or more during the monsoon months, the plain gradually slopes south to an apex some twenty-five miles inland where the Pattani River comes out of the higher hills. Alluvium is accumulating rapidly along the northern coast of the province, as this area is protected from the erosive action of the sea by a range of sedimentary hills [4] closely paralleling the east coast and ending in a thousand-foot promontory a few miles to the east of Panare. Beyond Pattani, to the south, jungle-covered mountain ranges rise gradually to peaks of over five thousand feet on the border between Thailand and Malaya; to the west, an extensive area of mountainous jungle separates the Pattani agricultural region from Songkhla province.

The climate is tropical, with a well-defined rainy season brought on by the northeast monsoon from the middle of Octo-

[2] G. William Skinner, *Thailand: Population Density, 1947* (map).
[3] Information provided by the Office of the Governor, Changwat Pattani, Pattani, Thailand.
[4] Joseph E. Spencer, *Asia East by South*, pp. 24–27.

ber through the middle of January; more than 50 per cent of the annual rainfall occurs in these three months (see Table 1). Temperature is uniformly high, with less seasonal than diurnal variation. Mean annual temperature is 80 degrees Fahrenheit, although during the three months of monsoon the mean is 78.5 degrees.[5] The velocity and direction of the winds and offshore sea currents are summarized in Table 1.

Table 1. Rainfall, temperature, and wind and sea movement

	Jan.	Feb.	Mar.	Apr.	May	Jun.	Jul.	Aug.	Sep.	Oct.	Nov.	Dec.
Rainfall (inches)	8.9	3.2	6.0	3.0	6.2	5.7	4.0	5.8	6.2	12.0	24.0	23.0
Temperature (degrees Fahrenheit)	78	80	81	81	82	81	81	80	80	81	78	77
Wind speed *	4NE	1NE	1NE	1NE	—	1SW	4SW	1SW	1SW	—	1NE	4NE
Sea drift (mph)	16S	17S	14S	9S	11N	13N	17N	19N	17N	15S	21S	19S

* As here used, "1" indicates winds from 1 to 38 mph, "4" winds from 13 to 38 mph, and the dash little or no wind and variable direction.

Sources: Rainfall and temperature are from Government of Thailand, *Thailand, Nature and Industry: Physical Features, Geology, Climate* (Bangkok: Ministry of Commerce, Department of Commercial Intelligence, 1951), Table 4; wind speed and sea drift, from W. L. Dale, "Wind and Drift Currents in the South China Sea," *Malayan Journal of Tropical Geography*, 8:1–35, 1956.

The Village

The political unit of Rusembilan (see Chapter VII) occupies about ten square miles in the central delta of the Pattani River. It is on the coast of Pattani Bay and the Gulf of Thailand, about three and one-half miles from the town of Pattani. During the dry season the road into the village is open to motor traffic, but the monsoon rains flood it and make it impassable. Within the administrative division or township of Rusembilan (see Figure 2),

[5] Government of Thailand, *Thailand, Nature and Industry: Physical Features, Geology, Climate*, pp. 39–40, Table 4.

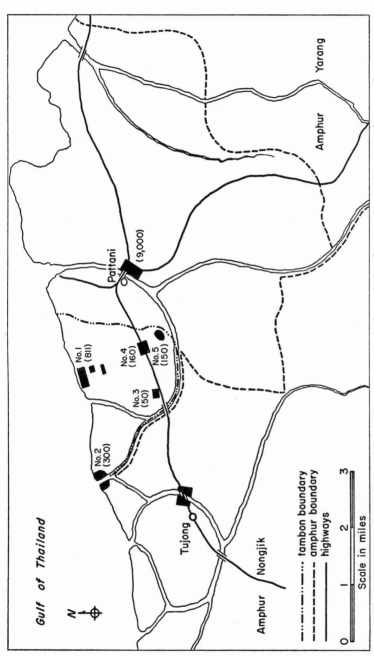

Figure 2. Pattani *amphur*, with location and population of the five sections of Rusembilan *tambon.*

there are five sections, with a total population of about 1,500.[6] Two of these sections, 2 and 5, are in no way except politically a part of the community of Rusembilan. Sections 3 and 4 are considered by the residents of the main village (section 1) to be distinct villages that to some extent participate in the activities of Rusembilan. Such participation includes using the beach at Rusembilan for their separate fishing activities, attending the Rusembilan mosque, and, along with other sections of the township, contributing labor to community projects.

The community of Rusembilan, for the purposes of this study, is limited to the area actually called Rusembilan by the Malay villagers and thought of by them as the community. This includes the main village and two hamlets, or section 1 of the township, as well as a scattered group of houses to the south and east of this, in a few instances extending over the boundaries of the township into the Pattani municipal area.

The main village, Kampong Pata (from *pantai*, beach), comprises ninety-four houses and a population of 548. The village also includes the *balaisa* or chapel and four coffee shops. Kampong Surau (mosque village),[7] a hamlet about half a mile south of Kampong Pata, contains seventeen houses and has a population of ninety-four. One coffee shop is located here as well as the village mosque and school. Kampong Baru (new village), located a half mile farther to the south, contains sixteen houses and ninety-three persons. There are in addition approximately sixteen houses and seventy-six persons included in the community as a whole but not gathered into any definite village or hamlet. (See also Table 2.)

Kampong Pata is situated along the beach, which is usually flooded during the monsoon season. Behind the first cluster of

[6] Based on an estimate by the *kamnan* or official headman of Rusembilan.

[7] Although *masjid* is the correct word for "mosque," the *surau* at Rusembilan is considered by the villagers to be almost a true mosque; see pp. 152–153.

I. View of Rusembilan from the east. The beach is to the right.

II. Central section of Kampong Pata. The *balaisa* is on the far left.

III. *Perahu pukat sinyoh* beached at Pattani Cape.

IV. Woman beaching a *jokung* through a mud channel. Drying racks for *kempong* nets are in the foreground.

V. Harvesting padi.

VI. Small coconut plantation at the edge of padi fields.

VII. Split coconuts drying for copra. In the left background padi is spread on buffalo skins to dry.

VIII. Vegetable stands in the Pattani market.

IX. Village women selling fish outside the Pattani market.

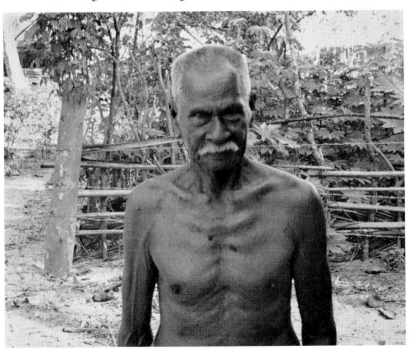

X. Waw Me, one of three Rusembilan men over ninety-five years old.

XI. Old Rusembilan school and assembled roof section for the new school building.

XII. House with woven bamboo walls and atap roof in Kampong Pata.

XIII. Poorer houses in Kampong Baru.

XIV. *Bomo* and musicians performing in the first portion of a *peterana*, here held in the *bomo*'s house.

XV. *Bomo* (right) and patient acting in a trance during a *peterana*.

XVI. *Balai* with offerings of food for the spirits after a *peterana*. The tray at the left warns mortals that the food is for spirits.

houses is a low muddy area of ground about fifty yards across and running almost the entire length of the village, or not quite half a mile. This area becomes flooded whenever it rains, even during the dry season. It is here that the village boats are moved for protection from storms during the monsoon. Beyond this

Table 2. Population of Rusembilan (section 1)
by sex and age group, 1956

Age group	Males	Females	Total
0– 4	62	75	137
5– 9	61	75	136
10–14	35	25	60
15–19	40	57	97
20–24	27	45	72
25–29	21	22	43
30–34	41	17	58
35–39	18	16	34
40–44	18	22	40
45–49	16	10	26
50–54	16	16	32
55–59	8	5	13
60–64	16	4	20
65–69	9	4	13
70–74	5	4	9
75–79	2	1	3
80–84	3	7	10
85–89	1	1	2
90–94	1	2	3
95–99	3	0	3
Total	403	408	811

Source: Government of Thailand, *Census BE 2499* (1956).

area is another cluster of houses (see village plans given in Figures 7 and 8). At either end of the village the shore is fringed with coconut trees. To the east of the village they form extensive and well-tended plantations; to the west there are smaller plantations interspersed with areas of mangrove swamp. Outside this palm fringe and the village settlement are the padi fields of Rusembilan and other villages. The village road leaves the community near its eastern end and runs out along the padi fields to meet the main highway near Pattani. Kampong Surau, south of the main village, is on a slight rise of ground on both sides of this road; Kampong Baru lies somewhat off the road on an angular strip of land representing the boundaries between padi fields. Several of the outlying houses are located along the road, and others are on the beach to the east of Kampong Pata. A few are scattered along paths that crisscross the area.

The People

The villagers of Rusembilan exhibit all the physical characteristics of the typical Deutero-Malay of the coastal regions of northern Malaya.[8] They stand, on the average, about five feet four inches, although men as tall as six feet are not uncommon. Skin color ranges from very light tan to dark brown, and only a few individuals exhibit the yellow tones more characteristic of the Thai and Chinese population in the area. Head hair is usually wavy, and face hair, though not abundant, characterizes most men. This population seems to stand closer to Hooton's Indonesian Subrace than it does to his Malay-Mongoloid Subrace,[9] although culturally and historically the people correspond more closely to the latter.

Malay villagers have the reputation for being little interested in work, preferring to sit idle all day; this is not, however, an accurate picture of the villager of Rusembilan. True, the men of the community are often to be found in the coffee shops during the morning hours, but it is merely their period of relaxation after spending the night engaged in relatively strenuous fishing operations. Aside from fishing every night that he is able, the villager also cultivates his padi fields and frequently owns rubber estates or coconut plantations as well.

[8] Richard O. Winstedt, *The Malays: A Cultural History*, p. 15.
[9] Earnest A. Hooton, *Up from the Ape*, pp. 639 f.

Both men and women wear the Malay sarong tied at the waist. Women usually wear a thin blouse, and men an undershirt or T-shirt. On ceremonial occasions women wear batik sarongs, fancier blouses, and their gold jewelry. When a man is dressed ceremonially, his sarong is white with colored lines and his shirt is the collarless, long-sleeved broadcloth garment typical in Malaya and Indonesia. He also wears the round, flat-crowned black Malay hat or, if he is a haji, a similar white hat.

The diet of Rusembilan villagers consists mainly of fresh fish or other sea foods and rice. Raw and cooked vegetables and fruits in season and sweet cakes and biscuits are part of everyone's diet. Meat is usually reserved for large feasts, when it is cut into small pieces and cooked in a curry to be served with rice. Coconut in some form is used with almost every cooked dish. Curried chicken is also a typical dish. There are almost no dietary deficiency diseases in Rusembilan.

Because of village exogamy and large ceremonial feasts held throughout the area, the villagers of Rusembilan have relations with people and communities covering a large part of southern Thailand and northern Malaya. During the cholera epidemic in the village in the early 1920's and at the time of a smallpox epidemic in 1953, large groups of people migrated from Rusembilan to other parts of southern Thailand and into the state of Kedah in Malaya. Ties of kinship and friendship established in the village are maintained when one party moves away, so that the villager has an ever-widening circle of people on whom he may rely for friendship and hospitality when he is away from home and in whose village he may find mates for his children.

The Language

As pointed out in the Introduction, all Malay words used in this study will be written as they would be found in Standard Malay.[10] Although this does not represent the dialect actually

---

[10] See R. J. Wilkinson, *A Malay-English Dictionary*.

spoken at Rusembilan, it was thought advisable to use this system as there is an accepted English orthography for the Malay language and also as the terms in this rendition would be more easily comparable with other Malay studies.

Even though none of the villagers of Rusembilan normally speaks the Standard Malay language, almost all of them are familiar with it and understand to some degree the relationship of their own dialect with it. Everything that is written in Malay is in the Standard Malay using *Jawi* (modified Arabic) characters. On certain formal occasions, such as reading from the *kitab* or religious books, speaking to Europeans and Thais, and reciting certain parts of myths and stories, the villagers commonly use the Standard Malay rather than their own dialect.

In its phonology and morphology as well as in vocabulary (except in cases of loans from the Thai language), the Pattani dialect is similar to that spoken in Kelantan, Malaya.[11] In many instances, however, the changes from Standard Malay found in the Kelantan dialect are carried even farther in Pattani.[12]

[11] See C. C. Brown, *Kelantan Malay.*
[12] See Appendix B.

CHAPTER III

Historical Background

THE area of Pattani and of southern Thailand in general is one
which has been neglected by historians. During the first two
decades of the seventeenth century, however, when factories
were occupied by the British and Dutch in Pattani, accounts
were written dealing mainly with their commercial activities.[1]
Histories of Thailand are chiefly concerned with events in the
central portion of the kingdom, mentioning the southern provinces only when they came in conflict with the Thai capital.
The histories of Malaya treat only the former British Malaya and
occasionally make reference in passing to the Siamese state of
Patani (i.e., Pattani, Yala, Narathiwat). Although a detailed historical account of the area is beyond the scope of this study, a
summary of historical references to the area, together with the
narrative account of residents, is presented in the following sections.

[1] W. H. Moreland, ed., *Peter Floris: His Voyage to the East Indies in
the Globe, 1611–1615*, chs. iv, vi–viii; Samuel Purchas, *Hakluytus Posthumus, passim*; H. Terpstra, *De Factorij der Oostindische Compagnie te
Patani.*

Early Documentary History

From the middle of the second century A.D. until the middle of the sixth, the kingdom of Ch'ih-t'u, comprising the area of Pattani and Singgora (Songkhla), is, according to Briggs, reported to have been a colony of the Funan empire.[2] Briggs finds no actual history of Ch'ih-t'u until the years 606–607, when it was arranged that an embassy should be sent to China. The Chinese ruler sent a group of mandarins to the capital at Pattani to make final arrangements. The Buddhist king of Ch'ih-t'u sent Brahmin priests with thirty boats to meet the Chinese in the harbor.[3]

Although the Srivijaya empire established a stronghold at Ligor (Nakorn Sritamarat) as early as 775, it apparently did not extend its control south from there to the kingdoms of the Pattani area, at least until almost the thirteenth century, by which time Hindu settlements had sprung up as far south as Pattani.[4] Briggs thinks it possible that the Srivijaya empire had been supplanted on the peninsula as early as 1183, but, at any rate, the Malayu empire must have held control for a short time before 1292, when the Siamese king Rama Khamheng conquered Ligor and pushed on to Pattani.[5] By 1365 the Majapahit empire reached the height of its control on the peninsula, extending to the north as far as Pattani. This control was short-lived, and by 1402 the raja of Pattani assisted in the ouster of the Majapahit consort governing at Singapore.[6] Although peripheral to all the great empires, Pattani, in the light of its later importance, probably did serve

[2] Lawrence P. Briggs, "The Khmer Empire and the Malay Peninsula," *Far Eastern Quarterly*, 9:264, 1950.

[3] *Ibid.*, pp. 265–266.

[4] *Ibid.*, pp. 273, 283–286; K. A. Nilakanta Sastri, *South Indian Influences in the Far East*, p. 96.

[5] Briggs, *op. cit.*, pp. 291, 301–302.

[6] Brian Harrison, *South-East Asia: A Short Cultural History*, p. 48; D. G. E. Hall, *A History of South-East Asia*, p. 235.

as a port for the commercial activities of both the Srivijaya empire and the Majapahit empire particularly during the time of the latter's alliance with Siam.[7]

After the territorial expansions of Siam at the end of the thirteenth century, relative stability ensued, with the Siamese in the north and the Majapahit in the south of the peninsula. By 1350, however, the Siamese under King Rama Thibodi moved south through Kedah and conquered the nascent kingdom of Malacca.[8] With the rise of Malacca during the fifteenth century, Siamese control was pushed back, and by 1460 the Pattani kingdoms had become vassal states of Malacca.[9] According to local tradition, it was at this time that the strongest Islamic influences reached the area and that Malacca sent missionaries along with its envoys to the Pattani palace. Harrison's evidence that the ruler of Kedah had embraced Islam by 1474 [10] would seem to confirm this opinion. Siam regained control by 1511, when the Portuguese captured Malacca. At this time the Portuguese envoy to the Siamese capital concluded a treaty with King Rama Thibodi II, giving the Portuguese rights to the rich China and Japan trade at Pattani.[11]

During the next century and a half, Pattani served as an important European trading station, and references to the area find their way into the writings of Europeans more often at this time than at any other period of history. Writing as early as 1516 after a voyage to the Far East, Tomé Pires describes Pahang, Trengganu, Kelantan, Say (Saiburi, now part of Pattani province), and Patane (Pattani) as belonging to the Siamese

[7] G. N. Steiger, *A History of the Far East*, pp. 194–196, 330–333.

[8] Virginia Thompson, *Thailand: The New Siam*, pp. 20 f.; Phra Sarasas, *My Country Thailand*, p. 26.

[9] Chester F. Roberts, Jr., ed., *Area Handbook on Malaya*, p. 21; Harrison, *op. cit.*, p. 59.

[10] Harrison, *loc. cit.*

[11] Roberts, *op. cit.*, p. 23; Hall, *op. cit.*, pp. 158, 205, 239; W. A. Graham, *Siam*, I, 201.

king.[12] The rulers and population of the northern parts (Pattani area) were either "Moors or heathens" at this time. Pattani is described as being an important commercial center, its harbor always crowded with junks.[13] By this time, the Siamese hold over Pattani was reasonably well established, and the daughter of the raja of Pattani had been sent to Ayudhya as a concubine of the king of Siam.[14] Tomé Pires indicates, however, that Pattani was still sufficiently independent of Ayudhya to be able to form an alliance with Trengganu (including Kelantan) and Pahang in order to contest, although unsuccessfully, the control by Malacca of the Bintang Channel.[15]

Later History of the Pattani Area

The following data in narrative form were supplied by Haji Wan Jussof, a greatly respected *guru*, or teacher, in the Pattani area. He spoke of a book produced locally which set forth the history of Pattani in great detail; to his knowledge, however, he had possessed the only copy of the work, and that had been recently destroyed by fire. Except where otherwise specifically indicated, all the information contained in this section was supplied by Haji Wan Jussof and must be considered legend rather than history.

Pattani province was at first just a high sandy jungle area. The first settlement was built at Telaga Sembilan (nine wells), about twenty-five miles south of the present town of Pattani. Each of the nine wells there was restricted to a different category

[12] Cortesao, trans., *The Suma Oriental of Tomé Pires and the Book of Francisco Rodrigues*, pp. xxx, 105 f.

[13] *Ibid.*, p. 110.   [14] *Ibid.*, p. 232.

[15] *Ibid.*, p. 244. Although there was a considerable amount written about Pattani during this time, particularly by the English and Dutch in the first two decades of the seventeenth century, most of it concerns the administration of their factories there, and very little is about local events. Therefore pertinent information from these sources will be included in the following section rather than being set down at this point out of local context.

of people (e.g., the raja, his ministers, wise men, soldiers, servants, slaves, and so on). The raja, who was fond of hunting, was told one day of strange animal tracks some distance from his settlement. After verifying the information, he set off with a large entourage in search of the animal. In the evening, after a day of fruitless searching, a white deer passed the party. The raja took up pursuit and, on reaching a spot on the coast and almost capturing the animal, saw it vanish. The deer, it is said, was a *hantu* or spirit. The raja returned to Telaga Sembilan disheartened and after much thought gave his ministers a plan to found a new capital on the spot where the deer had vanished. Forthwith, the raja and his people moved to the shore, and the commoners began clearing the jungle. Part of what they cleared was to belong to them, and the rest to the raja. After the city had been established, the raja again consulted his ministers. "What shall the city be called?" he asked his chief minister. The minister in turn asked the raja, "Why was it built here?" "Because the white deer disappeared on the beach." "What beach?" again queried the minister. The raja replied, "Pata ni" (from *pantai ini*, this beach).

For a long time Pattani grew both in population and in prosperity until the city was second only to Singapore in the whole of the Malay Peninsula.[16] Although the raja at that time had no religion, there were a number of business and professional men in the city who were Moslems. During this time the raja contracted a long and serious illness. He summoned all the residents of the city and promised half of his kingdom to anyone who could cure him. A Moslem doctor, Haji Sai or Tok Besar, came to the raja and promised that he could effect the cure and that all he demanded of the raja in return was his conversion to Islam. The raja was cured, but refused to keep his bargain. A year later

[16] It is probable that this reference to Singapore should be to Malacca, as there was no major city on this island until the time of the British East India Company. This is undoubtedly the period when the Malacca empire extended to the Pattani area during the fifteenth century.

he fell ill again and the same arrangement was made, this time the raja making his promise before all his trusted ministers. He was cured, refused to be converted, and a third time fell ill. This time he promised before all his idols, ministers, and children that he would be converted, but for a third time he failed to keep his word. Later, the raja, fearing that he might fall ill again, consulted his ministers, although he did not wish to be converted. They advised it, however. He called together all his people and told them of his decision to embrace Islam, and they replied that, whatever he did, they would follow. The Moslem doctor was called in and, after securing assistants, converted all of Pattani, which afterward grew and prospered. A small group of people, however, held out against conversion and established a village of their own away from Pattani. These people can still be found at Kampong Kedi practicing their old religion.[17]

Among the laws passed by this raja was one that required the captain of any ship desiring to anchor in the harbor to present the raja with an unusual gift before permission would be given. This system proved satisfactory to the raja until the captain of a Chinese ship presented him with forty liters of musket shot. After consultation with his ministers, the raja decided that the Chinese had wanted to prove that his country had many guns, whereas Pattani was defenseless. So it was ordered that a large gun be built and that all the iron ore in the kingdom be supplied to the gunsmiths and none to foreign traders. Shortly after production was begun on the gun, Shehali, a trader from Malacca, came to Pattani to buy iron ore.[18] Shehali was met in the harbor

---

[17] These villagers are Buddhists. Another source, a Thai, explained the presence of this village by saying that the villagers are descendants of a group from the royal Siamese court at Nakorn Sritamarat, who had been ordered to capture a certain elephant on pain of death. After searching as far as the border of Kelantan, they gave up. Rather than return to face death, they settled among the Malays of the area, adopting their culture and language, but retaining their old religion.

[18] At this time, probably near the end of the fifteenth century, Pattani

by his Pattani agent, Segomo, and was told of the situation. As Shehali was preparing to leave empty-handed, Segomo informed him that he had a small private stock of iron ore and that, if Shehali would wait aboard ship until night, it could be loaded aboard. This conversation was overheard by one of the raja's spies, and when Segomo set out at night to deliver the ore, he found soldiers stationed at a point in the river to stop him. Realizing that, if he stopped, the ore would be found in his boat, Segomo paddled as quickly as he could past the soldiers. The soldiers took up pursuit and captured both Segomo and Shehali in the process of loading ore onto the latter's ship. The two men were brought before the raja, who, on ascertaining the source of the ore, ordered both men killed. Both were strangled with rope rather than decapitated by long swords, the traditional method which had been discarded after several men with invulnerability charms had escaped death. Their bodies were thrown in the river.

It is believed that Shehali was *keramat* (unusually blessed by God), for his body continued to float in the river in an upright position, out of water from the waist up, and it moved in a direction opposite to the tide. One of the raja's ministers suggested that, as the fish nibbling at the body might be eaten by the people of the city, all would be safer if the body were taken from the river and buried. The raja, at first opposing this plan, later relented and ordered the body buried far from the city cemeteries. Prior to the burial, white cloth was measured and cut to fit the body. But when the dressing began, it was found that the body had grown three inches and was too large for the piece of cloth. All together, three pieces of cloth were cut and had to be discarded, until the people, observing the proceedings, said, "If Shehali is really *keramat*, he should stop growing and allow himself to be buried." And on the fourth attempt he was

was still under the domination of Malacca, which was then building up its newly acquired arsenal.

successfully wrapped and buried. Just before he died, Shehali had placed a curse on the raja to the effect that neither he nor any of his children would produce further heirs. Although each of the raja's five children succeeded to the throne, the line was not continued.[19]

After leading a long and prosperous life the raja died, leaving three daughters, Biru, Hija, and Kuning,[20] and two sons who jointly succeeded their father as raja—Raja Tua (older) and Raja Muda (younger). The Siamese king, hearing of the prosperity of Pattani, invited the Raja Tua to come to his capital to marry one of his daughters. Suspecting the motives of the king, both rajas, together with their army and guns, proceeded to Ayudhya, leaving behind only a handful of men to guard the kingdom. Siamese ministers came to the rajas' ship daily to discuss matters of state, but after six months no mention of the marriage with the king's daughter was made. Raja Tua felt shamed that he was being treated this way, and so he stormed the king's palace with his trusted and invincible force. The gates were thrown open unresisting, and Raja Tua proceeded into the palace from which the king had fled.

Raja Tua found the king's daughter and walked with her hand in hand throughout the palace while his army slept outside. He later married the princess and remained with her in the Siamese capital. As soon as peaceful relations were established between the rajas and the Siamese king, Raja Muda sailed back to Pattani.

[19] The information of Peter Floris (Moreland, *op. cit.*, pp. 59–66) indicates that this is not strictly true. The youngest of the three sisters married the ruler of Pahang with whom she lived for twenty-eight years, until 1613, and the daughter whom she bore married the brother of the sultan of Johore.

[20] It is possible that one of these daughters may have been the concubine of the king of Siam referred to in Cortesao, *op. cit.*, p. 232, and in W. A. R. Wood, *A History of Siam*, p. 167, who mentions a long succession of queens of Pattani throughout the seventeenth century.

According to Wood, King Chakraphat of Siam was engaged in war with Burma in 1556 and called upon the vassal state Pattani for assistance. The raja of Pattani, in this account, prepared a large army and a fleet of two hundred boats and set sail to give assistance. Arriving at Ayudhya, he found that the Burmese had gone and that the Siamese forces were in a weakened condition. The raja saw this as an auspicious moment and attacked the city. Although the king had fled, the invasion was easily put down and the raja's forces were sent back to Pattani.[21]

Meanwhile, the narrative continues, the *ratu* of Java had heard that all the forces of Pattani had been taken to attack the Siamese, and he considered it a good time to attack Pattani. He did not realize that Raja Muda had returned with all the troops. The Javanese invasion ship landed some distance from Pattani, and, meeting little resistance on the beach, the attackers marched on the city. Here the guns had been readied, and most of the Javanese force was wiped out. Those that were able to return to Java told the *ratu* of the situation, and he then ordered his most successful general to reattack Pattani. Equipped with two ships, the general made two attempts to land at Pattani, but both times he found the beach blockaded with sharpened bamboo and sand barriers. He was forced to return to Java and announce to the *ratu* that Pattani was invulnerable.[22]

[21] Wood, *op. cit.*, p. 119.
[22] Although there is no historical reference to such a war with the Javanese, it is possible that this account may refer to the Achinese. As reported in Federation of Malaya, *Annual Report, 1951*, p. 279: "Early in the 17th century a great and sinister figure made his appearance in the Archipelago: Iskandar Muda, Sultan of Acheh, in North Sumatra. His piratical hordes swept through Malaya massacring, pillaging and carrying away into captivity many thousands of Malays. Malacca was the only place he failed to capture, but no other territory as far north as Patani was immune from his depredations. He completed the conversion of the Peninsular Malays to Islam by compelling conversion at the point of the sword." In 1629, Pattani and Johore joined with Malacca and defeated the Achinese fleet off Malacca (Hall, *op. cit.*, p. 286).

During the latter part of Raja Muda's reign, the king of Siam asked for the hand in marriage of one of the raja's sisters. Three times Raja Muda refused the king's request, and on the third refusal, the king declared war on Pattani. Typical of wars in those days, the battles were fought only as long as the wooden war gongs were beaten. When the gongs stopped, all fighting ceased, and the opposing sides would frequently sit together, talking and sharing each other's food. During this war, the army of the raja ate so much of the Siamese food, to show that it did not fear poison and to shame the opposing side if it ran short of food, that the Siamese forces were obliged to retreat to their capital because their supplies of provisions had become exhausted.

On the death of Raja Muda, he was succeeded in turn by each of his three sisters. The narrative of Haji Wan Jussof leaves blank the important period between the death of Raja Muda and the succession to the throne of his youngest sister, Raja Kuning, shortly before 1632. According to history, in 1602 Dutch traders were given permission by the queen of Pattani to establish a trading post in the city. This was destroyed three years later by Japanese rivals, but was soon rebuilt and was followed by a British factory in 1612.[23] Although the British traders were not faring well in the area, in 1619 three Dutch men-of-war attacked the British ships "Sampson" and "Hound" in Pattani harbor and seized them. Had it not been for the intercession of the queen, it is reported, all of the British in the city would have been massacred by the Dutch. Because of trading difficulties, the British factory was closed in 1622, and the Dutch factory shortly thereafter.[24]

The narrative account continues with Raja Kuning's succes-

[23] Steiger, *op. cit.*, p. 459. See also Moreland, *op. cit.*, ch. vi. In addition to the Japanese burning of the factories, Floris reports that in 1613 there was a revolt of the Javanese slaves in the town, which resulted in the complete destruction of the town except for the royal court, the mosque, and a few houses (*ibid.*, pp. 94–95).

[24] Steiger, *loc. cit.*; Wood, *op. cit.*, pp. 167 f.; Hall, *op. cit.*, p. 300.

sion of her sister as queen of Pattani. The king of Siam asked for her hand in marriage, but she refused the alliance. Subsequently, however, marriage was proposed by the raja of Johore, and she accepted.[25] When this news reached the Siamese capital, the king dispatched his forces to attack Pattani. The raja of Johore had brought his army with him to Pattani and offered to help his wife, but she refused him saying, "Pattani will fight alone until it is very weak." The Siamese forces were obliged to retreat again because of food shortages, and thereafter relations remained peaceful for a long time.

Wood describes this situation without any mention of an alliance with Johore. In 1632, at the beginning of the reign of the Siamese king Prasat Thong, the queen of Pattani refused to pay the usual tribute to Siam of a gold and silver tree, declaring her kingdom independent. She is reported to have described the king to Dutch advisers in Pattani as a "rascal, murderer, and traitor."[26] Later that year, Wood continues, Prasat Thong launched a force of fifty to sixty thousand men, elephants, and guns to recapture Pattani. He also arranged for naval support from six Dutch ships. The Siamese forces attacked the town prior to arrival of the Dutch ships and were severely beaten before they were able to retreat to Songkhla. When the Dutch ships arrived, they found no Siamese support, so they too retreated to Songkhla. In 1636, in view of further Siamese military preparations, a Dutch adviser to the queen recommended that she accept the demands. Thus, in April of that year, envoys were sent with gold and silver trees of tribute to the court at Ayudhya to ask forgiveness and to resume the status of Pattani as a vassal state.[27]

With the death of Raja Kuning, the narrative continues, the

[25] This is probably the marriage of Raja Kuning's daughter with the brother of the sultan of Johore. See note 19.

[26] Wood, *op. cit.*, p. 177; Steiger, *op. cit.*, p. 68.

[27] Wood, *op. cit.*, pp. 179 f.

dynasty of Pattani rajas came to an end. Relatives of the family
were appointed to act as rajas, but there were trouble and death
in the land. Finally, the largest political units were one or two
towns presided over by a *datu* (ruler of lesser status than a raja).
When the Siamese king again decided to attack Pattani, he met
with no organized resistance and stormed through the area burning villages and taking back to his capital as hostage one child
from every family. Descendants of these hostages today make up
the populations of several Moslem villages in the central area
of Thailand.

After the Siamese invasion of the area, one of the younger
sons of the raja of Kelantan came into the area and to a certain
extent reorganized Pattani along its former lines. Although he
never achieved his goal of total unification of the area, his rule
and that of his descendants maintained peace in Pattani. The fifth
and last raja of this line was Raja Abdul Kadir. In 1892, King
Chulalongkorn of Siam ordered that all areas under Siamese control were to be governed directly under the central Ministry of
the Interior, rather than by their local princes.[28] In the south
the Siamese authorities offered to support, in return for Siamese
administrative jurisdiction, the local rajas as titular heads of their
areas with an annual salary and part of the rice tax. All of the
rajas in the area, except Raja Abdul Kadir, agreed to this plan
and were given Siamese names and appointed to positions under
the Ministry of the Interior. Raja Abdul Kadir was called to
Bangkok, and the king personally requested him to submit to the
new organization. He was offered a higher salary and promised
exemption of his people from police duty and, for a certain number of them, exemption from the national head tax. He still refused, however, and on his arrival home, he told the crowds of
people who had come to greet him to prepare for war with the
Siamese. Preparations for defense were begun, but when the raja's
ministers told him of the force being readied against him, Abdul

[28] See Thompson, *op. cit.*, p. 46.

Kadir decided that flight to British-controlled Kelantan was his wisest course.

In 1901, nine years after Chulalongkorn's decree, the central administration was set up in Pattani province, in essentially the same form in which it operates today (see Chapter VII).[29]

History of Rusembilan

According to tradition, many years ago a party of eleven arrived in Pattani from China. The leaders of this party were a brother and sister who were very close to one another. During their stay in Pattani, the brother became converted to the Moslem faith against his sister's wishes. After vain attempts to make him give up his new religion and return with her to China, the sister committed suicide. The nine other members of the party set sail for China shortly after the funeral, but were shipwrecked and drowned just off the beach which is now Rusembilan. In memory of the shipwrecked sailors, the Chinese residents of Pattani planted nine (*sembilan*) casuarina trees (*ru*) on a high sandy portion of the beach, and each year in Pattani they celebrate the anniversary of the death of the sister with a fire-walking ceremony.

During the reign of Raja Abdul Kadir, sometime before 1860, one man and his son moved from Pattani and started to clear the jungle from the land behind the beach at Rusembilan. As more people moved into the settlement, the raja appointed this first settler *kueng* (headman). The settlement at this time was not on the beach, but about one-half mile inland at what is now Kampong Surau. Somewhat later, a family moved to the spot on the beach where the nine casuarina trees were growing. By 1900 there were four or five houses on the beach, and the settle-

[29] At this time the commissioner or governor of Pattani was Chinese (G. William Skinner, "Chinese in Thailand," *Journal of Asian Studies*, 16:241, 1957). Probably the fact that the governor was not Thai made the centralization of government authority easier for the Malays to accept.

ment at Kampong Surau contained possibly twenty houses. Although the sea has been gradually encroaching on the beach, washing away a few houses along with the casuarina trees, the population of the beach settlement grew rapidly at the expense of Kampong Surau. The villagers explain the rapid growth in population as due to the fact that a living was much easier to make at Rusembilan than at inland villages, and in addition to the families who moved to the beach, almost all children of residents would settle in the village upon marriage instead of taking up residence in the village of their spouse.

Shortly after the family of the *kueng* had moved to Rusembilan, another unrelated family took up residence on adjoining land. These families lived amicably side by side until about 1935, when the ownership of part of the land being used by a member of the second family was disputed by a member of the first. This led to a bitter quarrel and finally to court action. The judgment was awarded to the first family, forcing his opponent to move from his house on the original land and establish, along with a group of supporters, a settlement farther to the south, Kampong Baru.

Between 1925 and 1930, the first *perahu kolek*, the large fishing boat commonly used in the village today, was purchased from Taluban. At that time the crew of eighteen used paddles to propel the boat, a method that is common in the area today although oars are now used at Rusembilan. In 1940 the road from Rusembilan to the highway into Pattani was constructed by the Thai government.

During World War II, Japanese forces using southern Thailand as a base from which to launch their invasion of northern Malaya set up a transient camp at Rusembilan. The villagers report that, for the month that the camp was used as a landing base, there were two or three thousand troops moving through constantly. Rather than use the village road, the Japanese vehicles cut directly across the padi fields, using quantities of lumber from Pattani when the fields were wet. They cut down coconut trees when they wanted the nuts (and when a villager would not climb the tree for them), commandeered fish from returning boats, and consumed all the village fowl. Many of the village boats were used by the Japanese for recreation purposes, and most of them were badly damaged. The people of Rusembilan greatly feared the Japanese, many of them hiding in the jungle until the camp closed.

During this period there was considerable activity on the part of the Malay population in Thailand supporting the Allied resistance in Malaya and directed toward union with Malaya. To help suppress this agitation, the Thai government offered supplies and food to various Malayan-Chinese guerrilla groups operating near the Thai frontier, even though these groups were fighting the Japanese, Thailand's allies.[30] Developments since the war are summarized in Chapter VII.

[30] *Straits Times*, April 9, 1948, quoted in Victor Purcell, *The Chinese in Southeast Asia*, pp. 189–190 n.

CHAPTER IV

Maritime Economy

ALMOST every family in Rusembilan either owns or works a padi field, and until very recently enough rice was produced for the community's needs and at times even a surplus. The chief occupation, however, and indeed the major economic orientation of the village is fishing. Making one's living from the sea is a strenuous occupation, and although men past sixty are still able to plow and tend the padi fields, many of them have neither the strength nor inclination for any sort of fishing. Young men who have not been chosen for a boat group will also be put to work in the fields when there is much work to be done. And because the fishing at Rusembilan is seasonal, in that these activities cease during the three months of monsoon rains, and because most fishing is done at night, even the most ardent fishermen are able to devote a considerable amount of time to purely agricultural and social pursuits. But it is fishing that comes first to the minds of the villagers when they are asked to name the chief occupation of the community.[1] It is fishing that the men talk about as they sit in coffee shops during the morning hours, and it is the fishing activity that takes precedence over everything but the observance of Friday as a day of rest.

[1] See Table 3 in Chapter V.

Fish and the Fishing Cycle

By far the most important fish in terms of community energy and tradition is *kembong*, a small species of mackerel (*Scomber kanagurta*).[2] This fish swims in schools of up to ten thousand in the waters of the Gulf of Thailand from approximately the first of April to the end of September or the beginning of October.[3] (See Figure 3.) Depending upon the condition of the wind

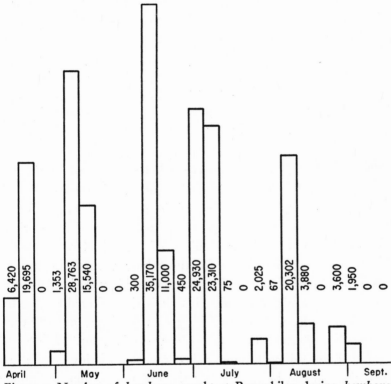

Figure 3. Number of *kembong* caught at Rusembilan during *kembong* season of 1956.

[2] R. J. Wilkinson, *A Malay-English Dictionary*, I, 550; Raymond Firth, *Malay Fishermen: Their Peasant Economy*, p. 341.

[3] From the end of April through September the northerly movement of wind and sea requires the schools of *kembong* to pursue their food

and sea and their effect upon the pelagic planktons and small fish which make up the diet of the *kembong*, these schools may be found anywhere from four miles offshore to fifteen or twenty miles out. One of the skills demanded of the steerer of a successful fishing boat is the ability to determine from weather conditions the probable location of these schools. In some years, such as the one when this study was made, the *kembong* seem to be very scarce or, for periods of almost a month, entirely absent. No matter how skillful the steerers, most of the fleet will come back night after night with no fish.

Within the annual cycle of the *kembong* is a lunar cycle limiting the periods when the fishermen will go after *kembong*. Since the *kembong* are netted almost exclusively at night, the fishermen rely for finding the fish upon the glow created as they swim through the highly phosphorescent water. Under ideal conditions, when the sea is calm and there is no moon at all, this glow can be seen for as far as a mile away. When the moon is full and high in the sky, however, it is impossible to see the fish at all; thus, all *kembong* fishing ceases for a week or ten days each month depending on the phase of the moon and its position in the sky. Likewise, fishing operations stop when offshore winds ruffle the sea and hamper visibility of the fish. Ordinarily the fishermen prefer to set out for the fishing grounds in the late afternoon before sunset and return to the village with their catch as early as possible. But their schedule is also affected further by the lunar cycle. Since the waxing moon sets later and later each night, the fishermen must postpone their departure in order to arrive at the fishing grounds when the moon is low enough so that the fish can be seen. After the full moon, they may once again go out early and fish before the moon rises. Particularly

north into this area, whereas the food supply is driven south during the period of the northeast monsoon and southerly sea drift. See Table 1 and W. L. Dale, "Wind and Drift Currents in the South China Sea," *Malayan Journal of Tropical Geography*, 8:23–35, 1956.

during poor runs of *kembong*, other fish may be taken into the nets, either along with, or instead of, *kembong*, and sometimes unintentionally. These other fish are usually *ayoh* (a bonito, *Thynnus* sp.) [4] and *pelaling* (a horse mackerel, *Carnax* sp.) [5] and occasionally *bawal* (a pomfret, *Stromateus* spp.). [6] Not too infrequently various types of sharks which prey upon *kembong* are caught in the nets. They often tear through the nets before being landed in the boat.

During the six-month *kembong* season, there is also a small amount of daytime fishing. In the past it was strictly limited by the fact that the fish feed far offshore during the day, and the prevailing winds are unfavorable to setting out in the morning and returning in the evening. With the introduction of motorboats during the summer of 1956, there was an increase in daytime fishing, particularly during periods when the *kembong* seemed scarce at night or when the full moon precluded night fishing altogether. *Kembong* is still the favored catch, but *kerisi* (sea bream, *Synagris* spp.) [7] is frequently sought and taken. Location of the fish during the day is also relatively simple if the sea is calm, as both these species keep within a yard or two of the surface and the school appears, from quite a distance, as a dark, reddish area of water.

Between the end of the wet monsoon period in late December or January and the middle or end of March, *udang ako* or large prawns measuring up to ten or twelve inches in length are netted. A diver locates these prawns by listening for their movement along the bottom, and thus the phase of the moon does not affect the operation. [8] During their short season, the large prawns are

---

[4] Firth, *op. cit.*, p. 342. [5] Wilkinson, *op. cit.*, II, 230.

[6] *Ibid.*, I, 93; Firth, *op. cit.*, p. 341.

[7] Wilkinson, *op. cit.*, I, 574; Firth, *op. cit.*, p. 342.

[8] The diver or *juru selam* in Kelantan and Trengganu is employed to locate and identify all types of offshore fish (Firth, *op. cit.*, p. 101). Villagers of Rusembilan claim that this was once their practice, but that now the diver is employed only in locating *udang ako*.

very plentiful, and this fact, as well as the high price they command in the market, usually makes this time of year the most prosperous for the community. Throughout the prawn season, however, the fisherman is impatiently waiting for the first indication that he may begin the more dramatic and exciting, if less certain, pursuit of the *kembong*. On the rare occasions when the prawn and *kembong* seasons overlap, prawns are immediately forgotten, and the attention of the whole community is turned to *kembong*.

Except during the monsoon period, men who do not care to fish for *kembong* or large prawns go netting any other types of sea food they can find within a mile or two of shore. During the day older men work up and down the shore, either wading or in small boats, netting shrimp (*udang baring*). Along with these small shrimp is a large variety of other small fish, most of which have very little value as food or as commercial products. Some fishermen net crab in the currents running not far offshore. The most numerous and valued type is the blue crab (*ketam ungu*), which is caught in large quantities from January through July, but which continues to be important until the monsoons in October. There are also the *ketam yima*, having pink and purple markings on its shell and not considered edible, and the *ketam batu*, a very large and much desired hard-shelled rock crab.

Besides net fishing, there is at all times a certain amount of fishing by hook and line. During the main fishing seasons, men will go out to sandy shoals, and there between two poles they will stretch a line which suspends up to two hundred hooks for catching *sembilang* (catfish, *Plotosus canius?*).[9] Some will take their boats an hour or two offshore and fish for *kerisi* with a triple line and three hooks. Occasionally sharks and the larger skates and rays are trolled for, particularly after the *kembong* season begins to slack off. During the monsoon season when the surf is

[9] Wilkinson, *op. cit.*, II, 423.

not too rough, men will cast from the beach for *anding* (a large gray mullet, *Mugil borneensis*) [10] and *lanu* and *lupat*, similar unidentified fish.

Other fish which are taken irregularly, usually by the men who prefer small-scale fishing, are another species of catfish, *dukang*; another gray mullet, *belanak*; a small squid, *sutung*; a sea pike, *kachang*; jewfish, *gelama*; cuttlefish, *ketang*; and *keng* (Thai), a horseshoe crab, which is never eaten by the Moslem villagers, but is given away to the rural Thais who consider it a great delicacy.

Fishing Boats

Although the villagers of Rusembilan are familiar with many kinds of Malay fishing boats, the community has only three types to serve for all its fishing activities. By far the most common type of boat in the village is the *jokung*, ten or twelve feet long with a three-foot beam. Because of its simplicity and cheapness, either to build or to buy, most families in the village have at least one *jokung*. Originally such boats were simply dugouts with or without added planks to raise the freeboard or with some form of stabilizers. Now, however, they are of conventional plank construction with keels made of larger timbers which have been hewn convex on the outside and concave within. To build one of these boats at the present time costs about seven hundred baht ($35), although good secondhand boats can be bought for much less. The boat is usually handled by one man and is used for setting crab nets or in conjunction with a push net for catching small shrimp near the shore. The fisherman will push his net and either push or pull his boat alongside him, using it as a movable base of operations and storage space for the catch.

The *perahu pukat sinyoh* (literally, shrimp-net boat) is usually from twenty to thirty feet in length. This boat, like the *jokung*, is always individually owned, although a crew of three or four

[10] *Ibid.*, I, 30.

is required to handle its nets. The boat is used mostly for various kinds of fishing near shore, but can be taken into deep water for netting prawns. It is used for prawns only when its owner is not a regular member of a larger boat crew and is not satisfied with the commercially less valuable inshore catches. The *perahu pukat sinyoh* is fast and easy to handle, so that it is used for transportation when a few people only want to go to some other coastal village or to a beach abundant with clams or conchs. The *perahu pukat sinyoh* is characterized by upturned pointed ends always sheathed in brass, in distinction to the blunted ends of the *jokung* and the large removable end boards on the *perahu kolek*.

The *perahu kolek*, although relatively few in the village, are the most important boats both socially and economically. They range in length from thirty-five to fifty feet and in fishing are used only for *kembong*, other deep-sea fish, and the large prawns. Large groups of people also travel in the *kolek* for feasts and ceremonial occasions in other coastal or river villages. Because a new *kolek* costs up to fifteen thousand baht ($750), only a few men are able to own one. Of the fourteen *kolek* at Rusembilan, seven are individually owned, two are shared by partners, and five are owned jointly by the crew members. Contingent upon both the size of the *kolek* and the number of men wanting to join the boat group, the crew numbers from twelve to eighteen men, although fourteen is the usual number. These boats are rarely made in the village. Most are bought new from Taluban, a village which is recognized as far as Trengganu as the center for building the most seaworthy and fastest *kolek*.[11] Several of the boats at Rusembilan were bought secondhand from fishermen in other villages; one was built in the village. The builder of this *kolek* was in the process of building a new one with the occasional aid of a builder from Taluban when this study was made. Much better care is taken of the *kolek* than of the smaller boats in the village, each *kolek* being brightly painted with many dif-

[11] Firth, *op. cit.*, p. 46.

ferent colors at least once every two years. Several of the *kolek*
have inscriptions in Malay and Arabic painted on their high bows
and including quotations from the Koran (e.g., "In the name
of Allah, the Beneficent, the Merciful"; "There is no God but
Allah, and Mohammed is his Prophet,") and Malay proverbs
(e.g., "The moon is full in the middle of the month"). The
brightly striped *kolek* are further decorated with traditional Islamic motifs for beauty's sake alone.

Boat and Net Groups

Before the end of the monsoon period, boat groups are organized for the coming prawn and *kembong* seasons. The steerer
of a *kolek,* whether he is the owner or not, is responsible for
choosing the crew and will try to pick the strongest, most diligent men. Men looking for positions in the boat groups naturally
try to get a place in one of the "lucky" boats (i.e., with a record
of better catches); the chances of such a position are relatively
small, however, as the same crew tends to remain with a successful boat and steerer year after year. The most-specialized role
among the crew of a *kolek* is that of the steerer, who is required
to have a good knowledge of wind and weather. He must know
where to find the fish and must have "good eyes" to sight the
school of fish. The steerer is also responsible for maintenance of
the boat though not for the cost unless he is also the owner.
Usually it is the owner or the owner's son who is steerer, but in
three of the nine *kolek* owned by one or two persons at Rusembilan, the steerer is a man with a good reputation for fishing ability
who is chosen by the owner to take command of the crew. Two
men of the crew are permanently stationed at the bow paddles.
Their special job is to assist when the boat turns in a tight circle
to drop the nets around a school of fish and to be lookouts when
scouting for fish. The rest of the crew rotates at will or by
plan between oar and paddle, and they rotate for the job of net
handlers or of bailer and washer.

The organization of the boat groups in the co-operatively owned boats (*perahu serikat*) is identical with that of an individually owned boat except that the steerer receives no extra share of fish for his position. (See "Distribution and Marketing," below.) Although he is theoretically in a position of authority, his actual ability to command the crew members may be limited by the fact that all the crew own an equal share in the *kolek*.

Common among the Malay fishermen along the shores of the South China Sea is the net group, which is made up of a group of boats all handling the same large net.[12] The fishermen of Rusembilan, though aware of the use and organization of such groups, have never utilized them to any extent in their own fishing operations. The reason for this, they explain, is that it requires too much co-operation and that the responsibility for successful fishing, as well as the distribution of the catch, would be spread among too many people.

With the introduction of motorboats[13] during the summer of 1956 to tow the *kolek* to the fishing grounds, fishing during the daytime first became practicable. Daytime fishing was considered desirable as a means of increasing the number of fish caught daily and also necessary in justifying the expense of the motorboats. During the daytime, the schools of *kembong* are more dispersed, and apparently the fish are more able to detect the presence of the fishing boats. Thus, the circumference of the netting circle must be increased so that the fish can be surrounded before the school disperses. In order to increase this circle, some form or organization beyond the individual boat group became necessary. The nets of three or four *kolek* are combined into one large circle, each *kolek*, with its own nets, being responsible for its own arc of the circle. The catch is evenly divided among each of the *kolek* if the net group is a temporary arrangement or is divided in the prescribed manner (see "Distribution and

[12] See *ibid.*, pp. 114–120.   [13] See pp. 45–49.

Marketing," below) if the co-operating *kolek* tend to fish together habitually or are usually towed to the fishing grounds by one motorboat. It quite frequently happens that a net group may be formed on a temporary basis and consist of boats from different villages. As in the case of the men in the boat groups, the more successful *kolek* tend to form the most organized and stable net groups, whereas the less successful boats circulate from one impermanent grouping to another trying to increase their "luck."

Nets and Traps

Each member of a boat crew is usually required to supply two *kembong* nets (*pukat kembong*), but sometimes the steerer of a co-operative boat is required to provide only one, and a nonfishing boatowner may send one or more of his own nets out with the boat, thus receiving a share of the fish for his nets as well as for his proprietorship. These gill nets are made of twisted twine knotted into about a one-inch mesh. They have draw lines on the top with six-inch oval wooden floats and on the bottom with three-ounce iron sinkers. Each net is approximately forty feet deep and sixty feet long. During the period when the moon is dark, all the nets of a boat (usually thirty) are tied or sewn together so that the net is forty feet deep and approximately a third of a mile in length, or circumference. When a school of fish is sighted, the crew, with loud and prolonged shouts, will take down the sail and stow it in its crutch, or cast off the tow if they were towed out by a motorboat, and start rowing and paddling with all their energy toward the school. As they approach the fish, an end of the net is dropped overboard. Attached to the upper corner of this end is a float of crossed planks supporting a small tree which is a marker. This tree must always be green and is therefore often replaced. As soon as the net is dropped, the boat quickly changes course so that it lets the rest of the net out encircling the school of fish. Almost always, though it is frequently pitch dark, the tree and float are met just as the end of the remaining net is reached, thereby closing the circle. With the net down, kerosene flares made of tin cans filled with cotton waste are lighted. Four to six members of the crew take long beaters with convex rounded blocks of wood on the end and begin shouting and violently beating the water inside the net circle. The tumult causes the fish to disperse and catch themselves in the net. With the float attached to the boat so that the circle will not open, the crew begins pulling the net back into the *kolek*, quickly but steadily. The net is managed by two or four net handlers and is pulled in so that the vertical plane of the hanging net becomes horizontal as it is drawn into the boat, thus minimizing the dropping back of the catch. The rest of the crew try to pick as many fish from the net as possible and stow them under the deck. When the net is completely hauled in, it must be carefully put overboard again as the remaining fish are extricated. During this process, only the end of the net with the floats is put overboard, the weighted end remaining in the boat so that the net may more easily be hauled in again. On the last netting of the night, the fish are often kept in the nets and taken out by the women after the boat returns to the village.

All the villagers repair their own nets which are frequently torn either by sharks or by the submerged pilings of abandoned fish traps. Few, however, make their nets, saying that it takes too much time. One man, the father-in-law of the imam, buys quantities of nets in the Pattani market, equips them with draw lines, floats, and sinkers, and sells them in the village at a small profit. The price he pays for a plain net is three hundred forty baht ($17); his sale price is three hundred eighty baht ($19). If a net is properly mended and cared for, it will generally last for four *kembong* seasons.

The nets used for large prawn (*pukat udang ako*) are much the same as the *kembong* nets, but have a smaller mesh which varies from one-half to three-quarters of an inch. When a diver locates by sound a group of prawns, the weighted end of the net is dropped, and the remainder is let out in a circle. The nets are recovered in the same manner as *kembong* nets.

Small shrimp nets (*pukat udang baring* or *pukat sinyoh*) are the highest-priced nets used at Rusembilan. Such a net, usually twenty feet long by twelve feet wide, has a quarter-inch mesh and costs five hundred baht ($25). Before using this net, it is cut in half so that it may be more easily handled by one or two men. The half piece or the double piece sewn together to make the width twenty-four feet is usually held by one man in shallow water while another, either paddling or pushing a *jokung*, lets out the rest of the net into a circle. Whatever is caught is hauled into the boat, to be sorted later on the beach, and the net is put out again.

The *jala* or throw net may be used by one man for catching small shrimp and other small fish living close to shore. It is a circular net with mesh a quarter inch or less and light chain around the circumference. The fisherman throws it from the beach or shoal water. He then draws it in from the center of the circle as a tube about nine feet long (radius). The shrimp and fish are tangled in the last three feet of the tube or in the chain. Before shaking the catch out onto the beach, the fisherman shakes his net in the water to rid it of excess mud, sometimes also losing much of the catch. The *jala* must possess a certain degree of stiffness so that it will open evenly into a circle when it is thrown. In order to keep it in this condition, it must be restiffened after six or seven days of use by kneading into it the whites of ten eggs mixed with a little water.

For the smallest shrimp (*udang belachan*) a net almost as fine as burlap is used. This net or *rawa*, made of woven grass imported from Nakorn Sritamarat, is suspended from two converging shafts each with a slide or shoe. The fisherman wades through shallow water, pushing his net like a wheelbarrow, and scoops into the body of the net any small fish and shrimp that may be in his path.

Nets used for crabs and cuttlefish (*pukat ketam*) are often made in the village, and even the ones bought from Pattani lack the standardization of other nets. Because of lighter twine and one and a half inch mesh, these nets rarely cost over one hundred baht ($5). The nets are taken out by boat in the late afternoon and anchored on the bottom perpendicular to the direction of the tide. Simple floating markers are attached to each end of the string of nets so that they can be found the next morning when the fisherman returns to collect his catch. Crabs are always badly entangled in the nets, and even with the greatest care and patience, the nets are torn when the crabs are removed. Unless the damage to the nets is extremely serious, they can be repaired before setting them out again in the afternoon, although if one man is using twenty or thirty nets, he needs the services of his whole family to have them ready on time.

The villagers of Rusembilan, like most of the other Malays of the east coast, do not place much emphasis on trapping fish.[14] Perhaps the commonest type of trapping is that done with the basket trap. This conical rattan trap is used in shallow salt water for species of catfish and in the flooded padi fields for any fresh-water fish found there. The fisherman sights a fish, quickly places his trap over it, and then spears the fish with a three-pronged spear through a small hole at the top of the trap. Fresh-water fish are also trapped by digging pits in the flooded fields. When the water recedes, the fish remain in the deeper pools and can be taken out easily. There is little interest in building weirs on the river which is just west of the village. One weir was in operation during the period of this study, but it belonged to a resident of a nearby village. The most important commercial trap is the *kelung*,

[14] Firth (*op. cit.*, p. 7 *et passim*) indicates that traps are used to a large extent along the coast of Kelantan and Trengganu, however.

a semipermanent deep-sea trap with a diameter of fifty to seventy-five yards and an entrance channel of a hundred yards or more diverging from a narrow opening in the circular trap. These traps are built and operated by the Chinese merchants in Pattani, and although the Malays speak frequently of the desirability of such traps, none are even serviced by Malays in the Pattani area. The traps are unloaded once a day, and an average catch is worth one or two thousand baht ($50–$100). But the villagers say that these traps are too expensive to build as they cost ten to fifteen thousand baht ($500–$750), and after being in use for a year, the traps are abandoned, since it is more economical to build new ones than to maintain the old traps. As the poles rot down to the surface of the water and below, they become impossible to see at night, and they are responsible for a great deal of damage by ripping the villagers' nets.

Motorboats

As in the case of any new venture which requires considerable capital expenditure, the villagers of Rusembilan and particularly the important fishermen and boatowners spent many months discussing the advantages and disadvantages of purchasing a motorboat to be used for towing the *kolek* out to the fishing grounds and bringing them back. Various men went to investigate motorboats[15] as far away as Nakorn Sritamarat and to observe fishing operations employing motorboats at other villages. Discussion ranged from the advantages of outboard motors for the *kolek* themselves at eight thousand baht ($400) to those of towboats large enough to tow all the *kolek* of the village and costing sixty to eighty thousand baht ($3,000–$4,000) secondhand and from the increased number of fish that could be caught by fishing in the daytime also to the lowering of market prices when a large quantity of fish arrived at market at the same time. One

[15] An outline of the major events and of the roles played by different individuals in the introduction of motorboats is presented in Appendix A.

formal meeting was organized in the village chapel (*balaisa*) on the evening of the feast day of *Hari Raya Enam;* it was decided then that if any of the villagers purchased motorboats, either individually or co-operatively, the price for towing a *kolek* would be two shares (i.e., one-seventeenth) of the boat's catch. The eventual decision, made in a manner which seemed almost to ignore all previous deliberations, was that at least one motorboat should be bought. Many men said that it would be desirable for purely economic reasons. Many others, however, expressed what was probably the major factor in the decision, namely, that by having motorboats much of the strenuous work of rowing the *kolek* would be obviated, that the *kolek* crew could sleep on the way to the fishing grounds and on the way back, and that as a consequence these men would have more leisure time during the day. In spite of the previous demands of several steerers for daytime fishing to justify the investment in motorboats, in actual practice the boats went out infrequently during the day.

The first motorboat to arrive in the village was bought co-operatively by the crew members of two *kolek*, each man putting up one thousand baht ($50) toward the total price of thirty-two thousand baht ($1,600). The difference was made up by the owners of the *kolek* and the steerer of one of them. The motorboat was bought with little or no mechanical inspection and then run at full speed for fourteen hours from Nakorn to Songkhla, where it was to be registered. On the way from Songkhla to Rusembilan "the sound of the engine changed," and it shortly developed a crack in the crankcase through which all the oil drained out. Finally, it was towed into the village for one hundred seventy baht ($8.50). A Malay repairman (rather than a Chinese) was fetched from Pattani who guaranteed to weld the cracks and to train a man from the village in the maintenance of the boat.

Extensive discussions followed the breakdown of the motorboat as to whether it was better to have the crankcase repaired or whether a new engine should be bought, the damaged one to be used for a village rice grinding mill. (The damaged engine was built to be a mill engine and had been mounted in the boat by the original owner.) The father-in-law of the imam, one of the men who put more than a thousand baht into the boat, said that the whole venture had been "unlucky" and that the signs were against success. He had had a fever during the time that it was decided to buy the boat, six hundred baht was found missing from the funds collected to pay for the boat (the amount was later found), and the imam had been advised strongly not to buy this particular boat.

The course of events over the rest of the summer of 1956 bore out the more pessimistic points of view. The crankcase developed cracks twice again. The first time it was rewelded, and the reverse gear on the boat was removed so that, with direct drive only, there would be less strain on the engine. After the next crack, it was decided to buy a whole new engine, rather than repair the old one or try to replace the crankcase. The new engine (the same type of mill engine) was sold by a Chinese merchant in Pattani for a total cost of twenty-two thousand baht ($1,100). The merchant allowed seven thousand baht ($350) for the old engine. The father-in-law of the imam put up eight thousand baht ($400) in cash, and it was agreed that the remaining seven thousand baht ($350) could be paid back, without interest, out of income derived from operating the boat over a period of five months.

Once one villager has made a capital investment, no matter how long or bitter the prepurchase discussions may have been, other individuals are apt to follow his lead uncritically, without waiting to evaluate the results of the original investment. Shortly after the arrival of the first motorboat, three others were bought and brought into Rusembilan. One was bought with the understanding that an engineer from Nakorn Sritamarat would come with the boat and stay in the village for at least two months to run and service the boat. The other two were bought from nearby villages, and informal service agreements were made with their former owners.

Although the villagers decided before the motorboats were bought that they should be used extensively for towing the *kolek* to fishing grounds during the daytime, they found, in spite of the greater distance they could travel, that daytime catches were too small to warrant the expense of towing the *kolek* out twice a day. For about a week, some of the fishermen tried going out for twenty-four hours at a time, returning to the village for twelve hours and back to sea for another twenty-four. But they found that even with this system, their catch was not appreciably improved. Aside from towing the village *kolek* to the fishing grounds, two of the motorboats made a practice of doing jobs on hire for other villages, such as hauling wood from Pattani to a coastal village or transporting people to the clamming grounds outside Pattani Cape.

Ordinarily a motorboat would tow three *kolek*, though one of the motorboats regularly towed two. Position in the tow rotated so that each *kolek* would have a chance at being last in tow and thus first to be released on sight of fish. The motorboat waited in the vicinity of the fishing grounds until the last *kolek* had made up its catch or until it was considered time to go ashore either because of the rising moon or in order to get the fish to market early enough to command the higher prices. If one *kolek* caught sufficient fish early in the evening, it could not expect to be towed in alone and would usually sail home rather than wait for other *kolek* to be ready.

Although the crew of some *kolek* owned a share in the towboat, each *kolek* in a tow was charged the same for a round trip so that a cash reserve could accumulate for supplies and services to the motorboat. After a certain level, excess funds were divided monthly among the shareholders in proportion to their investment. The standard charge for each *kolek* was three shares of the catch (i.e., about one eleventh of the total) or, if they failed to catch any fish, four baht (20 cents) per crew member. The fishermen calculated that one and a half five-gallon cans of diesel oil costing twenty-four baht ($1.20) were needed to run each boat for one night. Thus, a motorboat towing three *kolek* could expect to make a profit of about one hundred thirty-two baht ($6.00) even if no fish were caught.

Scientific Knowledge and Ritual

When questioned about their fishing activities, the villagers of Rusembilan assert that fishing is one area in which religion and belief in spirits play no part, that every step of the operations is based on purely practical considerations. Questioned further about the specific steps involved, the fishermen admit, some with an embarrassed laugh but always with sincerity, that there are areas where it is necessary, or at least advisable, to enlist the aid of the spirits. There are many related sea spirits who are, on the whole, indifferent toward men. If these spirits are offended in any manner, however, they not only will keep the fish from the nets and cause sharks to tear the nets, but will cause specific troubles to the offending fisherman such as stomach-ache or fever. In the past, many of the successful fishermen and divers maintained one of the sea spirits as a familiar and were able, with the spirit's aid, to amass fortunes through abundant catches and to perform unheard-of feats of skill and daring at sea. At present, at the beginning of the *kembong* season, the crew of each *kolek* prepare a *kenduri*, or feast, to be eaten aboard the *kolek*. The *kenduri*, consisting of *pulot kuning* (yellow glutinous rice) and strips of fried egg, is eaten entirely by the crew. The purpose of this ceremony is to make the crew remember the spirits and, by remembering them, inform them of the fishermen's presence.[16]

[16] See Firth, *op. cit.*, p. 123.

Each time a *kolek* is launched after being kept on the beach during the bright moon, a small ceremony is held by the steerer and crew. The steerer rubs lime juice and commercial face powder on the inside and outside of the *kolek* and decorates the end pieces with flowers and ribbons to please the sea spirits, the fish, the boat, or the wood of the boat, which has a spirit or "extra something" [17] although it is actually "God who gives us the fish."

Boats are considered good or "unlucky" on the basis of their proportions and measurements. Pleasant decorations and sound construction are secondary considerations. It may happen that two identical boats will differ in performance. This is because the man who owns the boat, or its steerer, and the boat are not *sekon* (in harmony with one another). *Sekon* connotes a permanent relationship between things, between people, or between things and people. When a man finds that he and his boat are not *sekon*, it is wise for him to get rid of the boat as soon as possible because he has no chance of having luck with it, although another man probably will.

It is true, however, that in the actual activities of fishing the Rusembilan fishermen are guided by sound practical knowledge of their local conditions. As their fishing is done mostly at night, some form of celestial navigation must be known. The villagers claim that they have names for all the stars, but generally use only two for navigating: *Bintang Pagi* (literally, morning star) is used to set a course to the village from the usual fishing grounds, and *Bintang Selatan* (south star) is used for the home course when they have been fishing along the coasts to the west toward Songkhla. They set their outward courses by sighting back at these stars. On a cloudy night, they wait until daybreak in order to steer back by *Bukit Besar* (big hill), a three-thousand-foot hill inland behind the village. Their knowledge of the wind and weather is extremely accurate, and any fisherman standing on

[17] *Ibid.*

the windless beach can tell when it is too rough and windy at sea to be able to sight the schools of fish. Movement of the tides is considered when timing the beaching and launching of boats, and they realize that the tide cycle and the height of the tides is related to the lunar cycle.

A few of the villagers have made relatively long sea voyages following traditional directions. One man has sailed to Bangkok following a star which he was able to point out but not name. It is very simple—one "just sails straight out from the village for seven days." This man has had considerable sailing experience along the east coast of Malaya and at one point made a trip to central Java.

The knowledge, both ritual and scientific, required by a fisherman and particularly a steerer is never formally imparted to a youth. At about fifteen, a boy is taken out in a fishing boat, and within ten or fifteen days he learns from observation and questioning all there is to know. It is said that a man must have a minimum of two years' experience before being chosen as a steerer, but as a rule all steerers are older men, there being only two between thirty-five and forty in Rusembilan when this study was made. Often, the son of a steerer becomes a steerer himself. This is not due to any formalized tendency to inherit roles, but rather because the young man has greater opportunity to observe and learn the skills of steering than an outsider. Frequently, also, the family will be wealthy enough to be boat-owners, and one of the sons automatically takes command of the boat when his father retires.

Distribution and Marketing

After the *kolek* return to the beach with their catch and the nets have been spread on the drying racks, the men have finished their share of work. As soon as the boats arrive, the wives or mothers of the fishermen start unloading the *kembong* into baskets. The women make a rough estimate of the total catch, approximate the size of each share, and empty the baskets on the sand accordingly. Any surplus over the approximation is distributed among the piles of fish, or deficits are made up from the fuller piles. Before the use of motorboats started in Rusembilan, *kolek* owned by one or two persons divided their catch into "small shares" (*bagian kechil*); each *kolek* had a slightly different system of figuring shares, the total being between twenty-eight and thirty-four depending on the number of crew members and also upon what extra services a boatowner thought fitting to pay for. A typical distribution for a *kolek* with a fourteen-man crew consists of one share for each man and one-half share for each net (thus each crew member gets two shares as he must provide two nets), one extra share for the steerer, one-half share extra for the bailer and washer and for each of the four net handlers, and one and a half shares "for the boat" (i.e., the boatowner), giving a total of thirty three shares. If a man steers his own boat, he gets four and a half shares, whereas the steerer in another's boat gets three shares. The co-operatively owned boats use a system of "big shares" (*bagian besar*), in which the catch is simply divided into as many shares as there are crew members, each receiving an equal amount.[18]

When the motorboats first started towing the *kolek* to the fishing grounds, the number of shares for each *kolek* which was individually owned or owned in partnership was increased to include three small shares for the motorboat. Later, a system of pooling the catch of all the *kolek* in a tow group was adopted, distributing the total catch from three *kolek* into one hundred eight shares, nine of which would be for the motorboat and the rest allotted to the crew members and owners of the three *kolek*.

---

[18] Compare the *bagi* system of the Melanau of Sarawak, a complex and meticulous system of sharing the proceeds from sago production which is based on ownership of the palms and work put in on felling and processing them (H. S. Morris, *Report on a Melanau Sago Producing Community in Sarawak*, pp. 32–33).

Because this system required so much space for distribution and because the *kolek* in a tow group were not always beached adjacent to one another, they soon adopted the large shares of the co-operative boats. The following system was used by the two *kolek* of one tow group: three shares for the motorboat, one share for each crew member (including one man from each *kolek* left ashore each night for the village patrol), one-quarter share for each of the four net handlers, one-quarter share for each steerer, and three-quarters share for each *kolek*. This system was in effect in all the tow groups during most of the *kembong* season in 1956. But as the season wore on and fish became less plentiful, the women connected with *kolek* which had made good catches began to complain about having to average their share of the catch with those of the less fortunate *kolek* until finally, at the end of the season, each *kolek* was distributing its own catch among its own members and paying for the services of the tow boat on the basis of its own catch only.

Distribution of the large prawns follows the same pattern as for *kembong*, although when the catch is small, it may all be taken to the market by a few women and the proceeds rather than the prawns divided into proper shares among the crew members or their wives and mothers.

Distribution of fish, crabs, and shrimps caught from *jokung* or *perahu pukat sinyoh* is far less formalized than that of *kembong* or large prawns caught by *kolek*. Again, it is entirely the women who are responsible for the distribution and marketing of the catch, and in general, if three or four men have been fishing together, the wife of the boatowner has a somewhat larger share than the others or the choicest part of the catch.

A woman usually takes a small number of fish from her share for her family's needs, and if the catch was large, she will take the rest of the fish to market herself. If the catch was small, one or more women will volunteer to carry all the fish to the daily market in Pattani for a fee of five baht (25 cents) for each consignment. A woman prefers to sell her fish directly to whole-salers (Chinese) rather than to retail the fish unless her share is small and the supply in the market is scarce. The dealers either take it inland to large daily or weekly markets or pack the fish in ice for shipment to Bangkok and Singapore. The final price will usually vary between seventy and one hundred twenty baht per hundred fish with one hundred baht ($5) about average.

Irregularly, Thais from inland villages will come directly to the village to buy fish, usually for important celebrations of their own. In such cases a number of Thais will come together and sit in a circle in a conspicuous location on the beach. When the village women have loaded their fish baskets on their heads and started for the market, the Thais will hail them and com-mence bargaining by means of sign language. The price of the *kembong* is always a very exact figure and always for units of one hundred fish. Although in the bargaining a woman may ar-rive at her price and refuse to come down a half baht per hun-dred, after the price is settled, she will frequently make a present to the buyer of four or five fish, half as many as he has already bought. Usually, the price arrived at on the beach is about ten baht (50 cents) less per hundred fish than the price in the Pattani market. Often, buyers will be waiting at the point where the village road joins the main road to Pattani. These people will be from inland villages, both Thai and Malay, but never towns-people. The price here is usually about five baht (25 cents) lower than at the market, but occasionally will be the same as the market price or even higher.

All other fish caught by the villagers are marketed the same way as *kembong*. Except for the large prawns, the volume of fish and money is never as great. Whereas an average-sized catch of *kembong* will be worth two hundred baht ($10) for each woman, the proceeds from shrimp and small fish will range between thirty and fifty baht ($1.50–$2.50), and crabs about twice that.

The only sea food caught by the villagers of Rusembilan which has a market but is not sold is the horseshoe crab (*keng*). These are forbidden by the Koran for use as food, and therefore the villagers will not sell them for this purpose.[19] When they are caught with other fish, they are either thrown back into the sea, buried in sand, or given to Thais who may be on the beach and to whom they are a great delicacy.

[19] According to village interpretation amphibians are forbidden as food. As a horseshoe crab may live for as long as twenty-four hours buried in the damp sand, the villagers consider it an amphibian and will not eat it.

CHAPTER V

Economy of the Land

TRADITIONALLY, Malay culture, in common with other cultures in Southeast Asia, is based on rice cultivation. Because of the well-defined rainy season, peasants in the Pattani area and southward along the east coast of the Malay Peninsula plant and harvest only one crop of rice a year. For the growth of this wet rice crop, the planter relies on the annual inundation of his padi fields; and in years when the rainfall is small or it is abnormally delayed, his harvest may be seriously reduced. Although irrigation systems have been employed to some extent in the higher interior country and although the coastal villagers are familiar with the principles of the system, it has not been attempted on the coast. This is due primarily to the fact that fishing plays a far more important part in the economic system of the coastal villagers than does rice, and maintenance of irrigation canals and dikes would require time and labor during the fishing season. The villagers also point out that in order to keep the irrigation system free of salt water, ditches would have to be led off the rivers and major streams from as far as five miles or more inland, above the point where the monsoon tides may back up.

Cultivation other than rice plays a very minor role in the economy of Rusembilan; however, ownership of coconut and rubber plantations is increasing. Although many inland villages maintain extensive orchards of rambutan and durian, the land at Rusembilan is not suitable for these crops, and the villagers regard fruitgrowing as an occupation decidedly inferior to fishing.

Agricultural Cycle

Fishing and rice cultivation are therefore the two most important economic activities in Rusembilan, and because of the seasonal nature of the height of these activities, many men in the village can be both full-time fishermen and full-time agriculturalists (see Table 3). This seasonal division is caused by the

Table 3. Occupational distribution of males at Rusembilan

	Fishing	Fishing & agric.	Agri- culture	Fishing & other	Agric. & other	Other	Total
Household head *	58	50	10	7	5	15	145
Dependent male	43	9	4	2	2	17	77
Total	101	59	14	9	7	32	222

* In a very few cases, a widow with employment has been entered in the official records as a household head.
Source: Government of Thailand, *Census BE 2499* (1956).

monsoon, which brings the rains needed to mature rapidly the young rice plants and also the high seas that prohibit any fishing activities except just inside the surf line at the beach. Thus, the greatest amount of time required for rice cultivation, that is, the time of transplanting, comes at a period when there is virtually no fishing activity. Likewise, the major part of the *kembong* season falls between the time rice is harvested and the time when the next intensive rice cultivation activity, transplanting, takes place.

Plowing (*bergaloh*) is usually begun in July, though some

farmers may begin as much as a month earlier or a month later. Landowners with several padi fields may stagger their plowing at weekly or two-week intervals so that each field will develop in a way that will bring the peak of work at a time different from the others. Sowing of the seed (*bernaboh*) is done as soon as the fields have been plowed. The peak of activity is reached during October and November when the new plants are taken up (*menyabu*) and replanted (*menyadung*) in other prepared and flooded fields. During February and March the rice is cut (*mengate*) and taken to the graneries. Except for these three periods of activity, plowing-seeding, transplanting, and harvesting, the villagers do nothing to maintain the padi fields,[1] their only interest in them being when they occasionally become flooded during the dry season and collect fish from adjacent watercourses.

Most garden crops are planted during March and April and harvested before the rains begin in September or October. Wild plants are collected any time they are ripe, but this time usually falls during the six months before the rainy season. The same is true of fruit-bearing trees, either planted or owned near the village or growing wild. Coconuts are picked throughout the year, although they may be somewhat neglected during the rainy months because the villagers are busy transplanting rice and also because drying the coconut meat for copra presents a greater problem at this time.

Rice and Padi Field Cultivation

Roughly three-fourths of the households in Rusembilan own their own padi fields. Most of the remaining householders use the fields of another either on the basis of share cropping or a small yearly rental of not more than fifty baht ($2.50) or in return for some past or future service to the landowners. There are 175 plots of padi field distributed among eighty owners, as

---

[1] See pp. 62–64, below.

well as twenty-eight other plots which are used partially for rice cultivation. (See Table 4 and Figure 4.) The average size of one

Table 4. Land utilization at Rusembilan (section 1)

Type of land	Resident owners	Plots	Acres	Nonresident owners	Plots	Acres
Padi field	80	175	154.6	150	201	141.4
Coconut	28	31	42.4	47	47	86.8
Padi and coconut	19	20	33.0	18	24	265.4
Padi (planned)				1	1	1.8
Coconut (planned)	1	2	1.3	2	4	3.8
Coconut and garden				1	1	5.5
Undeveloped				1	1	.04
Undeveloped and padi				1	2	1.6
Undeveloped and coconut				1	1	.13
House site	19	19	4.8	2	2	1.9
House and padi	7	7	6.3			
House and coconut	4	4	2.4			
House, padi, and coconut	1	1	7.0	1	1	.48
School site	1	1	.41			
Grave site				1	1	.58
Total		260	252.2		286	509.4

Source: District Tax Records, Pattani District Office, BE 2498 (1955).

of these plots is somewhat less than one acre, which is quite large for this area.[2] Until about 1950 Rusembilan had been entirely self-sufficient in terms of its rice production and in some years had had a marketable surplus. Because of the construction of a navigation canal nearby, however, and the channeling of inland irrigation runoff into it, the river mouth to the west of the village became too large to block off during the monsoon season.

[2] Figures are based on statements of villagers at Rusembilan and other communities in the Pattani area. But compare C. W. S. Hartley's statement (in "Establishment of New Rice Areas in Malaya," *World Crops*, 3:171–175, 1951) that peasants in Malaya require six or seven acres to subsist on agriculture and stock raising and Paul M. Kattenburg's finding (in *A Central Javanese Village in 1950*, p. 5) that the average padi plot in Kalibening, Central Java, is just over one acre.

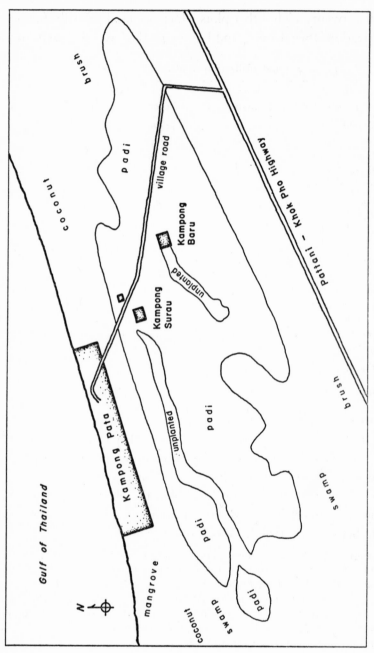

Figure 4. Plan of Rusembilan area showing settlements and agricultural land.

Consequently about seventy-five acres of padi field are flooded with salt water when the monsoon tides back up the river, spoiling any seedlings that may be planted in those fields. As a result, by 1956 most families in Rusembilan were forced to purchase retail one-third to one-half of their requirements of rice.

Cattle are kept for plowing purposes only. They are purchased for about fourteen hundred baht ($70) when three or four years of age and used until they are thirteen or fourteen, whereupon they are slaughtered and eaten. Although cattle are relatively expensive, almost all of the landowning householders in Rusembilan have one or more head. Maintenance is no problem, as the cattle are allowed to forage freely except in vegetable gardens, which are usually kept fenced. Young boys and old men take the cattle out of the village in the morning to an area suitable for pasture and return for them in the evening. Water buffalo are never used for plowing in this area as it is said they plow too deeply. Plowing is almost always done by men, although there is one instance in Rusembilan of a widow who supports her family by share cropping and does her own plowing. The first plowing is with the *nanga* (from *nanggal*, shaft of a plow) or steel-bladed plow. The blade is wedged into a curved piece of wood which is mounted on a vertical shaft so that the blade is at approximately a 110-degree angle to the shaft. The shaft, which also serves as the guiding handle, is attached at right angles to another shaft leading to the plow animal. Poles are joined by means of holes or notches and tied together. The yoke is tied to the crossbar near the forward end of the plow shaft; the two prongs fit in front of the animal's hump. (See Figure 5.) Plowing is usually done in the early morning between seven and nine and only occasionally between five and seven in the evening. Ordinarily it takes a man two or three days to a week to break the soil in his fields. After the heavy plowing and just before planting the seed, the field is again plowed with a *gurah*. This is little more than a heavy rake and is used to break up the remaining chunks of sod. Plowing with the *gurah* rarely takes more than one morning for an average-sized field.

Immediately after plowing with the *gurah* and before the rains come, the rice seed saved from the last harvest is broadcast over the plowed field. This process takes only a few minutes, including the time spent in thinning out some of the spots where the seed fell too thickly. The seeding is done by both men and

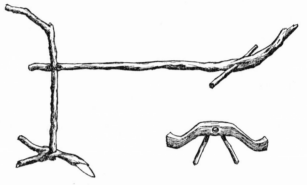

Figure 5. Plow (*nanga*).

women. After the rains have come and flooded the fields and the young rice plants have grown to six inches or so, they must be transplanted or thinned and transplanted. Other fields have been prepared between the time of seeding and transplanting. With a group of ten to fifteen people working, all the rice plants from one seeding bed can be transplanted in about three days, although the period of labor is to some degree limited to the cooler portions of the day. According to the villagers, transplanting the seedlings not only acts to save the plants thinned out of the original field, but also increases the yield of those moved. Inez Adams agrees that transplanting increases the yield per acre: "The seedling develops new grain-bearing tillers when it is transplanted." [3]

[3] Inez Adams, "Rice Cultivation in Asia," *American Anthropologist,* 50:286, 1948.

Between transplanting and harvesting, the villagers do nothing to maintain their fields. Weeding is largely unnecessary as the padi fields are covered by four or more inches of water, and birds which might feed upon the ripening grain are discouraged by the rain that falls during most of the day. In the same article, Inez Adams summarizes the similar farming techniques of the Malays of Kelantan:

In the district of Kelantan, "dry-land" nurseries are used for "wet padi." The site is plowed and harrowed twice, the seed broadcast thinly and harrowed in. Usually the single transplanting takes place forty days later, though adverse weather conditions may delay it as much as three months. The main fields cannot be cultivated until the July rains soften the soil. Preparation of the land and planting proceed from then until November. . . . The transplanted rice crop is drained if there is an excess of rain. The crop is not weeded.[4]

After the rains have stopped, the then mature rice must be harvested. This is a long-drawn-out operation, and the average family tends to put it off for almost any reason. Large landholders and those working on another's land are more conscientious, but still require two or three weeks to harvest the entire crop. The stalks are cut just below the rice-bearing tassels with a special knife blade, which is held perpendicular to the palm of the hand. The catching and cutting of a stalk are done in one motion by squeezing it against the blade. The cut rice is tied into bundles of about the equivalent of two quarts of winnowed but unmilled rice. The average-sized field will produce between seventy and eighty quarts of rice, though the yield ranges from about twenty-five quarts to over two hundred fifty. The bundles are taken home whenever the harvester leaves the field. There they can be stored either in a special granary or in a corner of the kitchen to keep them from marauding animals and thieves. About 5 per cent of the harvested rice is saved for

[4] *Ibid.*, p. 271.

seeding the fields in the next season. After a field has been harvested, the stalks are either left standing for cattle to feed upon or cut and sold to the nearby government quarantine station to be used as fodder for the buffalo kept there.

Winnowing is done, at almost any time before the rice is needed, by women using wide shallow trays. The winnowed rice is heaped on a cowskin and later collected in five-gallon kerosene tins. Milling used to be done by the villagers at Rusembilan, and a few of the old mills can still be seen under some of the houses. Now all the winnowed grain is taken to a privately owned rice mill at Pakhago, a settlement at the junction of the road to Rusembilan and the highway into Pattani. It costs one baht (5 cents) to have one kerosene tin of rice milled.

The villagers claim that it takes about two hundred quarts of milled rice to maintain a small family at a level at which they are able to work efficiently. The largest and most productive family holdings would just about satisfy this requirement, as there is about a 10 per cent loss in volume when the rice is milled. But because the larger holdings almost always belong to large families, deficiency in rice production is practically universal for the families of the community. With rising prices in the south of Thailand, rice now costs six and a half baht (32½ cents) per quart, so that the average family must spend about six hundred fifty baht ($32.50) annually to make up its rice deficit.

Plantation Economy—Coconuts and Rubber

Table 4 indicates the amount of land in the community of Rusembilan used for the growing of coconuts. It is roughly one-third more than the land used for growing rice, as the greater part of the padi and coconut land is planted in the latter. Approximately four-fifths of this coconut land, however, is owned by people not residing in the village of Rusembilan. One hundred sixty-eight acres out of approximately 265 acres owned by nonresidents for plantations is held in two plots by one Thai.

The remaining ninety-seven acres are owned in various small plots mostly by Thais and Chinese from Pattani, but also by some Malays from neighboring villages. There are about forty village families owning plantation land, with an average holding of about one and one-quarter acres.[5] On this they support from one hundred to three hundred coconut palms. There is very little interest in starting new plantations, although many villagers have land which is suitable for coconuts but not for rice. The reason given for this is that, whereas a tree will bear fruit in three years, a salable yield cannot be obtained for many years. A few far-sighted villagers, however, have since 1945 started extensive plantations for the benefit of their children.

In the case of the nonresident plantation owners, villagers are hired to pick the ripe coconuts and deliver them to the dealer in Pattani for processing into copra. The usual payment for this is one-third of the proceeds as well as any green coconuts the caretaker of the plantation may wish. In actuality, any villager who does not have access to other coconut trees will usually help himself to green coconuts from the trees of nonresident owners.

The owner of the largest plantation, mentioned above, has built a substantial house on the plantation for the caretaker and given a guarantee that if the plantation is sold the caretaker will take title to the house and the immediately surrounding land. The usual arrangement on coconuts obtains here also. The total proceeds from the sale of his coconuts is only six or seven thousand baht ($300–$350) annually, because the caretaker is apt to neglect his duties during the fishing season and because the nuts are sold whole rather than as copra. This landowner has also allowed the widowed sister of the caretaker to build a compound in part of the plantation farther away from the village

[5] Compare the average Malayan coconut small holding of about ten acres (Ungku Abdul Aziz, *Some Aspects of the Malayan Rural Economy Related to Measures for Mobilizing Rural Savings*, p. 11).

with the understanding that her son is to watch over that end of the property. No payment is made for this service other than the use of the land for the houses, except that the family is allowed to use all the green coconuts it needs.

Aside from the domestic uses of green coconut and the occasional ceremonial use of ripe coconut, usually collected from family trees growing sporadically along the beach or from a family's plantation, the villagers grow coconuts for sale as copra. There is one man in the village and one man in the hamlet Kampong Baru who own monkeys that are sent up the trees to pick the coconuts. Training such a monkey, male or female, requires about two months. The animal is taught to go up a tree at a given command and to kick down all the ripened coconuts. If green coconuts are desired, the handler will give the command "Muda-muda" (young), and the monkey will obey. The monkeys are generally bought fully trained from Kedah in Malaya or Bandon farther north in Thailand. The price will range from seven hundred baht ($35) for the Thai monkeys to twelve hundred baht ($60) for the best from Kedah. A well-trained monkey can pick about four hundred coconuts in a day—unless there are biting ants in the trees. The handler is paid eight baht (40 cents) for every hundred coconuts his monkey picks, and he is kept occupied throughout most of the year.

Village plantation owners try to have the nuts picked from each tree about once every month and a half, during which interval five or six coconuts will have ripened. On a plantation of two hundred trees, this produces a crop of about eleven hundred coconuts eight times a year. At the selling rate of fifty baht ($2.50) per hundred shelled and dried coconuts, this would amount to an annual income of about forty-four hundred baht ($220). To extract the meat for copra, the unhusked coconut is split open. Most of the year the split halves are simply spread in the sun to dry, but during the rainy season they must be placed on racks over a fire pit. After a day or two of drying, the meat can be pried out of the shell quite easily and is collected in burlap or woven marsh-grass sacks to be taken to the copra dealers in Pattani. Several years ago, some of the larger plantation owners hired women from other villages to husk the coconuts before splitting and drying at a price of thirty baht ($1.50) per thousand. This was because the husked shell is excellent as a cooking fuel, giving a long, clean, intense heat. At present, the shells and husks are used only to keep the daylong fires going under the dye-boiling pots for nets or to burn as smudges for keeping mosquitoes from the cattle during the rainy season.

Because people feel that making even a supplementary living by cultivating rice is becoming increasingly difficult and because they are discouraged by the relatively poor *kembong* seasons of the past few years, more and more are investing what capital they can in tracts of jungle land suitable for growing rubber. As buying land outside of the village is a new experience for the villagers of Rusembilan, there have been a certain amount of confusion and misunderstanding in regard to it and a small amount of shady dealing on the part of outside interests. The two usual methods of acquiring land are by taking title on paying up the defaulted taxes due on another's land, making sure the tax records in the district office reflect that fact as well as the transfer in ownership, or by claiming and paying for government land as it is made available for sale. The first method is difficult because most villagers are loath to appear at the district office for any reason at all—they are unable to read, or even speak, the Thai language, and they feel that they are not always treated as equals by the Thai officials. The second method presents similar problems, in that all land now being made available is in Yala province, and a resident from outside the particular district in Yala must obtain a letter from his own district officer certifying that there is no available government land in his home district. According to village reports, the average price paid for an acre of the government land is approximately one thousand baht ($50).[6] Land obtained through payment of back taxes is considerably cheaper. This land is bought with the private savings of an individual purchaser or with collective savings if it is a group enterprise; it may be financed by loans from several villagers who will be given proportional shares of the proceeds or by a loan from a single villager who will receive 50 per cent of the proceeds until such time as the owner pays back the initial investment. No interest is paid on these loans, and, so far, capital has always been available in the village without going to money-lenders in Pattani or Yala.

A total of twenty-six men from Rusembilan already have rubber land or were in the process of obtaining it in September 1956. The size of the present holdings ranges from about three to twenty acres, though some of the new estates may be as small as one acre.[7] Many other men from the village who do not have access to capital to invest in land go off for part of the year to work on the holdings of friends or relatives for a share of their proceeds or for wages on larger commercial estates.

Malaria is frequently contracted in the jungles, and up to half of the time a man is at his estate, he may be too weak to do any work. The villagers blame the cold mountain water for the disease and ordinarily treat it only with aspirin. If a man remains healthy, he is able to clear from one and a half to two acres of jungle in a month, and as he goes along, he will plant rubber saplings at about six-foot intervals. A rubber tree requires seven years to mature before it is ready for tapping, and it is the usual

[6] See James C. Ingram, *Economic Change in Thailand since 1850*, p. 210, and John E. deYoung, *Village Life in Modern Thailand*, pp. 185 ff.

[7] According to P. T. Bauer (*Report on a Visit to Rubber Growing Smallholdings of Malaya*, p. 9), "holdings up to about six to 10 acres each can be tapped by a family without recourse to outside labour." Average peasant holdings are given as from three to five acres by the *Area Handbook on Malaya* (Chester F. Roberts, Jr., ed., p. 428) and as about two and one-half acres for 99 per cent of Malayan small holdings by the Malayan Deputy Registrar-General of Statistics in 1931 (quoted in disagreement by Bauer, *op. cit.*, p. 8).

practice to plant vegetable crops between the saplings during the waiting period (see "Garden Crops," below). Occasionally a man buys and clears rubber land not for the purpose of growing rubber trees himself, but in order to resell the cleared land at a profit. A tract of cleared land suitable for rubber production brings approximately twice as much as uncleared jungle.

Although none of the rubber estates belonging to the villagers of Rusembilan is as yet producing rubber, the villagers are acutely aware of the fluctuations of the rubber prices. Before 1954, when many of the estates were started, the latex brought quite consistently twenty-five or twenty-six baht ($1.25–$1.30) per kilogram. During this period loans of ten to twenty thousand baht ($500–$1,000) were available on a villager's word alone. In the summer of 1954, the price dropped to six baht (30 cents) per kilogram.[8] Credit was almost impossible to obtain, and loans due at this time rarely could be repaid, often resulting in violence by one party or the other. Since 1954, the price has climbed slowly until at present it fluctuates between ten and eleven baht (50–55 cents) per kilogram. Laborers are paid according to the amount of rubber they tap, the rate being approximately half the market price of latex. As a laborer can tap only from five to seven kilograms a day and as he requires about twenty-five baht ($1.25) a day to live from labor alone, he probably would not work for large estates if prices, and thus wages, were to drop much below this point. The villagers of Rusembilan are sure that because of this situation the large estate owners will somehow be able to maintain the market price at the present level at least. Thus, they are working on their present holdings confidently, and more and more people are investing in new land whereas in the past they might have invested in new fishing boats or coconut plantations.

[8] Ingram, *op. cit.*, pp. 105, 226, indicates that prices in 1951 were approximately fifteen baht per kilo, whereas in 1953 they had fallen to five baht per kilo.

Garden Crops

In general, the people of Rusembilan have little interest in raising garden crops, preferring to buy what they need in the markets. Often, if a man does raise some crops other than rice, such as a fruit or a nut, he thinks of it as a plantation crop to be sold rather than for his own consumption, although he may have only one tree. In the case of coconuts, however, whether a man has one tree or a large plantation, his family will make free use of green coconuts for domestic purposes. Whenever the mashed meat of the green coconut is needed for cooking a curry, and this is almost every day, the wife of the plantation owner will simply request someone to climb one of the trees and collect whatever nut she may want.

Aside from the coconut, there are four crop-bearing trees of some importance in the village. One species of mango is grown in the village, though it is not very plentiful, and its fruit is considered a great delicacy. While the mangoes are ripe on the village trees or available in the market, hardly a child can be seen who is not sucking on a mango stone practically all day long. The fruit of the *sawahnillo* tree ripens in June or July. This is a soft, caramelly fruit with a rough brown skin like a potato. *Sawahnillo* trees are generally owned by less well-to-do persons, frequently widows, and the fruits are carried about the village in baskets to be sold at an average price of seven for one baht (5 cents). Papayas (*bete*) ripen in January and February and are eaten by the family who owns the trees. There is little interest among the Malay villagers in buying or selling papayas, although they are in great demand among Thais and the Europeans in Bangkok and the Malayan cities. The *jambu ketiri* (*Anacardium occidentale*),[9] though relatively rare in the village, is of considerable importance. In January and February it produces a round gray nut which is inedible but which is

[9] R. J. Wilkinson, *A Malay-English Dictionary*, I, 441.

collected by women and children and used as markers and counters in their games. From June through August the fruit of the tree is ripe. It is a bitter, firm-fleshed fruit related to the guava and important to the diet of the people as a fruit eaten whole or cut up with curries. Attached to the bottom of this fruit is the cashew nut, which is roasted to dry the nut and remove the bitter, toxic oil and is then sold to dealers in Pattani for shipment to Songkhla and Bangkok. One or two families have a few banana trees by their houses and use the fruit when in season as between-meal snacks.

As the cattle are allowed to wander about the village almost at will, one of the problems concerned with growing garden crops is that most plants must be protected by fencing or they cannot be grown at all. There are three crops, however, which the cattle will not bother, and these are grown on a small scale by about one-tenth of the village households. Such plants are never sold, but are used only to supplement the family diet. The most common is *ubi keladi,* a form of taro. Both the leaves and the tubers are eaten. One man in the village grows this in relatively great quantity, planting root cuttings in one bed, cultivating and manuring it, and later transplanting the young plants to another area. Pineapple (*nanas*) grows wild or is planted in otherwise unusable land bordering the village and along the dikes of some of the more peripheral padi fields. A few people plant *kache miong* or okra.

There are about a dozen men in Rusembilan who go to the trouble of erecting fences around fields in order to grow other crops. Because of the demand for these by the villagers who do not grow them, it is not uncommon to see even a padi field fenced off and planted in crops other than rice. The most common crop so planted is *ubi kayu* (literally, woody tuber) or sweet manioc. These are started in April in a small bed, usually near the house of the cultivator, and from this plot he takes a small number of the tubers for the use of his family and for replanting next year. The others he transplants to a large field in June or July and harvests them in early October. In other fenced plots, usually in the sandy soil along the beach to the west of the village, are grown *labu* or muskmelon and *timun China*, the common round watermelon.

Often, during slack periods in the fishing or agricultural cycle, the men of Rusembilan go inland to work on rubber plantations. While clearing the jungle or planting rubber trees, they sustain themselves by using wild foods extensively and by raising garden crops which either mature rapidly or which can be left safely from one visit to the next. Several men of the village have given up padi farming altogether and spend the entire monsoon season in the jungle, using their land for extensive gardens until the rubber trees grow up sufficiently to shade the ground. Pineapples, muskmelons, and *ubi kayu* are the favored crops. The practice of planting *padi omo*, or dry rice, on newly cleared ground is increasing. As this crop will produce only one good harvest on a plot of the thin jungle soil, the plantation owner will cut and burn the cover on just the amount of land he will be able to plant in rubber the next year and, without plowing, plant the rice grains in holes punched in the ground. He will then start planting rubber saplings and perhaps other vegetable crops on the land from which in the previous year he harvested his last crop of rice, and so on each year until he has exhausted his jungle holdings and is ready to tap his first rubber trees.

Wild Products

A variety of wild products is collected and used by the villagers at Rusembilan. Some are simply collected from their wild state when needed, no attempt being made to domesticate them. Others are by-products of commercial or garden crops, particularly the coconut palm. Various palm trees provide the villagers with many products they have come to rely upon. The coconut, as well as providing the coconut meat for copra and domestic use, supplies fibers which are twisted and braided into ropes and lines. Ropemaking is a commercial enterprise of importance in some of the neighboring villages, but at Rusembilan rope is either bought or made for personal use only. The husks and shells of the coconut, as has been mentioned above, are used for fuel. The leaves stripped from the stalk of the frond are used when green to make a low-grade atap or thatching; when dry they are fed to cattle during the monsoon season. The stalks themselves serve for a variety of temporary construction uses, notably fence posts. The young leaves of the nipa palm (*pohon nipah*) are stripped of their integumental covering and used as cigarette "papers" for the local tobacco. These cigarettes, though not as popular as commercial ones, are used on ceremonial and formal social occasions as well as in periods of economic hardship. The older leaves of the nipa palm are folded and sewn into sections to provide the best-quality atap. The fruit and young shoots of this palm are frequently eaten. The fruit of the palmyra palm (*pohon tal*) is considered a great delicacy and when in season is sought avidly. It is eaten with ice and sweetened with condensed milk. The palmyra also supplies an abundant quantity of clear sweet sap which is boiled down into sugar (*degan*). This is put into cylindrical molds three or four inches in diameter and about half an inch high and sold in the market at about five for a baht (5 cents). Rural Thais in the area, as well as in other parts of Thailand, ferment this sap into a palm toddy.

Roots and bark from various trees and shrubs are used for medicinal purposes (see Chapter X). Certain kinds of bark are also collected and used for dyeing nets and clothing. Wood for building is frequently collected from the jungle, different kinds being suitable for different jobs. These timbers are either used unworked with the bark removed as house posts or pole frameworks or else hewn into interior beams. Planking is never made in the village, but bought from the lumberyards in Pattani.

Coconut logs are considered to be excellent for house posts and for beams because of their great strength and resistance to rot, although their heavy grain prevents them from being hewn straight. The almost universal fuel in Rusembilan is *kayu batu* (literally, rock wood) or mangrove which is collected from the profuse growth just to the west of the village and allowed to dry in piles before being brought into the houses. Bamboo is often collected from the jungle. It is used for spars on the fishing boats, net-drying racks, poles for simply-constructed houses, and a variety of other purposes. Split, it is woven into flat sections used as inexpensive house siding. Rattan is also collected and used for many purposes in the village.

Fishermen, when they are unable to find *kembong*, sometimes wait till morning rather than come back to the village empty-handed and land at some distant beach to see what they can collect. Such parties may find various kinds of clams, conchs, and buried sea-turtle eggs, all of which can be sold in the market. They may also collect usable timbers washed up on the beach or a kind of edible sea grass which they call *sarang* and which is found growing in shallow tidal pools.

Many grasses and plant parts were used extensively as food during the Japanese occupation in the war, as padi fields were destroyed or taken over for Japanese use and other food was scarce and expensive. These are still remembered, but use is no longer made of any of them except a fleshy multileaved herb called *sepang* which grows abundantly on low, damp, salty soil. The pleasantly sour-tasting leaves are enjoyed boiled and served in curries.

Domestic Animals

Aside from cattle for plowing, discussed above, no domesticated animal is of much economic importance in Rusembilan. One man, living in the hamlet of Kampong Surau, pastures three or four bulls owned by a Thai in Pattani who enters them in the weekly bullfights. A few villagers also keep bulls for stud purposes, though ordinarily a male is castrated when he is about a year old. Two or three older men who no longer go out fishing are occasionally paid by the government quarantine station near the village to tend and water any buffalo quarantined for shipment out of the country.

Perhaps twenty families in the village own a few sheep. The sheep are allowed to wander about the village as they will, and the owner is frequently unable to tell his sheep from another's after the animal has been away for a few days. Sheep are kept only to be eaten, particularly on ceremonial occasions. To purchase a mature sheep for slaughter costs about two hundred baht ($10). One or two families keep goats as well as sheep which are also used only for meat and, like cows, are never milked.

Most families keep a few chickens and sell the eggs. Each year during the monsoon season, there is an epidemic which wipes out almost all the chickens in the village, and the people must either buy or get from the jungle new fowl to replace them. When a chicken dies, whatever the cause, it is eaten. Otherwise they are killed and eaten when egg production begins to fall off or whenever one is required for a special occasion. Ducks and geese are kept by a few families; unlike chickens, however, these must be fed. The ducks produce more eggs, but their market price is lower than chicken eggs. Wild birds are occasionally shot for food by boys with slingshots and clay pellets.

Dogs are never kept in the village; a wet dog is considered unclean, and anyone who touches it must be cleansed with ritually purified water as well as washed thoroughly with ordinary water. Cats are abundant, those with stubbed and crooked tails being favored, as it is said that straight-tailed cats will steal fish. Monkeys when they reach the age of about seven years are retired from coconut picking and may be kept as pets or let loose to live in and around the village.

The keeping of songbirds is a favorite pastime among many

of the men of Rusembilan. The birds are pampered, fed various kinds of oil, and hung in their cages on poles up to fifty feet high in order to improve the quality and volume of their singing. The most valuable type of bird is a variety of dove, bought for between one and two thousand baht ($50–$100) each. These doves are entered in periodic singing contests about the area. One bird from Rusembilan has taken a first prize and several seconds in these contests. A larger variety of dove is thought able to protect the house of its owner from fire, although not many are kept at Rusembilan for that purpose. One of these doves costs one hundred baht ($5). Quite common in the village, and among the Thai population in Pattani too, is a brightly colored bird local to the area. This is called by the Malays *mengabo* and in English simply "Pattani bird."

CHAPTER VI

Trade and Commerce

THE commercial activities most important to the total economy of Rusembilan have been discussed in sections on fishing and plantations. There remain, however, several areas of trade and commerce within the community and between the community and the outside world which are of importance, if not to the whole village at least to that group of people who engage in them often to the exclusion of more typical occupations. With the growth of the money market, which has always been more important in the south than in the central region of Thailand,[1] buying and selling and the accumulation of capital have assumed increasingly significant roles in the economy of Rusembilan and similar communities. Shortly before World War II, with the price of the baht rated at approximately 2.60 per U.S. dollar,[2] money was relatively scarce in the southern villages, and the

[1] Although this statement is contradicted by the figures given in Carle C. Zimmerman, *Siam: Rural Economic Survey, 1930–31*, p. 58, it was the impression gained by the author in talking to educated Malays and Thais in the southern area and to government officials in Bangkok.

[2] James C. Ingram, *Economic Change in Thailand since 1850*, pp. 149–174.

majority of families were able to satisfy almost all their needs by what they could produce themselves or obtain by barter. During and directly after the war, self-sufficiency became difficult if not impossible in most places because of damage to padi fields, coconut plantations, and fishing equipment and the enforced sales of fish and agricultural produce to the Japanese occupation forces. During the occupation, the value of the baht was artificially maintained near its prewar level, and this factor tended to drive products of other than local origin from the local markets.[3] After the war, the baht was put on the open market and has stabilized itself at around twenty to the dollar, with only slight fluctuations.[4]

Prices in the Pattani area more than compensated for the devaluation of the baht, with the result that Rusembilan, being able to sell more than it had to buy, was in the position of having a surplus of currency. A small group of families who had accumulated liquid capital before the war and had seen it virtually disappear with devaluation led the movement to invest a part of the community's increasing reserves in land and in new buildings and equipment.

With the greater availability of money in the village and the decrease in rice production, as well as a real or imagined fall-off in the supply of fish in nearby waters, more and more of the residents of Rusembilan are slowly turning from a predominantly subsistence-type economy to one wholly dependent upon money and the world market. Such a change cannot take place without having effects on, and introducing concomitant changes into, the structure of the society where it is taking place. The changes in the social structure resulting from such economic factors will be discussed more fully in Chapter XIII; the present chapter will deal with their manifestations in the economy of Rusembilan.

[3] *Ibid.*, pp. 163 ff.   [4] *Ibid.*, pp. 149–174.

Local Enterprises

Outstanding among the nonfishing and agricultural occupations in Rusembilan is the coffee shop (*kedai kopi*). Perhaps more important to the community than its function of selling coffee, tea, cigarettes, and other domestic necessities is the social role of the coffee shop. It is a gathering place for men and, at certain times of the day, for women. The coffee shops along the beach may be thought of as focal points of the community, to and from which individuals radiate according to the demands of activities elsewhere. Before the war, there were no coffee shops in Rusembilan, but shortly afterwards one of the villagers whose father was running a shop in the Pattani municipal area decided to open one. The shop was an immediate success. Since that time, quite a few other individuals have tried their hand at running coffee shops. Many have failed, and some have given up because they did not like the job. In 1956, there were three shops on the beach and one across from the schoolhouse on the village road to Pattani. During that summer, a fourth shop was built and opened on the beach.

In keeping with their social nature, the most important part of a coffee shop's business is selling hot tea with sugar and sweetened condensed milk or, less frequently, coffee. Two of the shops sell noncarbonated bottled fruit drinks, and another sells *ayer batu*, a glass filled with shaved ice over which is poured a sweet colored syrup. Aside from the refreshments served in the coffee shops, a variety of goods is also carried such as cigarettes and cigarette-making equipment, pencils, paper, wire, rope, nails, a few simple tools, cakes, sweets, and an assortment of local vegetables not likely to spoil. On the average, during good fishing periods, a coffee shop grosses from eighty to one hundred baht ($4-$5) per day, and most of the owners agree that their usual monthly profit is between two and three hundred baht ($10–$15). To supplement this income, two of the coffee-shop owners are members of boat groups during the *kembong* season, a third plants rice and is occasionally employed as a carpenter by other villagers, and the fourth is steerer of a *kolek,* holds the village office of *selawat* (see Chapter VII), and dabbles in other enterprises such as making concrete blocks on which to rest house posts and preparing and marketing cashew nuts.

Before the war, the villagers say, there was little business for the coffee shops. The men would rarely eat or drink anything before noon. Now they have "learned" to eat and drink during the morning, and these hours are the busiest for the coffee shops. When the fishing boats return to the village in the morning, the men will spread the nets to dry and then go to the coffee shops. One man may not frequent the same shop, or for that matter any shop, every morning. Generally, half a dozen older men tend to congregate regularly in each of the shops, whereas the younger men may be seen in any one of them. Unless there is work to be done, the older men will sit talking in the shops or on shaded platforms outside from about eight in the morning till noon. The younger men may stop for an hour or more, but rarely stay for the whole morning. Depending on how prosperous they feel, the men may have one or two glasses of tea and some cakes, or none at all. Tobacco and nipa palm leaves are always at the disposal of the guests, though they may buy commercial cigarettes singly. Much of the village business is accomplished at the coffee shops, as they are the only real assembly points in the village. Frequently in the afternoons, while the fishermen are sleeping, the coffee shops will be tended by the wives of the owners, and women with their children will gather there. Because the women's work is more continuous than the men's, they rarely remain at a coffee shop more than a half hour, and it is uncommon to see more than six women at a coffee shop at any one time.

Four or five people in Rusembilan make a business of preparing *belachan*, a salty paste made from the smallest shrimp (*udang belachan*). This paste is highly esteemed by both Malays and Thais and is used liberally in and with most of the foods they eat. The villagers engaged in this enterprise usually catch their own shrimp to use for the paste, though it requires a long time to accumulate enough shrimp to make up one picul (between 123 and 143 pounds) of *belachan*. One man, the steerer of one of the two most successful *kolek*, cannot devote the time necessary to catching the *udang belachan* and purchases them in large quantity once a month from dealers in Pattani. Although his profit is less because of buying the shrimp, his volume of sale of the finished *belachan* is great enough so that his net returns are probably not much smaller than those of men who provide their own shrimp. In the preparation of *belachan*, the whole, unshelled shrimp are allowed to soak in a saturated brine solution for three or four days, after which they are dried in the sun (or over fires during the rainy season) for a day or two. When the preparation is thoroughly dried, it is beaten with a wooden mallet until of uniform consistency. In spite of the drying, some moisture is retained, and the resulting product is more of a very dry paste than a powder. Now the *belachan* may be sold, or it may be salted and stored in jars until the manufacturer accumulates a large quantity or until the market price reaches its seasonal high near the end of the monsoon period. The stored *belachan* must be dried and pounded again before it is ready for sale. Although *belachan* is handled by the dealers in Pattani, all the manufacturers in Rusembilan prefer to transport their product some hundred miles by train and bus to Songkhla, where they can obtain higher prices than in Pattani. For small quantities of *belachan* the manufacturer generally is paid about four baht (20 cents) per kilogram, whereas if he accumulates a large quantity toward the higher market, he may get as much as four hundred baht ($20) per picul, or almost double the price paid on the small lot.

Transportation to and from Rusembilan has long been a favorite topic of discussion in the coffee shops. Each morning when the women have distributed the fish, they must get themselves and their loads to the Pattani market. Before the summer of 1956, except for one brief period, they walked the mile and a half on the village road to where it meets the main road into Pattani and there they could hire a trishaw, a three-wheeled cycle rickshaw, to take them the rest of the way to market. In 1954, a man from Pattani started running a bus into Rusembilan twice a day. The villagers, particularly the women, were happy to pay the fare of five baht (25 cents) per person and five baht for each bundle taken to market, as ten baht (50 cents) was the standard price paid to another woman to take one's basket of two hundred fish to the market before institution of the bus service. Although the bus owner undertook to maintain the village road and repair the three bridges, the service was stopped by the *kamnan*, the official village headman, within three months of its inception on the grounds that the bus was damaging the road. The villagers discount this reason and claim that the service was stopped because of a petition from the trishaw drivers to the district officer charging that the bus route had badly cut into their business.

In July 1956, a man who had just moved into Rusembilan bought a secondhand bus in Yala for twenty-nine thousand baht ($1,450) and started running between Rusembilan and Pattani. By September, no objection had come from the *kamnan* or district officer to the running of the bus. Fares were the same as they had been on the 1954 bus route. Because at the time this bus service was started the *kembong* were extremely scarce, the bus owner occasionally used the bus on a chartered basis, taking groups of people from Rusembilan and other villages to feasts or ceremonies in the area, or he waited in Pattani after the morning trip from Rusembilan to see if he could find a group of people wanting to go somewhere. During the periods when there were sizable catches of *kembong*, trips would be made from Rusembilan to Pattani and return as soon as there were enough people to fill the bus. With a full bus, the owner calculated that he could net between fifty and seventy-five baht ($2.50–$3.75) per round trip, making perhaps five round trips when "business was good." Aside from the bus, the transportation facilities of Rusembilan included six bicycles at the time of this study.

The few village businesses not already discussed are carried on only in a very limited way. The people concerned in these enterprises generally wait until there is a specific demand for their goods or services before devoting any time or energy to them. None of these is the full-time occupation of the entrepreneur, but is simply a means of occasionally supplementing income. The father-in-law of the imam buys *kembong* nets in Pattani, "rigs" them, and then sells them in the village, as mentioned in Chapter IV. Another man in the village buys low-grade iron bars in the market and casts net sinkers in the sand. These he uses on his own nets and sells to whoever may want sinkers. When a house is to be built, the *selawat* is called to mold concrete foundation blocks to go under the house posts. He has constructed three molds, each with a different Islamic design, and the housebuilder can have his choice. Another man in the village is very skillful at cutting out fancy wooden scroll panels which are placed between the tops of doors or windows and the eaves of the roof. These scrolls are cut out on what is apparently a unique invention of Rusembilan. This is a jig saw consisting of a long bamboo pole anchored at one end to the ground and at its midpoint to a tree so that it slopes up at about a thirty-degree angle. To the upper end of this is attached by wire a hack-saw blade, and below it, attached by another wire, is a foot pedal. The operator sits on a bench and works the saw up and down by a coaction of foot pressure and the spring of the bamboo pole. The work is held on a table through which the saw blade can pass.

One of the coffee shop owners and the wife of another one have recently acquired sewing machines. The woman is kept busy sewing sarongs for other women into the tubular form in which they are worn. She is also in demand to make women's blouses and to sew up funeral clothes whenever a person dies. The coffee shop owner decided in April 1955 that it might be a profitable business to make shirts for the men in the village. With a little experimentation, he learned how to make sturdy and good-looking shirts, and a year later had a backlog of forty orders for various types of shirts, each to be sold for twenty baht ($1).

Markets

To the villagers of Rusembilan the town of Pattani meant the market, and market meant Pattani. Thus, the word Pattani was almost never used, but rather *kedai*, meaning market. Except when there was a fun fair or carnival or when taxes were to be paid at the district office, the villager had no reason to go to Pattani other than to buy or sell goods. The market itself is a large, square, concrete structure covered with a multigabled, corrugated iron roof. Beyond the main structure on each side are rows of covered stalls, extensions of the selling space inside. In and around this market is sold all the meat, fish, and fruit and vegetable produce that comes into the town daily, as well as a great deal of nonperishable foodstuffs, dry goods, hardware, and so on. Surrounding the market and along the streets in Pattani are small shops, most of them run by Chinese but some by Malays and a few by Indians, each one of which sells a multitude of nonperishable products, some specializing more in one type of goods rather than another, but many apparently trying to sell everything that might be wanted. Scattered among these shops are the branches of three Bangkok banks, three gas stations, and perhaps half a dozen large importing firms. On the other side of the river from the business section of the town are the offices of the governor and other provincial officials, the district office, the hospital, the post and telegraph office, and, farther out from town, the customhouse. Until very recently, the Malay villager had nothing to do with any of these institutions except the district office, but confined his activities to the market itself or the small shops and Moslem restaurants of the town.

The women from Rusembilan generally sell their fish directly to wholesalers beside the market, but occasionally retail small quantities from their baskets while squatting on the pavement at the foot of one of the rows of market stalls. Women from other Malay and Thai villages rent stalls from the municipality and sit with their produce displayed above the ground level of the aisles. The Rusembilan women prefer not to rent stalls because of the uncertain nature of their daily supply of fish and the fact that they can frequently sell it to the wholesalers at a price higher than that established by the fish sellers in the market and also because by selling the whole lot at once they can get back to the village to carry on their daily activities there. After selling her fish, a woman will wander about the market bargaining for whatever she wants in the way of items not produced in the village. Before any of the major Moslem feast days, men as well as women are crowded around all the stalls and shops buying new sarongs. Everyone tries to have new clothes to wear for such festive occasions. The less well-to-do families will buy Thai or Japanese printed sarongs ranging in price from ten to forty baht (50 cents to $2); the more prosperous will buy the Indonesian batiks costing from sixty to one hundred twenty baht ($3–$6) or more.

In the Pattani area, on each day of the week a special one-day market is held which rotates among the towns. Thursday the market is in Pattani. This weekly market lasts only half a day and is not particularly large in spite of the fact that Pattani is the most important town in the area. Smaller towns in the region regularly hold larger and longer weekly markets be-

cause they lack the permanent market center of Pattani and because the weekly market must provide most of the supplies for
that community and its surrounding area for the whole week.
In Pattani, the Thursday Market rarely sells anything which
cannot be bought in the regular market for the same price, but
nevertheless it is considered an important event of the week.
Women from Rusembilan dress in their best clothes and are
apt to stay the whole morning. They do not try to sell their
fish in this market, nor do they buy more here than they
would other days in the main market. Thursday Market is
mainly a festive, social occasion on which women from different villages can congregate once a week and gossip. Occasionally, individuals from Rusembilan will travel to one of the
other nearby weekly markets, particularly when they desire
to purchase some product peculiar to or cheaper in that neigh-
borhood. Thus, if a coffee shop owner needs to replenish his
supply of nipa palm leaves for rolling cigarettes, he will try
to get to the Wednesday Market at Naperdu, where the leaves
are better and less expensive.

Working for Wages

Each year a large group of men from Rusembilan leaves the
community during the monsoon season to get temporary employment elsewhere. They reason that there is no fishing to
be done at that time of year and little else to do, so it is better
that they are away earning money rather than staying idle in
the village and consuming their families' food. Approximately
fifteen men go annually to Kedah state in Malaya to harvest
rice. Because the rains on the west coast of the peninsula come
earlier than on the east, the rice in that area is ready to be
harvested while the plants are still maturing at Rusembilan.
During this period, the Malayan immigration restrictions are
relaxed in order to attract additional labor from Thailand.
Villagers from Rusembilan either go to areas in Kedah where

they have friends or relatives or else go along with friends who know people there. Agents of some of the larger rice farms wait at the Padang Besar railroad station to hire laborers when they get off the train there to obtain their temporary Malayan immigration passes. On arriving at the area where he intends to work, the man from Rusembilan must surrender his pass to the *penghulu* (headman of the village). Then, while he is working, he is supplied with uncooked rice and other food. At the end of the job, he will be given his wages for the period in cash at the rate of fifteen to twenty Malayan dollars ($5–$7) for each *relong* (a little more than one and one-quarter acres) that he has harvested. The laborers from Thailand are glad to be paid in Malayan dollars rather than in baht as they are able to buy goods in Malaya cheaper than in Thailand and they also feel that they profit by having Malayan dollars to convert at nearly the free rate in Thailand.

Occasionally, the villagers, after being admitted to Malaya to harvest rice, will take other jobs instead. To do this, they must have friends in the village where they settle so that when they surrender their passes to the *penghulu* no official questions are asked. These jobs are almost always confined to fishing and to tapping rubber. Although these jobs are not as profitable as cutting rice, the villagers from Rusembilan prefer them, and, if they think they can avoid trouble with the authorities, they will first seek a fishing job and then a job on a rubber estate. As the immigration passes are issued for a period of thirty to forty-five days only, the villager, whatever job he has taken, must return to Rusembilan at the end of that period. Many of these men would like to stay in Malaya, but they realize that to do so would require a Malayan identity card, which is not granted without a passport and semipermanent visa.

A group of men from the village will sometimes travel to Satun during the east-coast monsoon period. Satun, also a Malay fishing area, is situated on the west coast of Thailand and thus has good fishing weather during the monsoons at Rusembilan. Although the people at Satun are Malay, they speak either Thai or the Perlis dialect of Malay which is difficult for Pattani people to understand. Enough men go from Rusembilan to form a complete boat group so that they can hire a boat and work as an independent unit. On the whole, however, the men from Rusembilan are dissatified with fishing in the Satun area, both because of the linguistic difficulties and because the price of fish there is very low, as it must be transported by truck to Phattalung, the nearest point on the railroad, some sixty miles away.

Before the war, many Malays from the Pattani area, including a few from Rusembilan, owned or operated small coastwise sailing craft. These boats were used for transporting rice from the ports of southern Thailand to Kelantan and Trengganu and even to Singapore and Malacca. They would return with cloth goods and biscuits.[5] Since the war, however, this occupation has been dying out, as the local sailing boats, even when equipped with engines, cannot compete with motor launches and small ships employed by the Chinese for the same purpose.

A very small amount of wagework is done in and around the village itself. Those who share-crop on others' padi fields consider themselves to be in the wage-earning category, whereas coconut plantation caretakers do not. Two or three men in the village are regarded as master carpenters, and occasionally someone in the village who is building a house will hire one of them to do a job requiring considerable skill. One of these men is frequently called to neighboring villages to direct and work on communal projects such as the construction of a mosque. Within the community itself, this type of work is handled as a form of *corvée*, but any outside labor is paid for at the standard wage rate of about six baht (30 cents) an hour. As the villagers of Rusembilan are getting more and more money, there is an

[5] See Raymond Firth, *Malay Fishermen: Their Peasant Economy*, p. 71.

increasing tendency to hire people from the outside to do hard or menial labor for them. In three instances during the *kembong* season of 1956, villagers who desired trenches dug around their houses or vegetable gardens hired laborers to do the job rather than attempt it themselves or call in their friends and relatives.

The Handling of Money

Although many villagers still would feel safer with all their capital invested in land or gold jewelry, most have come to realize that cash is necessary for daily marketing as well as for emergencies and also is needed to keep their local industries on a competitive basis with those outside of Rusembilan. The institution of money has been accepted, but many of the related institutions, such as banking, loans, and installment buying, have not been or are only just starting to be accepted. Children are trained in the handling of money almost as soon as they are able to walk. Usually, the father will give his son a one baht (5 cent) note to carry about with him and will impress upon his mind that it is a thing of value and not to be lost or treated carelessly. Children manage to earn small sums around the village by doing odd jobs and running errands for adult villagers. Such earnings are for the children to keep, but they are enjoined to spend them with care, weighing present desires against future contingencies. Adults are also extremely cautious about their cash and the safeguarding of it. Because of their suspicion of the Chinese and particularly the Thais, they do not trust the banking facilities in Pattani and generally keep their money, sometimes as much as fifty thousand baht ($2,500), in tin boxes hidden on one of the roof beams in their houses. As this is practically universal custom among the Malays of the area, thieves and robbers have little difficulty locating valuables in any house they choose.

Until very recently, the only contacts which Rusembilan had with the large merchants and importers were in connection with minor services and the delivery of goods by these businesses to Rusembilan or on occasions when the owners and managers came with their friends and families to picnic on the beach at Rusembilan. Now, particularly in connection with the motorboats at Rusembilan, the villagers have been forced to enlist the services of businesses in the area. They have signed a contract with one oil distributor for the delivery of bulk quantities of diesel oil at regular intervals. While discussions were taking place about the fate of the motoboat with the cracked crankcase, discussed in Chapter IV, one of the largest importers in Pattani was called in as he was experienced in the economics of such matters. When it was finally decided to replace the engine, a decision arrived at by the villagers without pressure from the importer, the arrangements were made with his importing firm. Fortunately, almost all the big businessmen in Pattani are scrupulously honest and realize that the Malay population will form an increasingly large proportion of their business, so that in most cases they have learned the Malay language and take a sympathetic interest in the villagers' business problems, sometimes to the point of giving them more advantageous terms in business transactions than they would to townspeople.

Rusembilan villagers have not been so lucky in their limited business contacts with people away from the Pattani area. But on the whole, they have gained valuable experience, if not profit, from unfortunate transactions. The fact that the first motorboat purchased for Rusembilan broke down before it arrived at the village led subsequent purchasers to have their boats more thoroughly inspected and to arrange various types of warranties and service agreements with the seller. When the villagers first started acquiring land for rubber estates shortly after the war, large estate owners who had not been entitled to buy the government land that was offered to the villagers often took advantage of the villagers' ignorance about tax laws and in a few cases actually encouraged tax delinquency so that they could acquire the land upon payment of the back taxes. Practices of this nature have been harder for the Rusembilan landowners to overcome, as it requires frequent attendance at government offices and a certain knowledge of the Thai law and language. Government officials, whose assignments change every few years, are not sympathetic to the Malay villagers as are the businessmen established in Pattani and occasionally will promise some form of action just to be rid of the villager. In spite of those problems, the villagers at Rusembilan are becoming increasingly aware of their rights in land ownership and in other business matters. There were no cases of tax sales in the three years before this study was made. During 1956, one man in Rusembilan was in the process of taking over a plot of rubber land belonging to an outsider delinquent in his taxes.

Although the actualities of credit and debt are recognized in most of Southeast Asia, the Malay population in southern Thailand have managed to remain aloof from the moneylenders and more recent credit institutions. In the past, and to a large extent at present, when the villager needed capital, he would borrow it from a relative or a friend. Interest as such was never charged, though frequently the borrower felt obligated to perform many small services for his creditor. Money was generally paid back as soon as possible, and it was not lent unless the chances of repayment were very good. Occasionally, the borrower would default, starting a family feud rather than litigation of any sort. But the feuds were generally forgotten within ten or fifteen years and the debt along with them.

With the increased interest in capital investment at Rusembilan, credit must sometimes be sought in Pattani. One or two men have taken out bank loans to finance land purchases, and it is understood that the interest rate on these is approximately 8 per cent. The new engine for the first village motorboat was being paid for on very favorable installment terms. The company that supplied the engine could have charged interest at the maximum legal rate of 15 per cent, but it agreed to let the village try to have the full price paid within five months with no interest whatever. If this obligation could not be met, it was agreed that standard interest would be charged on the remainder of the debt until it was paid. If perhaps not fully aware of all the implications of a credit system, Rusembilan was nevertheless actively discussing during 1956 various village projects which would have to be financed from outside of the village and was realistically calculating the probabilities of paying back such loans from the income to be made by the project itself.

CHAPTER VII

Rusembilan as Part of
the Thai Nation

SINCE 1901, when Siamese troops were sent into the Pattani area and government officials from Bangkok took over the political functions of the Malay rajas and their staffs, Rusembilan and the other Malay villages in the south have been administered under a system found throughout Thailand. Because they were, in a sense, a conquered people and because a system of government suitable for Thai villages was imposed upon their culturally different society, the Malays tended to dislike and fear the power of the men who were sent to administer them. Although at present the villager has almost no contact with any part of the adminstrative hierarchy above his local district and relatively little at the district level, he resents what he feels to be a superior and discriminatory attitude on the part of the officials. In speaking to Thais in general, but particularly to government officials, the Malays still employ the local courtly language, *Mata-ku*, formerly used only in speaking to royalty.

During World War II, the antipathy of the Malays toward

Thais and the Thai government reached its highest point. Not
only was the capitulation of Thailand to the Japanese side unpopular with the Malay population whose sympathies lay with
the people of Malaya, but the villages in the area, particularly
Rusembilan, were exposed to harsh treatment by the Japanese
forces themselves. In preparing for the offensive against northern Malaya, Japanese forces were landed on the beach at Rusembilan. Just to the east of the village, a base camp was set up where
units were assembled to be sent inland to larger camps or directly to the combat zone. Much village property was taken or
destroyed, notably coconut trees, boats, and padi fields. During
this period, the Thai government enacted a series of legislation
which was extremely unpopular not only with the Malay population, but to a lesser extent with the rural Thai villagers
also.[1] This legislation stipulated, among other things, that all
men must wear long trousers and topees, that school children
were to be dressed in uniforms, that the chewing of betel was
to be prohibited, and that loads were not to be carried on the
head (Malay style) but must be on the shoulder (Thai style).
For a time, enforcement of these laws was carried out rigidly,
any infraction subjecting the offender to heavy fines.

    In recent years, the Thai government has become increasingly
aware of the need for legislation that takes into consideration
the different cultural, religious, and linguistic behavior of the
Malay population in southern Thailand. Projects have been
launched by the central government to build mosques in the
large population centers and to translate the standard Thai
schoolbooks into the Malay language written in Thai characters.
Other projects to control flooding and increase irrigation
areas in the south as well as to link this area more closely with
Bangkok have been started.

    [1] John E. deYoung, *Village Life in Modern Thailand*, pp. 44, 46, *et
passim.*

Local Government Organizations

Thailand is divided into seventy-one *changwat* or provinces. Each province is administered by a governor, appointed by the Minister of the Interior, and a staff of officials, subordinate to the governor, representing the other ministries of the central government.[2] Four of the southern *changwat* are predominantly Malay, with as high as 80 per cent Malay population and, in rural districts, almost 100 per cent. Pattani, Yala, and Narathiwat form a block of Malay provinces on the east coast of the peninsula; Satun, on the west coast, is separated from the other three by Changwat Songkhla. Songkhla (or Singgora) was previously largely Malay, but because of its early development as a commercial area with excellent air, sea, and rail connections to the north and south and highways to the south, it has attracted a large Chinese and Thai population, and Malays in the province have been absorbed into their patterns of life. The three provinces on the east coast are isolated from the rest of Thailand, even from Songkhla province by uninhabited jungle, whereas they are in much closer contact with Malaya, upon which all but Pattani border. There is daily a train service to and from Haad Yai in Songkhla and one through train a week to Bangkok from this area, as well as a weekly boat to Bangkok from Narathiwat, Saiburi, and Pattani. A road being built from Pattani to the main highway into Songkhla had just been opened to official traffic in 1956. There is only one main road leading from these provinces into Perak and the west coast of Malaya and one rail line leading to Kelantan on the east, but the area near the coast is continuously populated on both sides of the frontier, and the land is relatively open, unlike the fifty miles of jungle between outlying villages of Pattani and Songkhla provinces. The proximity of Malaya and the racial, linguistic, and cultural affinities

[2] *Ibid.*, p. 13.

of the people on both sides of the frontier make communication and actual physical contact far easier and more frequent than with the other provinces of Thailand.

Changwat Pattani is subdivided into eight *amphur* or districts. The district officer, appointed by the Ministry of the Interior, comes under the direct supervision of the *changwat* governor. In the administration of the district, which closely parallels that of the province, the district officer is assisted by representatives of many of the ministries.[3] (See Figure 6.) In 1956, the district officer of the Pattani *amphur* had held his office for nine years. This is an unusually long tenure, as it is the policy of the Ministry of the Interior to rotate district officers throughout the nation every three or four years, so that, among other reasons, they do not develop too close personal and political associations with the people and institutions in one area. It is probable that the long term of office held by the Pattani district officer is due in part to the fact that he is able to speak the Malay language and is familiar with problems peculiar to this region of Thailand. As the *amphur* organization has been in effect since 1901 in Pattani province, few of the villagers at Rusembilan are able to recall any system of local administration other than this.

Villagers in Rusembilan have little actual contact with the district officer himself, though in other districts of the province the district officers, lacking the staff of Pattani district, are in closer personal touch with the residents of their villages. The villagers endeavor to have as little to do with the district office as possible, but for a variety of reasons they must appear there or meet representatives of the office at Rusembilan. Land and business taxes must be paid in person at the district office, and licenses for selling cigarettes and kerosene are obtained there. The villager must apply in person for permission to slaughter his cattle or change his residence, and twenty-one-year-olds together

[3] *Ibid.*, p. 14.

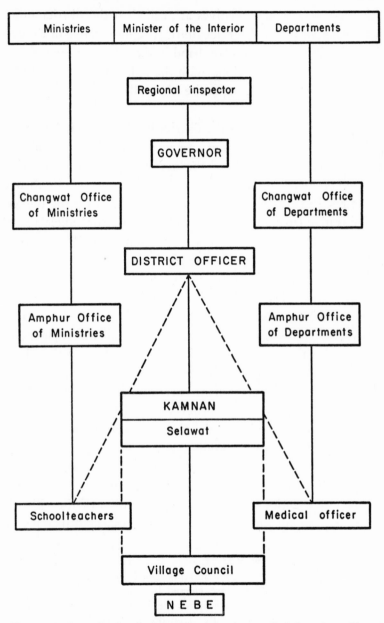

Figure 6. Organizational chart of government administrative officers, with heads of administrative units in capital letters.

with their friends and relatives are called to the district office once a year for national-service draft. A representative of the district office is required to be on hand in the village at each village meeting and is called in along with the police to investigate any criminal offense or to supervise the village registration and census.

Insofar as the officials at the district level are all civil servants appointed by the various ministries in Bangkok, they are almost always Thai. The officials of the next level below the district, the *tambon* or commune, are local people, elected in theory by the residents of the *tambon*.[4] In the south, this is the highest administrative (in contradistinction to legislative or judicial) level of government generally reached by the Malays. The head of the *tambon* is the *kamnan*. In a typical Thai village, the *kamnan* functions in a largely supervisory capacity; in Rusembilan, however, and other Malay villages, the *kamnan* assumes the duties of whatever administration is necessary in the smaller units of the *tambon*. It is his duty to know all the villagers, to take them to the district office for whatever reasons they have to go, and to make sure they get there to pay taxes. He is responsible for convoking village meetings, for assisting district and provincial authorities whenever they have business in the village, and for reporting with other *kamnan* of the district to the district office once a month.

To assist the *kamnan* there is the *selawat* (southern Thai and Malay for Thai *serawat*, secretary). In Rusembilan, most of the administrative duties requiring the co-operation of the villagers are carried out by the *selawat*, as he is a respected member of

---

[4] This situation is almost analogous to that reported by Robert Jay in "Local Government in Rural Central Java" (*Far Eastern Quarterly*, 15:121–122, 1956). There the *desa* and *dukuhan* (*tambon* and Thai *muban* or Malay *kampong*) officials are elected by the villagers, and officials of the subdistrict and above are appointed by the Ministry of the Interior and are rotated periodically from one area to another.

the community, whereas the *kamnan* is sometimes considered to be a puppet of the district officer and is not at all popular with many of the villagers. Until 1948, there were five subordinate village officers called *nebe* (Malay contraction of Thai *nai-muban*, head of village, used in Rusembilan instead of Thai term *pu yai ban*). Each *nebe* acted as the representative of the *kamnan* in one of the five *tempat*, or sections, of Rusembilan. Since the death in 1948 of the *nebe* in section 1 of Rusembilan, there has been no one else appointed, as the *kamnan* and *selawat* are both from that section. In Rusembilan, the function of the *nebe* is very limited; they are supposed to, but rarely do, report to the *kamnan* at regular intervals on conditions in their sections, and they are generally the first to be called for any village work projects. The *kamnan* receives monthly pay of forty-two baht ($2.10), but, unlike village officials in the rest of Thailand, subordinates of the *kamnan* at Rusembilan receive nothing.

To elect a *kamnan*, a representative of the district office calls together all the family heads of the village. The represent-ative, frequently the district officer himself, then asks the vil-lagers for suggestions on someone to become *kamnan*. Almost invariably, the Malay villagers at Rusembilan and other villages will not respond to this request for nomination, saying that re-gardless of whom they might nominate, the "district officer's man" would be given the position. In the rare cases of one or more nominations for *kamnan*, the choices are voted on by the villagers, but final authority to approve or disapprove the selec-tion rests with the district officer. Usually, however, a man is simply appointed by the district officer. The *selawat* and *nebe* are appointed by the *kamnan*, ordinarily at a village meeting called for the purpose of approving the selection. Both of these appointments are subject to the approval of the district officer. None of the foregoing village offices carries a specified term of office, the incumbents serving until they die or until they are considered unfit to serve. The *kamnan* of Rusembilan had held this office for twenty-one years when this study was made.[5]

In theory the villagers of Rusembilan have a right to take action to remove from office any village officer whom they feel is incompetent in his position; in actuality, they fear to exercise the right lest they incur the disfavor of the district office. In Rusembilan at the time this study was conducted, there was general dissatisfaction with the *kamnan*. The most usual complaint was that he is just a "yes man" for the district officer and that he should "do more for the village." A few individuals were more specific in their complaints and would frequently sit together discussing the possibilities of removing the *kamnan* from office. These people maintained that the *kamnan* was mainly a weak man who feared the district officer, never daring to make constructive suggestions concerning the village to him, but ready to carry out his slightest whim as law within the village. It was rumored that both the district officer and the *kamnan* were sharing the profits of projects detrimental to the village. The villagers had collected enough specific and general charges against the *kamnan* so that, if substantiated, the district officer would be forced to approve his removal from office; it is quite unlikely, however, that any of the charges would ever be brought to the attention of the district officer or that the villagers would in any way act on the basis of them.

In addition to the village administrative officers in Rusembilan, there are three schoolteachers appointed by the local office of the Ministry of Education. One of the two *bomo* or shamanistic practitioners (see Chapter X) has been appointed by the Public Health Ministry as the village medical officer. For a small salary, it is this man's duty to certify all births and deaths and be sure

[5] See Ruth Benedict, *Thai Culture and Behavior*, p. 6. Data from Rusembilan and Benedict's paper disagree with Carle C. Zimmerman's statement (*Siam: Rural Economic Survey, 1930–31*, p. 54) that the *kamnan* serves for a term of five years.

that they are registered with the *kamnan*. He is also responsible for seeing that people who need medical attention are sent to the hospital in Pattani. Although the teachers and the medical officer do not come directly under the authority of the district officer, they are required to attend the monthly meetings at the district office. As the *bomo* feels that he is primarily a member of the Rusembilan community and not of the governmental structure, he looks forward with displeasure and embarrassment to the time of these meetings when he must walk through the village wearing his civil service uniform.

The Kampong

The village in terms of social intercourse and organization is not the *tambon* or the section but the *kampong*. This serves as a framework within which various forms of group activity can be organized. And except for infrequent occasions such as the pilgrimage to Mecca, it is the largest organizing frame of reference for the Malay population of southern Thailand. Even in the case of marriages which perforce involve two villages, each village acts as a separate organizing unit with separate arrangements and ceremonies for the marriage. In practice at Rusembilan, the term *kampong* has two meanings. The first, based upon the settlement plan of the community, designates each of the hamlets of Rusembilan (section 1) as a *kampong*. Thus, by this definition, there are three *kampongs* comprising Rusembilan: Kampong Pata, the main village; Kampong Surau, the hamlet centering around the mosque; and Kampong Baru, the new settlement farther to the south of the first two. The second, more standard definition links the village with religion, in that it defines the *kampong* as that area falling roughly within earshot of the mosque drum. It is the first definition with which this chapter will deal; later chapters will treat the second definition more fully, though both types of *kampong* have much in common. As an example, men from each of the

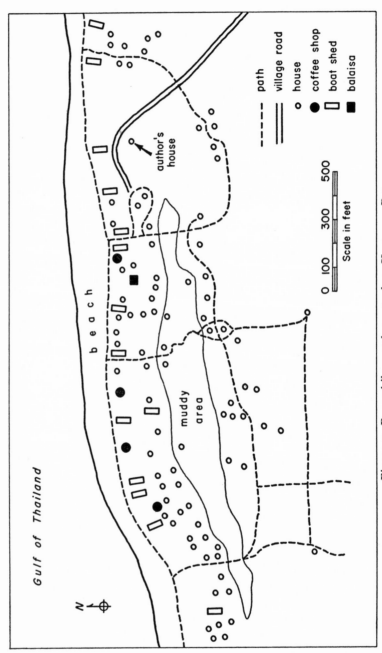

Figure 7. Rusembilan settlement plan: Kampong Pata.

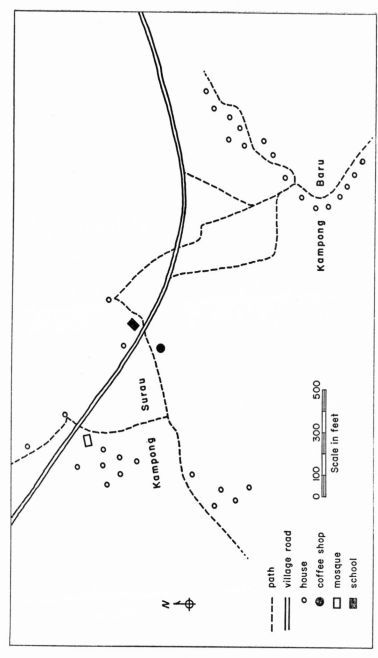

Figure 8. Rusembilan settlement plan: Kampong Surau and Kampong Baru.

Kampong Baru

Kampong Surau

N

path
village road
o house
● coffee shop
□ mosque
▨ school

0   100   300   500
Scale in feet

hamlets tend to form into the same boat group during the *kembong* season, referring to the boat as *kolek kampong,* but the *kolek* is still considered to be part of the fishing fleet of Kampong Rusembilan. The tendency to think of the *kampong* as a social unit is strengthened by the custom of married children to settle near their parents' house, thus creating a more or less closely related in-group. This is true both in the hamlet *kampong* in relation to the rest of Rusembilan and in the case of the larger *kampong* in relation to other communities.

The actual physical organization of the *kampong* can be seen by comparing the sketch map of the village area in Figure 4 with the settlement plans in Figures 7 and 8. Except for the village road and a few well-defined footpaths, there are no established routes within the village, each person making his own way however he thinks best. Since Rusembilan is primarily concerned with fishing, the main activity of the village is centered on the beach. Not only are most of the houses there, but also three of the four coffee shops and the *balaisa* or informal religious gathering place.

As building sites between the water's edge and the cultivated land and plantations to the south become scarce, people are forced to build away from the beach, on either their own or unclaimed land. The first people who moved away from the beach settled on family land near the present location of the Rusembilan school. With the erection of the mosque near this settlement, it became known as Kampong Surau. At present, this hamlet consists of a nucleus of nine houses, with eight outlying houses, including a coffee shop, considered as belonging to it. It was here that the former imam of Rusembilan lived, and at present his widow is looked to as leader of the settlement. All the residents of the main section of this settlement are active in religious matters, and several of them are hajis. Although most of the residents here are closely related, they maintain almost as close contacts with the residents of the beach as among those of their own settlement. This is in part because the present imam is from Kampong Surau, but is living on the beach with the parents of his wife,[6] and in part because of strong relationships established in connection with religious activities which cut across settlement delimitations.

A dispute over paying for land that he was living on in Kampong Surau caused one man and a group of supporters to move out of that hamlet some time before the war and settle on cultivated land already belonging to him. The dispute and the actual moving of houses created considerable hard feeling between the residents of Kampong Surau and those of the new settlement, Kampong Baru, and between the latter settlers and the *kamnan*, who was the father of the second disputant and whose injunction against the house moving was overriden by the assistant district officer. In 1956, not quite twenty-five years later, most people had forgotten about the quarrel, and even the disputants themselves were on friendly terms.

Kampong Baru, containing sixteen houses, is oriented more toward agriculture than any of the other parts of Rusembilan. Although there is on the beach a *kolek kampong* from this settlement and its crew is made up mostly of men from here, many of the men prefer to devote their energies to their nearby fields rather than to activities at the beach more than half a mile away. Since this settlement was founded because of the actions of one man, and on his land, his present role as leader of the settlement is accompanied by more authority than is usual for a *kampong* leader. Any questions in the settlement pertaining to more than one household are brought before him, and any suggestions he may make concerning settlement matters are usually acted upon without hesitation.

[6] Although community exogamy is strictly adhered to, marriage was arranged for this couple because they came from different settlements within the community and because the woman had been adopted and was not actually from Rusembilan.

Another group of thirteen houses immediately to the east of Kampong Pata forms a settlement started thirty years ago when there were no further shore-front building sites available in the main part of the village. This settlement is considered by the villagers as part of Kampong Pata, but it is set off from the rest of the village by a coconut plantation, and its residents are all descendants of the original settler plus their spouses.

Village Government

Although the villagers of Rusembilan accept formal governmental authority reluctantly, the pattern of their activities and the functioning of the village itself appear to be orderly and well organized. In the event of an unusual circumstance, outside of the normal patterns of behavior, the villagers will first seek the advice of respected, usually older men. (The criteria for a respected individual will be discussed in the following chapter.) If the problem cannot be solved in this manner, it is taken to the imam; if the imam regards the situation as falling completely within the sphere of government administration, only then will it be referred to the *kamnan* or the district officer. Frequently, however, such a matter will not be taken to the *kamnan* if the villager feels that it will not be received impartially. For instance, in the case of the theft of a cow, the man whose cow has been stolen will consult with respected men of the village as to what to do. Should it be decided that the *kamnan* has reasons for protecting the thief (e.g., if he is a relative), the villager will take matters into his own hands: he will steal the cow back again if he can find it, or he will take one of the thief's cows if he is reasonably sure of the culprit's identity. On rare occasions, when the theft has been important, the villager may bypass the *kamnan* and take the matter directly to the district office. In one instance when this happened during 1956, the suspect was a cousin of the *kamnan*. When the *kamnan* learned that the report had been made directly to the district office, he went to the office and removed the report from the records. Ordinarily, however, the *kamnan* will not take any action to interfere with decisions reached by villagers in concord with able and respected counsel.

On an average of four times a year, a representative of the district office will call together the villagers, usually at the village schoolhouse, to bring to their attention government policies which would affect them and to hear their complaints or suggestions about these policies or about any other matter they might wish to present. These meetings are never announced far enough in advance so that the villagers can prepare and organize any kind of suggestions or complaints, and sometimes the villagers are not informed of a meeting until it has already started. As the representative of the district office speaks only in the Thai language, and the villagers only in Malay, there is the further problem of translation. This is rarely solved satisfactorily, unless there is a highly respected villager who is fluent in both languages. At Rusembilan, the task of translation falls upon the *kamnan*, who is far from proficient in Thai. He is frequently unable to translate anything for long periods, and when he is able to, his rendition is a word-for-word translation which disregards the fact that sentence structure and the general mode of expression in the two languages are entirely different. The villagers complain that they are never able to understand specific points brought out in the meetings and only rarely able to comprehend the general idea. Attendance at these meetings is compulsory for all family heads. Usually no check is made, but if the number present is unduly small, names will be taken and those absent fined five baht (25 cents).

A typical village meeting in May 1956 included the following points: The representative of the district office outlined the plan to register all members of the village for voting in the coming election and for purposes of the national census. He stated that the following year (1957) there would be a special registration, and any person failing to register then would be denied the privileges of changing his residence, or obtaining permits to buy land, or making the pilgrimage to Mecca. He also pointed out that certification of death by the village medical officer, or by the Pattani government midwife in the case of still births, must be received at the district office before burial can take place. The *bomo* who had been appointed village medical officer called attention to the fact that according to Islamic practice the dead must be buried "immediately" and that fulfilling the government demands would take more time than their religion permitted. The representative said that ideas for the improvement of the village should be presented to the district officer on the second and twenty-fifth of each month. Any time that a thief is apprehended or a "bad character" is suspected, this information will be received by the district officer in the strictest of confidence. In the case of a reported bad character, the district officer will call him to the office and advise him to improve his conduct. The representative also announced that people born in the Buddhist year of the mouse deer (i.e., those who were roughly eighteen at that time) must register for the national conscription and that delinquents or their parents would be fined. The central government was urging that greater efforts be made in the villages toward cleanliness in matters of personal hygiene, housekeeping, and food preparation and that nursing of children in public should be avoided. Finally, the representative of the district office announced that land tax payment was now overdue and that any villager not paid up should do so at once, including the 10 per cent surcharge for late payment, or run the risk of having his land seized by the government.

In July 1956, a special village meeting was called to implement the central government plan of having a village council elected in each *tambon*. According to government publicity, the purpose of these village councils was to democratize village government and to make the villagers aware of their place in the national democracy. The council was to be made up of two men from each of the five sections of the *tambon*, with two assistant chairmen to be elected from this group. The chairman would be appointed by the district officer for each meeting. The *kamnan*, the four *nebe*, the schoolmaster, and the village medical officer were to be members of the council ex officio. The district officer had suggested to his representative at the meeting that the schoolmaster be made permanent secretary of the council as he could read and write the Thai language and could speak some Malay. It was explained that the council would meet once a year unless convoked more frequently by the district officer. Its duties would include the discussion of village matters such as protection, welfare, and building projects. The members of the council would receive a small salary at some time in the future, but the representative of the district office could not say when. Villagers at the meeting were asked to nominate men for the council. As they remained silent, the *kamnan* and one of the *nebe* suggested ten men and asked for the approval of the meeting by a show of hands. When no hands were raised, the *kamnan* questioned a few of the villagers about the choices; they hurriedly mumbled their assent. Several of the villagers said after the meeting that the people chosen were men whom the *kamnan* could count upon to go along with his ideas, rather than those who would present the village point of view. They explained that there would have been no point to their nominating men whom they considered able as all nominations were subject to the approval of the *kamnan* and the representative of the district office present at the meeting. The only result of the formation of the village council, most people maintained, would be an additional number of officials who could call the villagers out for work projects.[7]

[7] Paul M. Kattenburg (*A Central Javanese Village in 1950*, p. 12) describes a situation of similar village attitudes in Central Java. The villagers have no desire for elections and are not enthusiastic about instituting an elected village assembly. Their headman has held office for forty years.

During the spring and early summer of 1956, there was a minor wave of thefts and robberies in the Pattani area. On three or four occasions, while the men of Rusembilan were out fishing at night, homes were broken into and women and old men intimidated. This matter was presented to the district office, and more frequent police patrols were requested. When it was obvious that nothing would be done by the district office, the fishermen decided to organize a village patrol on their own. This operated every night that the men went out fishing (i.e., every relatively calm night except Thursday night when the Sabbath begins and during full moon). A different man was left ashore from each *kolek* each night, and he received his full share of fish in the morning for his patrol duties. The men operated in pairs, either both patrolling or each of them alternating between sleeping and patrolling. Each pair assigned itself a patrol area, if possible the area in which the men resided. The main village was divided into four areas, east, central, and west along the beach and the fourth area south of the beach. The two hamlets, Kampong Baru and Kampong Surau, were each assigned as patrol areas. As there were usually more than twelve men on patrol, one or more areas, usually along the beach, would have an extra patrol man. This patrol proved to be very effective, completely stopping thefts and robberies on nights when the men were fishing, whereas the crime rate in unpatrolled villages in the Pattani area remained the same or even increased.

Taxation and Community Projects

Almost all the households in Rusembilan are subject to some form of direct taxation during the year. All those who own cultivated land are required to pay one and a half baht (7½ cents) per rai (about 0.4 acre) while undeveloped land in the village is taxed at the rate of one baht (5 cents) per rai.[8]

[8] See Kattenburg, *loc. cit.* Land tax rate is 40 cents per acre (i.e., 16 cents per rai).

Each landowner is responsible for paying his taxes at the district office by a certain date each year. Each *kolek* as well as each of the motorboats is subject to annual registration and taxation. The tax on each *kolek* is fifteen baht (75 cents), but some of the villagers at Rusembilan complain that they have been charged up to sixty baht ($3) for their annual tax. The boat registration period lasts for three days each year, when agents of the Revenue Department are in attendance in Pattani. Each boat must be brought to the agents at this time (even if the boat is not being, and will not be, used during the year), and the tax paid. If this period is missed, the boatowner is liable to a three hundred baht ($15) fine as well as his back tax. In the case of both land taxes and boat taxes, the *kamnan* is responsible for notifying the villagers well in advance of the dates for payment.

The villagers of Rusembilan recognize that taxation is necessary to finance the various government projects that they see in the area, but they frequently forget to consider the expense involved in civil service salaries and government building maintenance in the district and province. They feel that, because of their taxes, the government should allocate funds to village projects or to projects outside of the *tambon* that would directly affect the villagers. In 1956, there were three such projects envisaged by the villagers: major repairs and new bridges on the road from the village to the main road into Pattani; construction of a road from the main village (section 1) to Kuala Prima (section 2) some four miles away, which would include building up a foundation above flood level and blocking off the mouth of the river between the two villages; and, finally, the removing, or enforcing the private removal, of the pilings of abandoned fish traps. If taxes, including land taxes of nonresidents, fees for permits and government services, and various fines are taken into account, the village of Rusembilan probably does not contribute more than four thousand baht ($200) to the sum of over two and a half million baht ($125,000) collected in the province annually.[9]

In order that essential projects may be carried out in the villages in spite of limited budgets, the villagers themselves are called upon to contribute their own labor. How often and how many men are called for work is dependent upon the number and kinds of jobs to be done in the village. This procedure is followed rather than a *corvée* system requiring work from each man for a fixed number of days. Before the war, this system was used on the district level as well as the village level. Many villagers recall the time that a canal was to be built and labor was recruited from most of the villages in the district. Each man was required to dig ten meters of the canal, thereby being forced to neglect completely his ordinary work for approximately ten days. A shack was constructed near one section of the canal, and it is reported that those who refused to work were either locked up there or shot. No pay or food was provided during the project. Now, when men are called up for labor, they may be excused if they have pressing enough personal reasons or if they pay someone else to do the work for them. Food is customarily provided even for a short job, as when a group of Malays is called in to help on a neighbor's or relative's house.

During 1956, three calls for labor were made at Rusembilan by the *kamnan* or the *selawat*. The first was to clear out the channels of the river to the west of the village. Because the villagers felt that by clearing the channels more water would back up during the monsoon season, they refused to work, and the *kamnan* let the project drop.

The major work project of the year was the construction of a new schoolhouse. It had been decided by the villagers, the schoolteachers, and representatives of the district office that the old school had been too small for all the children of the village.

[9] Information provided by the Office of the Governor, Changwat Pattani, Pattani, Thailand.

The Pattani office of the Ministry of Education is reported to have allocated two thousand baht ($100) for this purpose. The villagers maintained that this sum was nothing more than the school maintenance fund which had been withheld for several years and that in order to complete the school building the village would have to supply another two thousand baht as well as all the labor. For this project as well as most of the others, the *kamnan* undertook to supply and prepare the food for the men out of the funds allotted for the project. Most of the village men arrived for work the first day, and the old school building was quickly torn down and usable materials salvaged. As the next stage in the operation was putting together sections of the building to be erected later and required skill rather than a large labor force, chiefly the older men experienced in carpentry came to work for the next few days. When it was time to erect the prepared sections, it was difficult for the *kamnan* and *selawat* to find enough men to do the job. After that, manpower for the job became extremely scarce, since the remaining work consisted mainly in finishing touches such as putting tiles on the roof and planks on the wall studding.

More than a month later, when the school was scheduled to open for the new term, the roof had still not been completely tiled, and the walls were entirely lacking. School was begun, and a certain amount of time each day was devoted by the teacher and children to putting tiles on the roof. Two days after the school opened, a squall blew up while the children were in the building, and because there were no walls or supports for the uprights of the building, the wind toppled the building and its tile roof, seriously injuring one of the children. The villagers first petitioned the *kamnan* for assistance in the matter and finally sent a committee to the district officer to ask for some kind of government action. Three months later, the district office announced that the Ministry of Education had granted ten thousand baht ($500) and that with this sum the government would build a new schoolhouse. In the meantime, the village had constructed a slightly smaller school with the wood salvaged from the one that had collapsed. This they had braced securely and roofed with atap which they bought with the proceeds of selling the whole tiles that could be salvaged from the previous roof.

The road into Rusembilan was built in 1940 by the government and in theory should be maintained by the district and the province. As it is an unimportant road, however, it is usually neglected by the authorities, and maintenance falls upon the villagers. In 1956, with heavy trucks bringing oil for the motorboats, building materials for several new houses in the village, and a daily delivery of ice, the road became practically impassable after the summer rains. The *kamnan* prohibited all further truck deliveries to the village, but the villagers were quick to have this decision rescinded by the district office. Under the direction of the *selawat*, all the villagers were called out one Friday morning (on nights other than Thursday most of the men were out fishing and wanted to rest during the day), and by shoveling mud up from the padi fields onto the road, they managed to repair the whole length of it before the noon meal served to them by the village women. The bus driver had contributed one hundred baht ($5) toward the expenses, and another man who had been responsible for much of the truck traffic was asked for that much.

The School at Rusembilan

Primary education in Thailand is compulsory, and this is no less true in the Malay-speaking provinces. The Ministry of Education has tried to have a schoolhouse with a staff of teachers, if not in every village, at least within walking distance by most village children. Secondary education is also provided by the government, but these schools are to be found only in the larger towns. The school at Rusembilan is situated about a half mile from the main village on the road out of the village and between Kampong Surau and Kampong Baru. According to the statistics available to the headmaster, of a possible enrollment of one hundred forty children between the legal school ages of seven and fifteen (see Table 5) there are from sixty to seventy

Table 5. Children at Rusembilan of legal school age

Age group	Boys	Girls	Total
7–10	46	48	94
11–14	27	18	45
15 *	8	16	24
Total	81	82	163

* Four girls within the fifteen-year age group are married.
Source: Government of Thailand, Census BE 2499 (1956).

who attend. A large part of the difference between the number of children in the school-age groups and the actual attendance is made up by the fact that postpubescent girls are almost universally kept at home learning domestic arts until they are married. In Rusembilan and other Malay villages, one almost never sees a girl between the ages of twelve and sixteen except in her own home. Among the sixty or seventy children who do attend the school, there is very little absenteeism except during the time of the rice harvest, when all available labor is needed in the fields. At the time of transplanting the rice, the school schedules a recess so that this work may be done without having the children miss school.

The educational program is divided into four standards, each of which a child must pass. It is customary to spend two years in each standard and graduate at the age of fourteen. Many children, however, either pass through the standards faster than every two years or simply leave school before graduating from the fourth standard or reaching the legal age. At Rusembilan, all four standards are taught in the same classroom, one standard being given instruction while the others study. The curriculum in each standard is much the same, including the following subjects: history, geography, reading and writing (in Thai), dictation (in Thai), mental arithmetic, Buddhist morals, drawing, handicrafts, and physical training. Standards three and four add bookkeeping and letter writing to the curriculum. One of the major sources of dissatisfaction with the educational system, on the part of both the children and the adults and religious leaders of Rusembilan, is the inclusion of Buddhist morals in the curriculum. As all the villagers are Moslem, they feel that Islamic morals and law should be taught the children in the school or nothing at all. Another point of dissatisfaction deals with the language difficulty. Although the headmaster of the school maintains that almost all the graduates of the school know how to read as well as speak Thai, the villagers insist that this is not true, and as instruction is mainly in Thai rather than Malay, many of the children have learned very little during their stay at school.[10]

The headmaster of the school believed that the educational facilities of Rusembilan could be improved by having a more adequate school building (this problem was being worked on; see preceding section) and better educational materials such as blackboards, textbooks, and visual aids. He felt that the curriculum was satisfactory as it was. He admitted that there was a language difficulty, but that the children wanted to and did learn Thai, and that complaints to the contrary by the parents and religious leaders of the village were based on the fact that the adults took no real interest in school activities and curricula. This, he said, was made manifest in the response to a two-year adult education program which was offered at Rusembilan seventeen years before (1938–1939). The course included sub-

---

[10] A similar situation existed under the French administration in Indochina, where some Cambodian schools were staffed with non-Khmer-speaking Vietnamese teachers (Human Relations Area Files, Inc., *Cambodia*, Subcontractors' Monographs, p. 327).

jects in language (Thai) and civics, but there was almost no interest on the part of the adults of the village.

At present, the Thai government is taking a more realistic view toward the educational problems in the Malay villages. For several years, the Ministry of Education has been working on a project to translate the Standard Thai textbooks into the Malay language but with the Thai characters. This would form a basis for familiarizing the Malay-speaking children with the Thai orthography and would make learning the Thai language far easier if they had a background of literacy in their own. In place of the adult education program presented to the village in 1938–1939, the Ministry of Education about three times a year sends a cinema van into the village. The films deal with areas such as agriculture, industry, education, and explanations of some of the government's policies. The films are explained to the people in Malay over a public address system. These showings always attract a great number of villagers, and the films serve as topics of village conversation for some time afterward.

Law and Justice

The villagers of Rusembilan are, on the whole, little concerned with matters of law and justice. Within the village, individuals conduct their lives and business in accordance with Islamic principles, and when misconduct or disputes arise, they are generally dealt with or arbitrated successfully by respected members of the community or the imam in accordance with the Koran. With regard to national laws, as long as the application of them is limited to the village itself, the villagers take the attitude that they know what is best for their village, and if their ideas disagree with the law, then the law should be ignored. Such was the case when the *kamnan* was told (1955) by the district office that it was required by law to rotate village crops. The *kamnan* ordered the villagers to do this, but it was obvious to the *kamnan* as well as the villagers that rice is the only crop practical to grow in the padi fields as the cattle would eat any other crop. Furthermore, the villagers had no desire to grow other crops, either instead of rice or during the period after the rice is harvested and before the fields must be prepared for the next rice planting. Thus, there has been no attempt to rotate crops at Rusembilan, and no attempt to enforce the law. The village attitude was summed up by one old man: "People generally don't do what the *kamnan* says—they do as they want and say nothing about it."

When rubber prices dropped in 1954 and there was a tremendous upsweep of crime in the Pattani area, villagers of Rusembilan and surrounding communities, disturbed by increased thefts and robberies in their villages, decided to take action themselves. They realized that the legal processes of justice were extremely slow and frequently became stalemated by financial and political pressures brought to bear in the right places. "The law is good," they would say, "but the keepers of the law deal in money." When a criminal could be positively identified, a group of villagers would apprehend him and themselves administer punishment, sometimes, according to villagers' statements, even killing him. Each member of this vigilance committee would contribute one hundred baht ($5) to cover any costs incurred in the event of court action against the group.

When a Malay villager is indicted and brought before a court, the Thai government has set up certain institutions for his protection. Each court in the four Malay-speaking provinces is staffed with two Thai-Malay interpreters, and all proceedings are required to be translated into both languages. Furthermore, each Thai judge must have with him a Malay adviser of the same civil service rank. This adviser or *kadi* is responsible for counseling the judge on matters that bear upon Islamic religious beliefs and practices and upon Malay customs.[11] The judge is under no obli-

[11] In Malaya, the jurisdiction of the *kadi* is strictly limited to marriage, divorce, and alimony (E. N. Taylor, "Malay Family Law," *Journal of the Royal Asiatic Society, Malayan Branch*, 15 [pt. 1]:4, 1937).

gation to accept his advice. It is usually extremely difficult to get Malays to give evidence in court, as they realize that there are several ways for a man to escape conviction and to retaliate on the plaintiff or witness.[12] If a man is unable to bribe the judge to keep his case out of court, he is usually able to purchase witnesses for himself for as little as five hundred baht ($25) or pay four or five thousand baht ($200–$250) to have his name kept on the prison records for the term of his sentence without requiring him to be present. Political influence in most cases is as effective as cash.

Political Parties and Movements

Although no one in Rusembilan was active in political parties or movements at the time this study was conducted, there is a lively interest in these matters on the part of Malay villagers. Their interest stems in large part from the hope that one or another of the candidates for the national assembly would, if elected, be able and willing to obtain legislation beneficial to the Malays in the south. During 1956, political interest was at its height, as candidates were beginning their campaign for the national elections scheduled for early 1957. Previous to this election, Pattani province had sent only one representative to the national assembly, but because of population growth over the last five years, the province was now entitled to send two representatives to Bangkok. There were eleven candidates for the two vacancies (the incumbent was not running for re-election), five of them Thai and six Malay. It was thought probable that one of the Thai candidates would drop out of the race before election and that his campaign was being supported simply to take votes from another candidate.

Ordinarily, the political campaigns in Pattani and neighboring provinces are run in a standardized pattern. The election seeker

[12] Charles Brant (*Tadagale, a Burmese Village in 1950*, pp. 32–33) reports the same reluctance among Burmese villagers to give evidence or name suspects for fear of revenge.

will ride into all accessible villages in a jeep decorated with bunting and pictures of the candidate. He will usually buy any interested villagers ice cream or cold drinks, either from a village shop or from a supply in his jeep. He then gives a short speech, making exaggerated promises about what he will do if elected and criticizing his opponents. He shakes hands, says a few words to the village leaders, and drives off. One of the candidates for the 1957 election, however, was a young (age twenty-six) idealistic Malay, with no great financial or political connections. He conceived an idea for a new sort of campaign, with which he was convinced he could win the election. His method was to appear in a village, no matter how inaccessible, on foot and talk to the villagers, village leaders, and the imam about religion. He felt that religion is the most important part of a villager's life and that other candidates, being unable to "talk well" about it, would suffer on this account. He gave lectures about registration and voting procedures, trying to decrease voters' disqualification because of small technicalities. His platform included the following general points, toward which he would devote his energies if elected, rather than specific promises: improvement of the status of Islamic religion in Thailand; improved educational facilities and curricula; and improvement of local transportation and communication facilities with the understanding that, if the government supplied the materials, affected villagers would supply the labor. Influential Thais and Chinese in Pattani were certain that this man was destined to fail in his campaign, but villagers at Rusembilan who knew him well and other Malays in the area considered his chances quite good.[13]

Several years before this study was made, there had been a very active movement in the provinces of Pattani, Yala, and Narathiwat, which expressed the desire of the Malay population

[13] This candidate polled 2,828 votes, coming in fourth; the highest winning candidate polled 25,885 votes (personal communication, February 1957).

to be united with Malaya rather than Thailand. The leader of this movement resided in the next village (part of Pattani municipality) to Rusembilan, and his lieutenant was the owner of the rice-grinding mill at the junction of the Rusembilan road with the main road to Pattani. The organization drew up a petition to the United Nations requesting that the three provinces involved be ceded to the Federation of Malaya, and local Malay villagers were canvassed for signatures and thumb prints. It is understood that about two hundred fifty thousand names had been obtained, or about half the adult Malay population of the three provinces, before the Thai authorities discovered this movement and removed many of its leaders to Bangkok. In a thorough search of the area, the authorities found only a small number of the signatures and thumb prints and little information about the organization of the movement. Many Malays say that the remaining parts of the petition had been destroyed and that the organization has died down, but others feel that it may be revived immediately if political developments in Thailand or Malaya favor it.[14]

[14] This movement has been treated in a broader political framework by Barbara Whittingham, "Patani Appeals to UNO," *Eastern World*, 2(no. 4):4–5, 1948, and "The Singapore Conspiracy," *ibid.*, 4 (no. 2): 25–27, 1950, and by Virginia Thompson and Richard Adloff, chiefly in their chapter "Malays of Southern Thailand" in *Minority Problems in Southeast Asia*, pp. 158–165.

CHAPTER VIII

Community Organization

AS pointed out in the last chapter, there is no formalized machinery within Rusembilan for direction and control of individual or group behavior. If an individual or group acts in a manner detrimental to the community, no organization exists within the community itself that can demand and enforce appropriate behavior. To handle persistent infractions of good-behavior codes, Rusembilan must rely upon the legal and administrative institutions of Thai society which operate only on levels above that of the community. Thus, to maintain order and relatively close adherence to the behavioral norms of their culture without stepping into the framework of a different society, the villagers of Rusembilan emphasize the relationships of the individual to his family, to the mosque, to his boat group, and to friends in order to strengthen the principles of conformity and kindness (*hati baik*, a good heart). The villager always prefers individual activity to any co-operative effort. The success or failure of the venture then rests squarely upon him, rather than upon the unknown factors of other people's behavior. And, although he is always willing to give where help is needed, he demands strict adherence to the rights of ownership, even to insisting that a deficiency of one *kembong* in his share be made up the next night. Large projects, however, require the efforts of several men working together as a team. The villager reluctantly submits to co-operative projects and to working in groups, which stay together only as long as is necessary for their specific ends. Relationships of friendship frequently spring from such activities, especially from the boat groups, which stay together usually at least six months. These friendships often form the bases of further groupings for different purposes, and from them emerges a tendency toward reciprocal co-operative action.

The Family and Household

In Rusembilan, the nuclear family is the basic unit of social interaction. Ideally, each man lives with his wife and children in his own house, the children leaving to set up their own homes when they marry. It often happens, however, that the youngest child will bring his or her spouse to live in the house of the parents and that at some point a transition either implicit or explicit will occur so that it is the aged parents living in the house of the young family. As in our own society, there is little importance placed upon family relationships other than husband-and-wife, parent-child, and siblings. The fact, however, that two people are related in a certain degree, such as uncle-nephew, does enable the individuals concerned to set up a relationship between each other *as individuals* more easily than if they were not related. This relationship may just as easily be negative as positive. The important fact is that the society recognizes such a relationship in theory and facilitates its establishment. As in almost all cases where the nuclear family is important, the relationship between grandparents and grandchildren is usually one of pleasant informality and permissiveness on the part of the grandparents.

As long as the children are at home, they are expected to defer to the authority of their parents, although each child is treated with the respect for individuality due to any person. If the father or the head of the household wants the child to do something in the house, the child is expected to do it with no complaints. Once he is outside of the house, however, the child is to a great extent his own master and can, with a relative degree of impunity, ignore commands of his elders, even of his parents. Because outside of the home all adults are in a position of practically equal authority with regard to the children, it is common to see any adult in the village administering, or trying to administer, discipline to another's child, even when the parent is present. In most cases, however, the children are co-operative and ready to do any service that is asked of them.

When the parents reach old age and are no longer able to earn their living through active pursuits, the children are expected to contribute the food or money necessary to support them. Generally, this burden is light, as even the oldest can do a little gardening on their own or set their nets for crabs each night. But in almost every case, whatever support is necessary is given willingly and without the necessity of the community's invoking social or religious pressures upon the children.

The relationship between siblings, particularly siblings of the same sex and approximately the same age, is usually very close throughout life. Not only do brothers and sisters form the nucleus of, or at least join, the same childhood groups, but they take an active part in the ceremonies attendant upon marriage, childbirth, and death as these pertain to each of them. When a man or his family is in any sort of trouble, it is usually to the family of his elder brother or sister that he turns first for assistance, and there is a certain sense of obligation on the latter's part to offer the assistance.

Figure 9 illustrates in diagrammatic form the various kinship relationships which have sufficient importance in the Malay society of Thailand to be named. From the point of view of the individual, only the members of his family of orientation and his

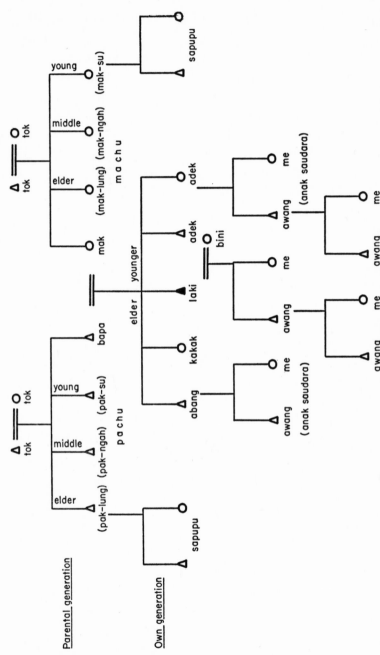

Figure 9. Rusembilan kinship terminology, with special terms used in inland agricultural communities in parentheses.

family of procreation are given descriptive names. He has different terms, used both in address and in reference, for his parents
(*bapa*, sometimes *pak*, father, and *mak*, mother) and for his
children (*awang*, son, and *me*, daughter) based on differences
in sex. On his own generational level, there is greater emphasis
on age differences in his terms of address and reference. Thus,
the individual will have a separate term for his elder brother
(*abang*) and his elder sister (*kakak*), but his younger brothers
and sisters will be called by the same term (*adek*). All cousins
are referred to as *sapupu*, but are usually addressed by sibling
terms.

Because of differences in the basic economy of Rusembilan and
other fishing villages in the area compared with Malay villages
farther inland, where their living is made from the land, a difference is beginning to appear in the kinship terminology of the
two types of villages. In an agricultural community, land must
be passed from generation to generation, and as a family's holdings descend, they become spread over an ever-wider group of
relatives. An attempt is made, therefore, to hold the family together in order to limit fractionalization and inefficient exploitation of the land. In a fishing village, with comparatively little
importance attached to the land, each man starts out individually
on his fishing career, and there is no danger of fractionalizing
the means of subsistence production. Consequently, there is no
advantage in attempting to weld a larger family group into a
social unit to avoid fractionalization. This difference in the nature of the economic systems and the attempted social solution
of the problem are reflected in the kinship terminology used in
the two types of villages. In an agricultural community, there
are classificatory terms for the parents' generation linking the
males with the speaker's father and the females with his mother.
As in the case of siblings, the age of the relative, in relation to
the speaker's mother or father, determines the appropriate term.
In these terms sex is also differentiated, but other factors are not

considered since descent is bilateral and location of home after marriage is optional. Thus, all related males of the parental generation, depending on their age relative to the person through whom they are related, are called either *pak-lung* (elder father), or *pak-ngah* (middle father), or *pak-su* (younger father). In the same way, all females in the parental generation are called *mak-lung, mak-ngah,* or *mak-su.* In Rusembilan, the people are aware of these terms, but never use them. They simply classify all related males of the parental generation with whom they have a certain degree of contact as *pachu* (from *pak kechil,* meaning little father) or uncle. Likewise, all females in that generation are called *machu* or *machi* (from *mak kechil,* little mother) or aunt. But if an individual lives in a village different from that of his father's brother, for example, he may on an infrequent meeting address him by his name rather than using the kinship term, *pachu.*

Whereas the agricultural communities have separate terms for grandfather and grandmother (the same for maternal and paternal) and even for the great grandparents, Rusembilan uses only one term, *tok,* which covers all relatives, male or female, above the parental generation. It is frequently extended to include respected nonrelatives such as the imam, who is always called *tok imam.* Inland agricultural villagers refer to children of their brothers and sisters as *anak saudara* (sibling's child), although the children must make age distinctions in reciprocating. Grandchildren, and occasionally even great grandchildren, are designated by special terms. In Rusembilan, all related persons below one's own generation are simply called *awang* or *me* (son or daughter) or *anak* (child). In-laws are referred to by adding the word *ipar* to the term that the spouse would use in addressing the relative. In Rusembilan, it is common to refer to both the older brother and the older sister of the spouse as *kakak ipar* (literally, elder sister-in-law), thus distinguishing only age and not sex among siblings-in-law.

The importance of kinship ties outside of the immediate family has been greatly diminished at Rusembilan, but it is still common, upon meeting a stranger, to spend a good deal of time trying to establish some sort of relationship on the basis of kinship. It is likely that a person from Rusembilan is related in some degree to people from all Malay-speaking regions of southern Thailand as well as areas in Kelantan and Kedah in Malaya. And on meeting a stranger, the villager will try to establish some bond, if not through a common relative, at least a mutual friend, to determine what degree of respect and what services are due the stranger and also to establish a common ground for conversation with him.

There are no fixed rules of postmarital residence among the Malays in southern Thailand, but there is a strengthening tendency in marriages in which one partner is from a fishing village to favor residence in that village. Until recently, as in agricultural communities, the bride and groom always had to be from different villages, and they and their parents would consider the advantages of residence in each of the villages. The couple would spend a few weeks living in each one before they made their final choice. Now, because of decreasing reliance upon rice cultivation at Rusembilan, the fact that a young man is familiar with fishing techniques and favors fishing as an economic pursuit heavily influences the deliberations toward settling in the man's village. In the case of the marriage of girls from Rusembilan to men from inland, probably 75 per cent settle at Rusembilan chiefly because the fishing village tends to be more prosperous than the agricultural village.

The domestic situation and family organization of a Rusembilan household can best be visualized by citing an example of a typical well-to-do family in the community. The house is elevated about ten feet on stilts, and this provides a work and storage space below as well as protection from monsoon floods. The house itself is built of wood with a clay tile roof. It has a large living, dining, and sleeping room with a smaller sleeping room at either of the back corners of the main room. The floor is built on four levels with a difference of about eight inches be-

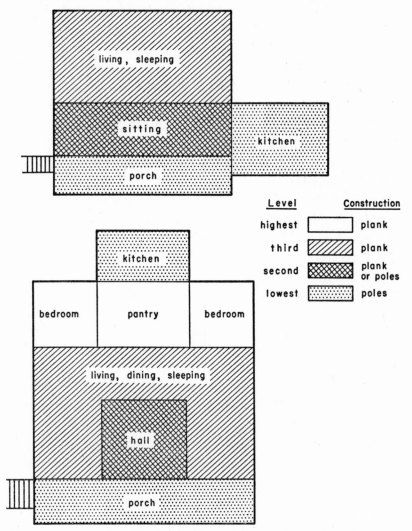

Figure 10. Plans of typical Rusembilan houses, the larger that of a well-to-do family.

tween each. (See Figure 10.) The corridor between the two smaller rooms serves as a pantry for the kitchen, which is erected against the back wall of the house proper. Over the doors and

windows in the main room are ornate Islamic designs similar
to those used on the *kolek*, and hanging on the wall are photo-
graphs of the family, quotations from the Koran, and pictures
of Mecca. This room also contains two tables, a storage cabinet,
two mirrors, a wall clock, and twelve to fifteen woven grass mats
for sleeping and sitting.

The head of the household, called *Pak Sa* (*pak besar*, big
father) by all the villagers, is sixty, and his wife *Mak Sa* is fifty.
In theory, they have authority over all members of the house,
but rarely try to exercise it. With them live one son, thirty, who
is attending a religious school in the area and who comes home
only for special occasions; a son, thirteen; and a daughter, eight.
The couple has, living in the village, one married son and one
married daughter whose children are often found in and around
the grandparents' house, where they are sure to find greater in-
dulgence and fewer chores. Another son, just recently married,
was at the time of this study spending some time at the home of
his wife and some time occupying one of the smaller chambers
in his parents' house before settling permanently in a house of
his own. *Pak Sa* says that he expects married children, before
settling permanently, to live with one set of parents or the other
in order to save money. His daughter and her husband lived with
him for several months, and his son lived with his wife's parents.
An average house for a newly wed couple costs about two thousand baht ($100).

Pak Sa supports his family by growing rice and by fishing.
He owns ten plots of padi field, three of which have been
spoiled by salt-water flooding, and the rice that he plants on
the remaining seven is sufficient for his family. He owns two
head of cattle for plowing, a *kolek* of which he is steerer, and a
jokung. He sums up his position by saying that he has many
things but no money and does not consider himself particularly
important in the community. Actually, although he holds no
formal position in the village, *Pak Sa* is one of the respected

individuals whose advice is frequently sought by people having difficulties. He believes that probably he will never make the pilgrimage to Mecca as he never has enough money. He is spending fifteen hundred baht ($75) yearly to support his son in religious school and has no surplus when the rice harvest and the fishing are poor. When his catch and harvest are good, he has no inclination to go to Mecca.

Respect and Authority

Because there are few well-defined formal roles of authority in the society of Rusembilan, members of the community must rely on roles defined in terms of different relationships and on informal relationships in order to regulate activities in the community. The role of the steerer in the boat group and the accretion to this role of group leadership will be examined in the next section. In the community as a whole, well-structured roles are absent, even within the religious organization. Consequently, the community has come to endow the role of a respected man with a limited degree of authority. This equation of roles is now so complete that when a man without the proper relationships of respect from the community is placed in one of the few formal roles structured for authority (e.g., *kamnan*) his authority may be ignored.

Different villagers give various criteria for establishing a man in a relationship of respect, but at the head of the list is always found *hati baik* (a good heart) or kindness, helpfulness, and judicious generosity. Within the household, the father or head of the house is respected by all members of the household, and he expects to be consulted before any project is begun. A well-respected man is accorded certain politeness by the whole community, such as being spoken to first upon meeting, being among the first to be invited to feasts, and being given aid and assistance by many when he is in need. The order of respect in inviting guests to a feast is strictly followed unless the feast is to be small and limited to a certain close group of people. The imam is first to be invited, followed by the hajis of the village, then respected relatives and men respected by the community. After these, other relatives, close friends, and neighbors are invited. The *bomo* is almost always invited to feasts because he is a well-known and helpful man, but he is accorded no special respect because of his position. Finally, other villagers, except those on bad terms with the feasting family, and people from other villages are invited.

Degrees of respect can often be ascertained from the names used for certain people. The term of highest respect for a man possessing no title is *tok* (grandfather). This is not used in Rusembilan except in addressing the imam and sometimes the *kamnan;* other villages reserve the term for the very respected, old men of the community. Similar to *tok,* but never used for officeholders, is *wak* (literally, old man, gaffer), applied to respected, old men who have not acquired a term of respect earlier in life. *Pak* (father) is used for respected men of middle age and older. It is generally this class of men who are consulted on various questions and problems that arise in the community. An especially respected man in this category is addressed as *pak te* (*pak puteh*, white father), whiteness in this case being associated with the lighter skin usually found in royal families. If the man is a haji, instead of being called by his name (e.g., *pak te Daut*) he will simply be called *pak te Haji*. Wives of men called *pak* and *pak te* are called *mak* and *mak te*. If a younger man, such as a very successful steerer, is respected in the community or if an older man is respected enough to be set off from others, but not enough to be *pak,* the villagers will call him *pachu* (uncle). Otherwise, it is general to refer to a person by his name and address him either by name or by a sibling kinship term, *abang* if he is older than the speaker, *adek* if he is younger. Children are usually called *anak* (child) and reciprocate with *pak* or *abang*. Chinese are all referred to and addressed as *toke* (merchant), and Thais as *abang*. The rare European that the villager meets is called *tuan* (master).[1]

Titles deriving from local royal families are common in Rusembilan but admittedly imprecise. It is claimed that many villagers assume lesser titles for their children to ensure that they will be respected when adults. There is one woman in the village who, it is said, is entitled to be addressed as *tuan-ku*, or a descendant of the last raja of Pattani in the direct line of succession. The woman herself neither confirms nor denies this; she maintains that such titles are meaningless in the present society and prefers to be treated as anyone else. The only other titles found in Rusembilan are *che*, defined in this area as belonging to one descended from a collateral branch of the royal family, and *wan*, a title even farther removed from the royal line. Many people having such titles are also placed in a position of respect in the community because of their personal attributes and usually prefer to be addressed as *pak* or *pak te* rather than *che* or *wan*.

Economic Co-operation

As was pointed out above, the villagers of Rusembilan avoid the formation of groups for co-operative economic pursuits whenever possible, and, when such groups are necessary, they tend to minimize the permanence of them. The formation of groups is essential, however, in three of the areas most important to the economic life of Rusembilan. Fishing for *kembong* and the large prawns could not be accomplished without the pooling of nets and effort. Rice could not be transplanted and harvested in short enough time to avoid spoilage and loss without a larger group than the family unit. And, with the limited capital re-

[1] Contact with Europeans is so rare at Rusembilan that the Standard Malay term *tuan* is pronounced as in Standard Malay rather than changed to *tue* (see Appendix B, phonological changes, 4). Because the villagers as a whole were unfamiliar with this expression, they adopted the use of *pak te* in addressing the author and *orang puteh* (white man) in referring to him.

sources of the community, a large part of the rubber-growing land owned by villagers could not have been bought without the pooling of funds either of a group of co-operating land-owners or at least of villagers willing to risk their capital on another's venture.

The unit of co-operation which is most durable and which also frequently serves as a foundation for other groups both economic and social is the boat group. Although the fishermen think of the boat group as completely disbanded at the end of the *kembong* season, to be formed anew at the beginning of the next season, these boat groups actually have far greater permanence, particularly those of the more successful *kolek*. At the beginning of the 1956 fishing season, more than half the *kolek* on the beach utilized the same crew as in the previous season. Viewed in this way, the boat group can be said to exist as an intermittently functioning unit of social organization for at least as long as the life of the boat. Groups periodically lose one or more members and gain others to take their places, some groups more than others, but the group itself remains, generally retaining its particular netting techniques and distribution procedures from one year to the next.

In the operations of the individually owned *kolek*, the boat group is limited to an organization for co-operative economic exploitation. In the *perahu serikat*, however, the co-operative organization also functions as a proprietary group to the extent that the *kolek* itself belongs to the group organization, belonging to it in spite of turnover in the membership of the group. Within the boat group, authority is exercised exclusively and regularly by the steerer (*jeragan*), even though he may be steering another's boat. The crew (*awak perahu*) may discuss among themselves, or with the steerer, matters such as when and where to fish, the need for motor tows, and maintenance of the boat, but once the steerer has committed himself to a decision, the crew must follow unquestioningly or else quit the group. It is customary in the boat groups that, no matter how inefficient a man has proved and how many other groups he has been forced out of, he will be taken on if a new group has a vacancy or if the group can be stretched to include him. Ordinarily, however, men such as this are unable to remain with a group for more than one season and therefore form only peripheral relationships with several group organizations. One or two men in the community actually affiliate themselves with two different groups at the same time.

Parallel to the boat group and functioning because of it is the distribution and marketing organization of the wives of the crew members of each *kolek*. In this organization the position of authority is held by the wife of the owner, and she is responsible for settling any dispute which may arise over the distribution of the shares of fish. Although the marketing operations are the responsibility of each woman herself, a group of women representing the same *kolek* frequently bargain collectively with the wholesaler in Pattani. If the total catch of a *kolek* is small, one or a few women take it all to market. The women's group also tends to retain its structure during the period when nets are being repaired, though each net is individually owned. If several nets are badly damaged and others not at all, there is a tendency on the part of all the women of the same *kolek*, as well as the men, to help repair the damaged nets. Without the distribution and marketing functions of the women's group the boat group would cease to exist in its present form. On the other hand, however, because of complaints and occasional organizational action on the part of a few or all of the women, some of the boat groups have been badly disorganized by large losses in membership and by the weakening, through criticism, of the authority of the steerer.

Stemming directly from the boat groups are the co-operative tow groups. These groups are generally proprietary, to a large extent, in terms of the motorboat, although the membership may be entirely from individually owned *kolek*. As these groups were first formed in the summer of 1956, their organization was not completely structured when this study was completed. There was some indecision when situations outside the normal routine arose or even when there was a simple set of alternatives within the routine situation. With no one to fill the undefined role of authority, the steerers of the component *kolek* in the tow were looked to for decisions, but sometimes they were unwilling to fill this role either individually or collectively. An example of this hesitation to exercise authority outside of a structured role occurred during one of the slack periods of the *kembong* season. A sailing vessel loaded with wood from Pattani and bound for a village ten miles to the west of Rusembilan was becalmed off the village. The crew of the vessel talked to representatives of four Rusembilan motorboats in trying to arrange to be towed and to set a price. Not until all the steerers of the eleven *kolek* "belonging" to the motorboats had discussed the matter both in terms of the tow group itself and in terms of defining a consistent policy for all motorboats of the community was even a tentative decision reached. By that time, more than twenty-four hours had elapsed, the wind had come up, and the vessel in question had sailed on.

Although the tow groups ordinarily functioned efficiently enough, with all *kolek* consenting to rotate position in tow and agreeing approximately when and where to fish, it is probable that the situations demanding the exercise of authority will force the establishment of a role for this authority. Whereas in the boat group the exercise of authority can easily be added to the role of steerer because of his personal qualifications, no such situation seemed to obtain in the case of the tow group. The qualifications of the personnel aboard the motorboat are chiefly mechanical and not ordinarily suitable for authority. In two of the tow groups, there were signs that authority was being vested in member steerers because of their personal qualities of leadership. Their assumption of the additional role could almost be expected. The other tow groups, however, lacked such able men, and in the future they will be faced with the problem not only of creating a role for authority on some logical basis, but also of filling it.[2]

To a certain extent, the co-operative groups formed for the transplanting of the young rice plants are based upon the relationships established among men in the boat groups. But more important are family connections. In most contexts wide family relationships play a small part in Rusembilan; however, in the context of agricultural co-operation they assume almost the same degree of importance that is found in the purely agricultural villages inland. Partly through tradition and partly because inheritance of land usually results in a physical proximity of the padi fields that reflects genealogical proximity, landowners generally call first upon their close relations (fathers, brothers, uncles, cousins, nephews) to help with transplanting. Next are called congenial members of the planter's boat group and his close friends and neighbors. If for any reason he needs more assistance than can be found among these people, he will call upon more distant relatives before calling casual friends, even though his relationships with the relatives may be more casual than with the friends. This is because kinship relations, though infrequently utilized, afford a convenient bilateral channel for reciprocal obligations in farming as well as in social and ceremonial contexts. There is a tendency to expect exact reciprocity for working on another's fields, and many landowners keep a written tally of how long they work and on which fields, balancing it against the work done for them.

Co-operative enterprise for buying rubber-producing land is usually based on boat-group relationships, but may also involve family ones. Frequently, these groups of land buyers are co-

[2] See the end of this section and also Chapter XIII (Sociocultural Factors) for a discussion of the disintegration of the tow groups.

operative only in respect to the difficulties attendant on acquiring the land. Once the land is bought, each man clears and plants his own share as sole proprietor. When the whole tract is undivided and run as a co-operative enterprise, little attention is paid to the organization of the working group. Each man will go to the plantation when his duties in the village permit, or all will go together and do whatever work each is inclined to do. In the case of the rubber holdings of Rusembilan, none of which is yielding a marketable product yet, these co-operative organizations will not be functioning fully until such time as they can regulate the tapping routine, the marketing, and the distribution of profits.

Organization of the village patrol system was possible only because of the well-organized boat groups. As was pointed out in the last chapter, there was no systematic organization in the patrol itself, and because of this lack of organization, a patrol member could decide for himself what area of the village he would watch and how conscientiously he would do the job when he got there. Basically, the patrol was just a coincidence of one of the organizational roles of each boat group, structured in terms of the boat groups and not in terms of the function of the patrol group itself. Some men on the patrol felt resentment because they had to protect the wealthier men who were not forced by economic necessity to fish and thus had no patrol duties. The fishermen probably would not have allowed themselves to be drawn into a patrol that was organized only in terms of community welfare. But because their patrol duties were defined as part of the boat-group membership and because they received equal shares of fish even when they were on patrol, the fishermen were willing, if not eager, to accept the additional role of policeman.

Lack of co-operation and the partial disintegration of co-operative groups are not unknown at Rusembilan. Frequently, a plot of land or two adjoining plots are worked jointly by descendants of the original owner. Occasionally, one of the land-owners wants to sell, or does sell, part or all of the land, destroying the co-operative farming group and generally severing any relationships the two individuals or families may have with one another. Boat groups, particularly in *perahu serikat*, are occasionally disrupted by a serious challenge to the authority of the steerer. In 1956, such a group split into factions, one loyal to the steerer and the other loyal to a man who had steered the boat on several occasions with apparently more success. Finally, the alternate steerer decided to leave the boat and got a job as steerer on a new boat. Most of his followers left with him, some being able to sell out their shares in the *perahu serikat* and others just accepting a loss, hoping to make it up through better fishing.

At several points during the formation of the tow groups, disorganization caused by lack of co-operation threatened to cause a return to the old practice of each *kolek* sailing out alone to the fishing grounds. The members of one boat group accused the steerer of another, who was beginning to assume authority in the tow group, of partiality to members of his own boat group in financial matters, and they actually left the tow group for about two weeks. The accused steerer carefully explained his position to the steerers of the other *kolek*, and the situation had almost been forgotten when the wives of the crew members began to complain about the distribution of shares. The complaint was not limited to this tow group alone. The basis of the complaints was that successful boats had to pool their catch with the less successful *kolek*, with the result that the crew members of the successful *kolek* had less income than they had had when they were fishing alone. For a short time, it seemed that it would be necessary to reorganize the tow groups on the basis of fishing ability of each *kolek*, but finally it was agreed that each *kolek* would contribute a proportion of its own catch to the motorboat regardless of what the other *kolek* in the tow had caught.

By the end of the *kembong* season in 1957, the process of

disintegration of the tow-group organization had proceeded even farther. Of the four original tow groups, only one was left intact, and two others had each lost one *kolek* from the group. Distribution of fish within the tow groups was strictly on the basis of the individual *kolek*, each paying a fixed number of fish or sum of money for the tow. *Kolek* which had left tow groups invested in outboard motors. These had the advantage, according to the villagers, of being faster than the motor tows, as well as the obvious advantage of returning to the individual *kolek* complete responsibility and authority in their own fishing operations. It is probable that, because of the ease with which the outboard motors can be incorporated into the structure of the boat groups, more and more *kolek* will adopt this form of mechanization as they are able to afford it, and the motorboats, if they remain at all in Rusembilan, will cease to function in fishing operations.[3]

Social and Religious Groups

The villagers of Rusembilan maintain that there is only a minimum of co-operation in areas of community life other than economic and that groups formed for co-operative effort are impermanent. To a certain extent this is a true representation of the situation. There is a standing committee to take care of the mosque and arrange for special ceremonies, but there seems to be an active avoidance of other situations requiring noneconomic co-operation, an avoidance of extending organizational patterns from economic groups into social and religious activities. The closest approximation of an extension of economic groupings, that is, a grouping which has a degree of stability, is the group of men found most mornings in each of the coffee shops. The organization of these coffee shop groups, however, is very fluid, and although it is common to find a small nucleus of elder men in the same shop most mornings, any or all of them may be absent

[3] Personal communication, September 1957. See also Appendix A.

or at another shop. It is the pattern in which the younger men enter temporarily into these groups that links them with the boat groups, as the men will usually come into the shops as a unit made up from a part of a boat group. The choice of coffee shop is usually determined by where the steerer or boatowner habitually goes or is expected to be. This is partly due to the fact that the *kolek* do not all get back to the beach at the same time of day, and even if a man has a closer friend on another *kolek*, he enters into the coffee shop group with his fellow crew members led by the steerer or owner because he happens to be with them at that time.

Later in the day and during the time the boat groups are not functioning, groups of men tend to be formed on the basis of friendship. These groups, like their counterparts among the women, are almost completely unstructured and are not recognized by the villagers as groups but only as the casual association of friends. The groups of children, of one sex or mixed, are somewhat more structured than the adult groups or associations because of the greater degree of disequality based on slight differences of age or strength. Even though leadership and even the definition of other roles may be apparent in children's groups, these groups dissolve at about the age of puberty, and whatever structuring they may have had is not carried over into adult life.

When constructing a Malay house, a large labor force is essential for a short period of time. The framework of the house is almost completely put together on the ground, and when all the parts are ready, the housebuilder calls together a group to lift the sides into position. This group, though involving reciprocal obligations, is unlike the agricultural groups in that there is no tendency to call upon relatives before friends. Usually, the group is made up of members of the same boat group, close friends and neighbors, and any other men who are obligated to the builder for some previous service. Twenty or more men are rallied for the average house. A feast, consisting in part of some of the *nasi pulot* (glutinous rice) offered to the spirits when the house is raised, is served to all the men at the end of the job. The head of this group is always the most experienced carpenter present. He is rarely the housebuilder himself, who is apt to be a young man. Even though the builder is the owner of the house, he must accept the authority of the head carpenter in the group. Ordinarily, the group labor is limited to raising the four sides of the house (eight sides if it is a large double house) and securing them with diagonal braces and roof beams. Sometimes the owner asks the group to return later to help with the slow job of finishing the tiled or atap roof.

Groups similar to those for house raising are recruited for the construction of public buildings and other community works. The building of the school was discussed in Chapter VII. The only other public building constructed within the last twenty-five years is the *balaisa* or chapel, built in 1954. Although the labor force required for these buildings was no larger than for a typical house, all men in the community were called to work on them so that each person's share in the work would be small. In the case of the *balaisa* but not of the school, one able carpenter was on the job throughout the construction, and he was considered the head of the group despite the fact that the imam was actually in charge of the building. At the school, the *kamnan* placed himself in authority. Because reciprocation was impossible in relation to either of these projects, food was supposed to be served to the workers throughout the construction period. During the construction of the *balaisa*, this was practical as the job was done quickly by a large group. The food was provided by the imam and a group of the village hajis and was prepared by their wives. As the construction of the school building was spread over a long period and a particular man might work on it only an hour or so each day, the *kamnan* did not provide food except on the first day and when the sides of the school were erected.

Work on community projects, such as mending the village road, is organized in the same manner either by the *kamnan* or by the *selawat*, and food is provided by them from whatever funds may be available.

The major noneconomic areas in which co-operative effort is required is the feasting (*kenduri*) which accompanies all ceremonial occasions. Feasts are given either in the home by the family if the ceremony is held for an individual or at the mosque or *balaisa* if it is for the community as a whole. According to the size of the feast, fifteen or twenty people may begin preparations three days in advance. The helpers are enlisted first from among close relatives and then from close friends, neighbors, and boat-group comembers, as is done in agricultural groups. There may be a large amount of work involved in preparing a feast, but the family has as few helpers as possible because each has to be fed for as long as he is working and some prestige accrues to the feasting household if it breaks even or makes a profit on the feast. The preparations for feasts held at the mosque or the *balaisa* are under the supervision of the imam and the mosque committee, and helpers are recruited from among those most active in mosque affairs. Other people are expected, and frequently asked, to help defray the cost of the feast.

Occasionally various other forms of social co-operation are found at Rusembilan. There are sports such as a kickball game played by young men, team competition in kiteflying, and boat races. A boat race is held annually on the Pattani River, and any *kolek* or smaller boat from the surrounding villages may enter. A *kolek* is paddled by a crew of twenty-five to thirty men. One woman in the village holds periodic lotteries in front of one of the coffee shops. For fifty satang (2½ cents) she gives each interested woman or child a numbered ticket. The winning number is worth a small prize. This lottery is considered more of a pastime than a money-making project both by the woman who runs it and by those who participate in it. There are several other games played frequently by groups of women and children and one or two games occasionally played by two men with a large crowd of onlookers.

Feasting and Intercommunity Integration

In connection with every religious ceremony or important event in the life of an individual or family, a feast or *kenduri* is held. On many of these occasions, such as the marriage ceremony, the guests are invited to partake of the feast only and not to witness the actual ceremony. Thus, it is common for the villagers to speak of *makan pulot* (eating rice) in referring to a ceremonial occasion and feast. At the feast, the rice served is not the kind used in the daily diet (*nasi, Oryza sativa*),[4] but a glutinous rice (*pulot, Oryza glutinosa*)[5] grown in the northern parts of Thailand and many other places in Southeast Asia.

During the first six or eight weeks following the fasting month, many people throughout the area hold *makan pulot* on almost any pretext and sometimes for no reason at all. A typical villager from Rusembilan may have to attend three or four of these functions in one day, often being required to travel fifty or sixty miles at considerable expense to get there. When the *makan pulot* is large, the host invites people from his own village and friends from other villages, and he asks all to invite as many people as they wish. Thus, the villager from Rusembilan may get an invitation from a man in another village whom he respects to attend a *makan pulot* being held in a third village by someone whom he does not know. To refuse an invitation would be a rudeness toward the respected friend, and except in the case of some important contingency, the villager must accept.

After estimating how many guests will attend the *makan pulot* and buying the necessary quantity of food, the host begins

[4] R. J. Wilkinson, *A Malay-English Dictionary*, II, 192.
[5] *Ibid.*

preparations by calling together all those people who are going to help with the feast. Usually the day before the feast, but sometimes three days in advance if it is to be a large feast, the cooking area is prepared. This is generally a shed which is used for storing food and in which the cooks may sit, and around it are the cooking pits. Each pit consists of a large hole dug in the ground for the fire; a tunnel to this pit from a rectangular cut in the ground about three feet away provides a draught for the fire and a means of adding fuel without removing the pot from the fire. The outdoor cooking is done by the men. This is limited to cooking the rice and the basic curry. For an average *makan pulot*, the cooks prepare from ten to twenty pots of rice, each containing twenty-eight quarts, and half as many pots of curry. Generally, the sheep or cow to be used in the curry is brought to the cooking area alive and is slaughtered shortly before it is cut up and added to curry, grated coconut, and other ingredients. Meanwhile, women work in the house, gathering together plates and bowls and preparing the many side dishes that go with the curry and rice. Groups of boys and girls are always to be found at these preparations, and they are counted on by the adults to perform a certain part of the work involved.

The feast itself usually lasts all day, with guests arriving at whatever time is most convenient for them. As two or three hundred people may be fed at the average *makan pulot*, overcrowding and waiting to be served frequently occur even though the meal is served throughout the day. Arriving guests are seated on the floor in groups of five around large trays holding bowls of curry and the side dishes. Men and women are in different rooms or are separated by a curtain. After the right hand of each person is rinsed over a basin, rice is passed, and each guest takes as much as he wants and puts it on his plate. Curry and the side dishes are then eaten along with handfuls of rice. After the meal and a final rinsing of the hand, the guest usually rises immediately, places some money in a box for that purpose, and leaves. At smaller ceremonies, usually connected with passage rites for children, and at the final serving of large feasts, those guests invited for the ceremony itself will either remain seated where they have eaten or move to a different part of the room.

The system of collection varies according to the occasion. Each guest at a *makan pulot* is expected to contribute ten baht (50 cents) or more for his meal if he is an intimate friend. Other villagers usually pay five baht (25 cents), and guests from inland villages pay two or three baht.

Before the war, it was common for a man to expect and realize a profit on a *makan pulot*. He would usually count on clearing nearly one thousand baht ($50) on a feast that cost three thousand baht ($150). Now, with higher food costs, both for the feast itself and for feeding the group called to prepare the feast, and with transportation costs cutting down the contributions of people from inland villages, a man considers himself fortunate if his receipts equal his costs.

Old men in Rusembilan complain that today the *makan pulot* has lost its meaning, and because of costs and the grand scale on which it is often held, it is a waste of time either to hold or to attend a *makan pulot*. The *makan pulot* held by villagers or by friends outside of the village are usually so large, and the actual feasting so crowded and hurried, that guests may not see the hosts during the feast or even know why the *makan pulot* is being given. Formerly, feasts were small, more informal gatherings where most of the people knew each other and where they could enter into the spirit of the celebration for which the feast was being given though they might not actually remain for the ceremonies. Even the *makan pulot* given by a stranger, to which the guest was brought by a mutual friend, was formerly a pleasant and socially worth-while event. Such *makan pulot* were usually small, and people were invited in order to bring together two sets of relatives or friends for mutual benefit. In this way, a man was able to build up a circle of friends on whom he could rely throughout the area; and marriage alliances were frequently formed in this manner.

Now, however, much of the original purpose of the *makan pulot* is lost. Instead of trying to increase his circle of friends throughout the area and renew old friendships, a man merely strives to have as many people present at his feast as possible. In the summer of 1956, a *makan pulot* was held for two days in a nearby village and was attended by over three thousand people from all over southern Thailand and northern Malaya. This emphasis on sheer numbers of guests attending tends to reinforce itself within the area and become an end in itself. Thus, if a man is talked about, though not necessarily respected, because he has held an extraordinarily large *makan pulot*, another man planning a celebration will fear adverse comparison if he does not attempt to surpass it in size. In this way, a large *makan pulot* has become a recognized symbol of prestige throughout the Pattani area.

CHAPTER IX

Rusembilan as a

Moslem Community

SINCE the fourteenth century or earlier,[1] the Malays in the Pattani area of southern Thailand have embraced the Moslem faith. Although retaining many elements of earlier Hindu beliefs[2] and local spiritual beliefs antedating even the Hindu elements (see Chapter X), the villager of Rusembilan is a sincerely devout Moslem. Religion, mainly in the form of precepts and proscriptions, pervades the villager's daily life. Most of the residents of Rusembilan lack any Islamic theological background at all, and those who to some degree understand the meaning of a few of the formal elements of the religion have great difficulty in trying to impart this understanding to others. In general, the villagers and some of those who officiate at the mosque are content with being able to display the outward symbols of the religion and to recite the Koran and passages from other sacred books. In spite of its historical connections with and its founda-

[1] Richard O. Winstedt, *The Malays: A Cultural History*, pp. 33 f.
[2] Richard O. Winstedt, *The Malay Magician, Being Shaman, Saiva, and Sufi*, pp. 27–38.

tion upon the Shafi'i school of the orthodox Sunna,[3] religion in this area readily embraced elements of the antipathetic Shi'ism later introduced from India.[4] Shi'ism served as a rationale to integrate into the Islamic structure the majority of the older animistic beliefs, the use of charms and other magical practices, and the Malay predilection for mystic names, numbers, and formulas. After the Koran, the most important books in use at Rusembilan are *Kitab al-kurbat ila Allah* (Book of Approach to God) and *Kitab taj al-muluk* (Book of the Crown of Kings). The last-named volume, including a complete almanac of auspicious days, types of divination, and rituals for curing and the prevention of bad luck, is carefully consulted by the villager before he undertakes any venture at all out of the ordinary.

The Villager as a Moslem

The Malay villager is seriously dedicated to his religion, but in spite of this puts certain basic Malay tenets before his Islamic precepts. The chief among these has to do with his treatment of women. In ordinary life there is no segregation of the sexes, women are not veiled, and there is a feeling of equality between men and women. If a woman seems to have a business sense superior to that of her husband, she will take over the handling of the family finances, and in one case a woman is listed in the official government census as being the head of the family.[5] For many years the rajas of Pattani were women.[6] Only when matters deal directly with the mosque and religion and when an unmarried girl has passed puberty does segregation of the sexes occur, and even here there is no feeling of disequality. In this connection, women may not hold office in the religious organization, although two women hajis have been among the most respected

[3] Winstedt, *The Malays*, p. 37.
[4] Winstedt, *Malay Magician*, pp. 72–80.
[5] Government of Thailand, *Census BE 2499* (1956).
[6] W. A. R. Wood, *A History of Siam*, p. 167.

religious teachers in Rusembilan. Attendance at the mosque is not compulsory for them on Friday; when they attend, they are assigned a separate section, with a curtain between them and the men. They are separated from the men during *kenduri* or feasts, generally eating after the men in the kitchen of the feasting household. A postpubescent girl is kept carefully secluded in her parents' house until marriage, during which ceremony she wears the veil traditional with Moslem women, as well as a pair of very dark sunglasses. Innumerable relatively unimportant Islamic laws are ignored or openly contravened daily by the villagers: except for religious feasts, flesh is rarely slaughtered in accordance with the Koran; spirits and ghosts are of considerable importance to the villager, and he is constantly propitiating them; daily prayers are frequently omitted, and the bathing ritual is seldom carried out as prescribed by law.

To the villager of Rusembilan, the most important area of his religion is that of prayer and reading the Koran. Prayer, like any religious act of value, falls within two of the three categories of obligation defined by the Malay Moslem. The first of these categories, *wajib* (obligatory), includes all religious obligations that must be carried out, such as the five daily prayers (*sembayang lima waktu*), the observance of Ramadan, the fasting month (*bulan puasa*), and the *zakat* or alms to be contributed to the mosque for distribution to various classes of needy. The second category, *sunat* (commendable), includes those religious acts which, though not obligatory, are considered to be of great virtue, such as the addition of two extra prayers to the five which are *wajib*, continuation of fasting for six days beyond Ramadan,[7] and the haj or pilgrimage to Mecca. The third category, *harus* (proper), includes only acts which are of no religious value one way or another, but which are not specifically banned by the religion, such as eating mutton on a feast day (rather than fish) because it is more valued.

---

[7] This is *wajib* rather than *sunat* if one has been forced to break the fast during Ramadan for any reason, for example, menstruation or illness.

The five daily prayers are required to be said by all adult men in the village, though on certain occasions, particularly when the men go out fishing, one or more of them may be omitted. The prayers (*sembayang*) include the following: *sembayang suboh* (dawn), *sembayang lohor* (midday), *sembayang asar* (afternoon), *sembayang maghrib* (evening), and *sembayang isha* (nightfall). In addition, two *sunat* prayers may be added: *sembayang loha* (forenoon) and *sembayang tahajud* (night). The time for each of these prayers is announced by the beating of drums at the mosque and the *balaisa*. Frequently, much of the prayer ritual is omitted, the supplicant simply performing the verbal portions of his prayer. Each prayer is supposed, however, to consist of certain definite elements. The supplicant stands *kiblat*, facing the direction of Mecca, and repeats a short prayer of aspiration or a specific request (*niat, hajat*). He then raises his arms and says several times the *takbir*, which consists of the phrase *Allahu akbar* (God is great). The supplicant now recites the *fatihah*, the opening verse of the Koran:

In the name of Allah, the Beneficent, the Merciful.
Praise be to Allah, Lord of the Worlds,
The Beneficent, the Merciful.
Owner of the Day of Judgment,
Thee (alone) we worship; Thee (alone) we ask for help.
Show us the straight path,
The path of those whom thou hast favoured;
Not (the path) of those who earn Thine anger nor of those who go
   astray.[8]

Following the *fatihah*, the supplicant performs the *rakaat* at least once. This consists of a prayer said standing erect, followed by a deep bow (*rukok*), full prostration (*sujut*), rising to the knees, and a repetition of the *sujut*.

The villagers usually think of their abbreviated form of prayer (with some of the ritual omitted) as the *hajat* and differentiate

[8] Mohammed Marmaduke Pickthall, trans., *The Meaning of the Glorious Koran*, p. 31.

it from the full *sembayang*. Another form of prayer is the *donga* or *doa*, which is an informal petition to God, usually for some specific end, said in a standing position with raised palms. Some authorities see in this a suggestion of white or religious magic.[9]

Friday prayers (*sembayang jumaat*) in the mosque are *wajib* for men if forty or more male residents can be gathered at the mosque. If less than forty arrive at the mosque, the ordinary *sembayang lohor* is performed. When the Friday service is to be performed, a call to prayer is made by the *khatib*, who is accompanied by loud beating of the mosque drum. The *khotebah* is read by either the imam or the *khatib*. Although the *khotebah* may include an extemporaneous sermon, at Rusembilan it is ordinarily confined to readings in Arabic, followed by Malay translations from a book of passages from the Koran and sayings of the prophets. Passages are chosen as appropriate to the season of the year or the religious calendar, such as what to avoid and how to live virtuously during the fasting month. After the *khotebah*, the *sembayang lohor* is repeated twice, followed by the *shahadat* or confession of faith. People may leave after this, or they may remain in the mosque to read from the Koran or say additional prayers along with the imam. On leaving the mosque, the men *salam* with a double handclasp and ask each other for forgiveness and blessing. Usually, a large group of men remains on the porch of the mosque talking quietly of village matters until the imam and those who have remained inside with him have finished their prayers and are ready to return to the beach.

The Mosque and Religious Organization

According to strict usage, the mosque (*surau*) at Rusembilan is not a true mosque of general assembly (*masjid*). The *masjid* must be of permanent construction, such as stone or concrete, rather than wood. It must contain a lectern pulpit for the imam or the *khatib* and must to a degree be sanctified by avoiding such acts as smoking and loud, irreverent talking in and around it.

[9] R. J. Wilkinson, *A Malay-English Dictionary*, I, 283.

The *surau* at Rusembilan fits none of these criteria, but the village is proud of it nonetheless as a place of worship, as many other villages in the area lack even this. The *balaisa* in Kampong Pata actually falls into the same category as the *surau* in Kampong Surau, but it is called *balaisa*, denoting an even less formal religious function than the *surau*, in order to maintain the significance of having one village mosque.

The mosque and the *balaisa* are cared for by the mosque committee, whose duty it is to look after the actual physical structures and to arrange for celebrations and feasts to be held there. The committee, made up of twelve men serving a four-year term, includes the imam, the *khatib*, and the *bilal* (muezzin). These three appoint the nine lay committeemen after consulting with other religious leaders in the community. The imam, *khatib*, and *bilal* are themselves appointed by the Moslem Religious Board (*Majalis Ugama*) of Pattani province from candidates suggested by the villagers. This board must notify the district officer of the choice and the date that the appointment is to be made in the village mosque. The actual appointment takes place right after the Friday service and is followed by a talk given by the district officer on the function of the government as well as religion in the villagers' lives. Other functions of the Moslem Religious Board include registration of the number of mosques and religious officials in the province, collection of the *zakat* or alms, and approval of the building of any new mosques in order not to have too many in a particular area. Frequently, this body is called upon to settle religious disputes or civil disputes involving Islamic law in the villages within the province. The board meets monthly with the governor and the district officers of the province to discuss matters dealing with both religion and administration, such as the government budget for building mosques and plans for joint Moslem-Buddhist prayers at civil functions.[10]

[10] Such joint Moslem-Buddhist civil ceremonies as the *Phud Mon Khon*, or blessing of the rice seed, are attended by Thai officials, a few Malay village officials, and a few Thai civilians.

Members of the Moslem Religious Board are chosen from men of wisdom and respect, usually hajis, by all the religious officials of the province.

The chairmen of the Moslem Religious Boards from all the provinces in Thailand having Moslem elements of population form an informal committee which is headed by a Moslem representative of the Thai national government, the *chakhul Islam*. He is supposed to be a wise and able man who will bring to the government's attention problems in the Moslem areas of the nation and actively work toward solutions of them. As he is appointed to his position by the political party in power, he is frequently no more than a spokesman for the government, whose duty is to explain to the Moslems of Thailand, through their Moslem Religious Boards, any government policy which seems to them to be counter to the interests of Islam.

Ceremonial Calendar

The villagers of Rusembilan, though having a tendency to abbreviate and simplify many of their ritual and ceremonial observances, are extremely precise in keeping track of them. Even the daily time for prayer is calculated from the position of the sun rather than according to Thai zone time (i.e., Rusembilan clocks are approximately forty minutes faster than local time). At the exact time for each prayer, the drums at the mosque and the *balaisa* are beaten. At sunset, the beginning of the new day, they are beaten harder and longer, particularly at sunset on Thursday, the beginning of *jumaat*, the Moslem Sabbath. Because of Islamic proscription of working for profit on *jumaat*, it is Thursday night rather than Friday night that the fishermen must not work. A few of the crabbers, however, put out their nets Thursday afternoon and bring them in Friday morning; and except when the men are attending the services in the mosque, the coffee shops are usually open all day Friday. Many of the fishermen have complained that, because other gainful occupations are carried out on Friday and because *kolek* from other Malay villages go out the night before, it is unfair that they must stay in. The imam, however, says that it is better for the villagers to live good lives than to have one extra night of fishing each week.

Most of the important Islamic holy days are celebrated at Rusembilan, although, except for a few, they are observed merely by a service at the mosque and perhaps the preparation of a simple meal to be served to friends. Religiously, the most important period of the year is Ramadan, the fasting month (*bulan puasa*). With very few exceptions, and those surreptitious, the villagers observe for the entire month the fast and the period of abstinence from sunrise to sunset. Two days before the beginning of the month of Ramadan, most families prepare *ketupat*, a triangular packet, wrapped in a banana leaf, of cooked glutinous rice with coconut. They distribute *ketupat* to all their friends, relatives, and neighbors. The fasting of Ramadan is not started in the Pattani area until the day after the first night that the new moon is actually seen, and in case of cloudy weather this may not be until several days after the official start of the month.

At Rusembilan during Ramadan, many people sleep during the day and remain awake at night, when they may eat and smoke. The usual waking time is about one in the afternoon, in time for the *sembayang lohor* or midday prayer. Later in the afternoon, some light work may be done by the men, but if it can be put off for the rest of the month, it usually is. Men will often prepare the sweets for the evening meal while the women make ready other food before the *sembayang asar*. At sunset, after prayers, the main meal is served, consisting of sweets and a sweet drink first and then rice and curry. Following the *menamat*, which is the point when one entire Koran has been read during the evening recitations of this month, a fast-breaking feast is customarily held in the mosque instead of the evening meal at home. In 1956, this feast was given for the people of

Kampong Pata by the residents of Kampong Surau; it was reciprocated at the *balaisa* in Kampong Pata two nights later. Later in the month, fast-breaking parties are often held in the coffee shops.

The people usually rest between the *sembayang maghrib* (evening prayers) and the *sembayang isha* (nightfall). *Sembayang isha* may be followed by *sembayang teraweh*, Ramadan prayers, which are *sunat* or optional. These consist of a repetition twenty-one times of the full ritual *sembayang*. Children are encouraged to be present at the *balaisa* or the mosque during the recitation, and each night a different family provides food for them. They add much enthusiasm to the shouting in glorification of the Prophet after each repetition. The more religious individuals remain in the mosque or the *balaisa* after the *sembayang teraweh*, reading the Koran with the imam or religious leaders. As each *jus* (or sura, chapter of the Koran) is finished in the consecutive reading of the Koran from the beginning of the month, the drum is sounded. After the last *jus* of the night, the drum is sounded longer so that the women will know it is time to prepare the next meal. The *sembayang suboh* (dawn prayers) are then said, and the villagers go home to eat and sleep. When the *kembong* season coincides with Ramadan, the fishermen must of course alter this routine, compromising as best they can between their religious obligations and their economic pursuits.

On the twenty-seventh day of Ramadan, the *zakat pitrah* is collected. This *zakat* is the only one levied during the year at Rusembilan, unlike the system in other Malay communities, where the *zakat pitrah* is collected only to provide the poor with plenty at the time of *Hari Raya Puasa* (see below), and another *zakat*, collected after the fasting month, is distributed more generally. The *zakat* at Rusembilan consists of gifts of four quarts of rice which must be given to one or more of the following: the poor, caretakers of religious properties, new converts to Islam, debtors, men who do not earn enough to support their families, religious organizations (i.e., the Moslem Religious Board), and widows. Frequently, the families at Rusembilan will simply give their contribution to the mosque for distribution.

As in the beginning of Ramadan, the fasting month is not considered ended until the next new moon is actually seen.[11] A representative of the Moslem Religious Board in Pattani announces this the next day from a truck equipped with a public address system, and the information finally reaches the more remote villages by word of mouth. Even in Rusembilan, some people complain that they are notified too late to enjoy fully the prayers that are said on this feast day. From the second to the seventh day of the month following Ramadan is a period of *sunat* or optional fasting. Fasting is forbidden on the first day of this month as it is *Hari Raya Puasa*, a feast day. At Rusembilan, about half the residents of Kampong Surau, a few hajis in other parts of the community, and any person who was forced by sickness or menstruation to break fast during Ramadan observe this six-day fast.

The first day of Shawwal, the month following Ramadan, is *Hari Raya Puasa* (great day [after] fasting). Of the three *hari raya* observed in Malay communities, this is by far the most important at Rusembilan, as it is a day of feasting and festivities following the month-long fast. All villagers dress in their newest and finest clothes and greet each other with the *salam*. Many of the village households prepare large quantities of food to serve to friends who may drop in, as visiting is common this day. A complete service is held in the mosque during the morning, and the daily prayers are said more assiduously on this day than perhaps on any other in the year. On most *Hari Raya*

[11] Actual observation of the moon by one person with two witnesses (four if the sighter is a woman) is required by the Moslem Religious Board as proof of the beginning of the new month. In the Federation of Malaya, an astronomical calendar is employed to determine the exact moment of the new month, at which time a gun is fired.

Puasa, a carnival opens in Pattani, and large groups of young men from the village spend much of the afternoon and evening watching the Malay dancing, Thai boxing, and bullfighting as well as enjoying the side shows and "rides" to be found there. During the evening, or the previous evening if the village has been notified by then of the end of the fasting month, children and adults alike set fire to great "candles" of coconut shells, which are placed one on top of the other on sticks, and set off firecrackers made in the village either from gunpowder or from water-filled bamboo sections which are heated until they explode.

On the eighth day of Shawwal, *Hari Raya Enam* (great day [after] six [days of fasting]) is celebrated. This feast after the six-day fasting period following Ramadan is never as elaborately observed as *Hari Raya Puasa*, and most of the village pays little heed to it. Unless a villager is to embark on a pilgrimage to Mecca, *Hari Raya Haji* (great day of the pilgrim) on the tenth day of the month of Zu'lhijjah is also of little importance. If a villager is going to Mecca at this time or later in the year, this *hari raya* may be celebrated almost as elaborately as *Hari Raya Puasa*. *Ashura*, on the tenth day of the first month, Muharram, derived from the celebration of the Jewish Day of Atonement,[12] is also noted, but is of no particular significance at Rusembilan. *Maulut*, the birthday of the Prophet on the twelfth day of the month of Rabia I, is considered the most important day after *Hari Raya Puasa*;[13] the *Maulut* celebration is very similar to this *hari raya*, except that both sexes sit together in the mosque to hear the history of the Prophet read by the imam.[14]

[12] Wilkinson, *op. cit.*, I, 50.

[13] In the Federation of Malaya, *Maulut* is celebrated as a national holiday, as are some of the Indian and Christian holidays, but *Hari Raya Puasa* is not.

[14] A comprehensive account of Malay festivals is to be found in Zainal-'Abidin bin Ahmad, "Malay Festivals and Some Aspects of Malay Re-

Religious Schools and Instruction

Starting at about six or seven years of age, every child in the village receives instruction in the Koran. Each morning and afternoon, except on Fridays and religious feast days, the children of the village assemble at the *balaisa*. Instruction starts at about seven and continues until nine, when the village school opens, and in the afternoon it generally lasts from three to five. The imam is in charge of teaching the boys, and his wife instructs the girls in another part of the building. The purpose of the instruction is to teach the children the entire Koran by rote. Frequently, however, the children will be able to associate the written Arabic characters with their sounds, and thus they learn to read rather than memorize the Koran. The instruction ordinarily consists of the reading of a passage by the imam, followed by a recitation of it in unison by the children. If the imam feels that some of the children are not learning as well as they should, he will single them out for individual recitations. Although the majority of the children of Rusembilan attends the lessons at the *balaisa*, there are two other religious leaders in the village who also give this instruction. Each of them has about ten pupils. Until early 1956, these instructions were also given by the son of the former imam of Rusembilan. This man is admitted to be one of the wisest men in the village concerning religious matters, but since his return from Mecca eighteen years before, he has been suffering from a mental disease which reached such a point of dissociation and occasional violence that the imam thought it best to discontinue his classes.

After a period of instruction lasting one and a half to two years, the student is given an informal examination on his knowledge of the Koran. When he passes this, his compulsory religious education is over. At this time, a small feast (*khatam Kuran*) is held by the family of the child. Friends and relatives of the family contribute money, and the closest of these are invited to the feast along with the most respected religious men of the community.

Many boys, instead of ending their religious education here, continue receiving instruction from the imam or from one of the other religious instructors. This advanced instruction attempts to impart to the child some understanding of the Koran; for although the child has memorized or learned to read it, the Arabic words are meaningless to him. To facilitate this understanding and to supplement it, the student is taught to read books in *Jawi* (the Malay language in Arabic script). Unlike his lessons in recitation of the Koran, the student now receives individual instruction, partly because his goal is understanding rather than recitation and partly because the books he must use can be found only in the private collection of his teacher, whereas each household and each learning child has a copy of the Koran. These instructions continue for as long as the child or the parent wish. There is no tuition charge for such instruction, but the student or his family is expected to contribute food or services to the teacher.

Whether or not they have had the advanced training in religion at Rusembilan, perhaps 80 per cent of the boys after their *masuk Jawi* (entering Malay-hood) ceremony are sent by their families to study in a religious school. At any of the dozen or more such schools in the area, the student may stay from one year up to ten depending on how long his family will support him there. The annual cost to the family is from twelve hundred to fifteen hundred baht ($60–$75). The schools are constructed on a monastic plan. There is one building larger than the others in which instruction is held if it cannot be out of doors. The *guru* (teachers) and the *murid* (students) alike live two or three together in small elevated houses encircling the school. Often the residents of the school raise some kind of crops for use at the school or occasionally for sale. Ordinarily, a student will have to beg for the food he prepares for himself daily, though part of a person's *zakat* can be given for the support of religious students. The student is not supposed to have money with him at school which he might use for buying food; he may not smoke; and in general he is expected to live an ascetic life. For the student who will stay at the school for only one or two years, the major emphasis in instruction is placed on learning how to pray and perform appropriate ritual, what is legal, and what is an infraction of Islamic law. Few people know the reasons for or the meaning of what they do, the prevalent attitude being, "Don't ask for reasons, just do as it says."

For students who plan to remain at the schools longer than two years and who presumably wish to become *guru* themselves and devote their lives to religion, the training is somewhat different. Although they are given instruction in the performance of ritual, they are also started on instruction in the Arabic language, with lessons in the grammar followed some time later by the vocabulary. In addition, they are given instruction in the interpretation and meaning of the Koran and other religious books, including the *Kitab taj al-muluk*, which consists of an intermixture of Islamic and indigenous Malay beliefs and practices mainly concerned with divination and magic.

During the fall of 1956, a young man in his fourth or fifth year at one of the religious schools was discussing his program with the owner of one of the coffee shops who had attended the same school for about seven years. Soon the discussion had turned to more general philosophical considerations. A summary of what was said in the conversation is set forth in some detail below, as it illustrates the manner in which Malay Moslems juxtapose in their thinking Islamic theological concepts with an animistic Malay philosophy:

"There are three elements in proper religious study: the Discipline of God, Islamic Law, and philosophical studies of the nature of man and things.

"Many fishermen know a great deal about religion, but may

sometimes forget and say, 'The fish were swimming in a particular direction; if we had been there, we would have caught many,' or 'This boat is bad—we would catch more fish with another,' instead of remembering that God alone controls our destinies.

"It is God, not medicine, that cures diseases. God may ordain that the cure will come about when another man comes to the sick man and gives him medicine. But this is the reason of the cure. It is like scratching an itch: it gets worse. Or it is like eating something sour: it disagrees with the stomach and the stomach aches. God is the cause; the reason is only intermediate (in the cause and effect relationship).

"Man must work for his own good although he has no control over his destiny; he must not be idle waiting for God to act.

"God's power cannot be separated from man's ability. When a man climbs a coconut tree, which is God's power and which is man's ability?

"Actually man's will and ability are part of God's power, though man is unaware of it. Thus, in spite of care, strength, and skill, a man sometimes falls when climbing a tree. This is God's power counteracting man's ability.

"Is man, then, like a shadow player, with all power in the hands of the operator? Or does God give man a quantitatively and qualitatively limited amount of power for his own free use?

"A man either walks or is still; all things on earth either live or die. Thus, there are only two states to any quality, existence and nonexistence. Only God determines which of these states will obtain.

"If God wants us to have more income, we have a 'feeling' to work harder and get it; otherwise any increase in effort will have no effect. There are limits set by God within which man can find his own level in whatever he does.

"Ji [disrespectful contraction of haji, referring to the insane haji in Rusembilan] learned too much about religion in school and at Mecca. A friend was jealous of this knowledge and performed magic to make him insane.

"People have specific 'gravelands,' not necessarily near their residence; but it is seen to it that they die near their 'graveland.' The length of time between death and burial is an indication of the weight of consideration of the good deeds and the sins of the man's life and of whether he is bound for heaven or hell.

"Some unsinning children take longer for burial than others.

"The *guru* says that this is untrue, that the length of time between death and burial has nothing to do with a man's virtues.

"There is a specific reason for everything that happens; but God alone is the cause of everything."

Although the later religious training is of much greater importance to the individual and to the community, there is no form of celebration, such as the *khatam Kuran*, to mark the completion of the individual's religious training. This omission is said to be due to the fact that a man is expected to get married or start on a pilgrimage to Mecca almost immediately after his training, and either of these events, marking a change in his life, will be celebrated. Marriage is by far the more usual of the alternatives, for the round trip to Mecca costs from ten to twelve thousand baht ($500–$600). When a man does travel to Mecca, however, on his return he is sure of being a respected man in the community. If he remains to study at Mecca or goes on to study at the Moslem universities in Cairo or Istanbul,[15] he is rewarded on his return by being given the position of *guru*, whether he actually teaches or not.

Religious Authority as an Integrating Factor

The religious leadership of Rusembilan is primarily in the hands of eight or ten people. Five of these are hajis, among them the imam and the *khatib*. The others, including the *bilal*, are

[15] A favorite story in Rusembilan concerns a Malay boy who was sent to Cairo to study religion. Instead of learning about religion, he learned

respected people in the community, who either because of inclination or training or because of family ties have become closely connected with religious activities in the community. Aside from their purely religious functions, the members of this group act individually as the highest level of mediation within the community. Questions that arise in the village, arguments and disputes brought to members of this group, are usually answered or settled by them or else are taken beyond the village to the Thai authorities or to higher Moslem authorities such as a *guru* or the Moslem Religious Board. Rarely would a question or a dispute be taken back to another villager for settlement after it had been brought to the attention of one of the religious leaders in Rusembilan.

One of the major areas of mediation by these leaders, particularly the imam, is that of steering the course of new marriages. Because a girl before she is married is secluded in her parents' house and is married to a boy without ever having seen him, there is generally a certain amount of tension during the first few months of marriage. If this tension becomes serious and cannot be handled by the young couple or their parents, the imam will be called in for advice. In the two such cases handled by the imam of Rusembilan during the course of this study, he first recommended a compromise on the part of the couple, urging them to try to stay together. He suggested that they and their parents say prayers for the continuation of the marriage and that they think more about and participate more fully in religion. Usually, the imam is able by these methods to avoid divorce. In both the cases mentioned above, however, he failed in his objective. In one case, it became obvious quite soon that the marriage was not going to last, and it was decided that the boy (from another village) was largely at fault, although he was a haji and should have been an exemplary husband. It was then

about politics and returned to Thailand to be second in command of the coup which first overthrew Premier Phibun.

up to the imam to decide on how the marriage money, contributed about equally by both sides of the union (see Chapter
XI), was to be divided. Because the boy was mainly responsible
for the situation, the imam finally settled on one-third or five
hundred baht ($25) for the boy and the remaining two-thirds
for the girl. Once a decision is made by the imam, it is almost
never contested by the couple or their parents, for to do so
would involve taking the matter to the Moslem Religious Board
or even to the Thai law courts, with resultant protracted litigation. In the other case, the couple stayed married for several
months after the first intercession of the imam, but finally, because of differences in their religious opinions, the couple decided that they must separate. In this case, although the girl was
a close relative of the imam, he felt that she was primarily at
fault and recommended that the marriage money be divided
equally.

Because these religious authorities frequently have more general knowledge than other villagers, even those who are highly
respected for knowledge of fishing or their leadership abilities,
they are often called upon to present village matters to government authorities or to act as intermediaries between the government and the people. Thus, if the villagers have a request which
they want to make at a village meeting called by the district
office, they will usually have the imam as their spokesman rather
than speak directly to the *kamnan* or allow the *kamnan* to present their case. It was the imam who was chosen to lead a party
of respected village men to the flooded padi fields to meet the
governor of the province when he was making an inspection
tour in 1956, in spite of the fact that the *selawat* was among the
members of the party.

Hajis are allowed to perform almost no manual labor because of their position of great respect in the community. About
the most menial job a haji does is the opening and drying of
coconuts from his own plantation. The fact that he was able

to make the pilgrimage to Mecca implies far greater wealth than average, and this prohibition of labor, which extends to both fishing and rice cultivation, is of no real hardship for the haji. Rather it allows him to devote more of his time to religious studies and instruction. In other communities in the Pattani area, some hajis purchase all the food required for their families, and some live to some extent off the contributions of villagers. In Rusembilan, however, all the hajis own large tracts of riceland as well as coconut plantations. Thus, it is to their benefit as well as that of the community to have the land worked for them. The usual system is for one man to be responsible year after year for one or more of the haji's fields and to divide the harvest equally between the haji and himself. Although there is no proscription of labor for those men who are considered religious leaders but not hajis, at Rusembilan they are all wealthy men and are therefore able to have their fields worked for them on the same basis as the hajis. These men, always the first to be invited to feasts and small family functions as well as large *makan pulot*, are never expected to pay for the food they receive there.

Religious leaders at Rusembilan, hajis as well as those who have not made the pilgrimage, have invested heavily in both land and capital goods. All these leaders own fair-sized to large coconut plantations in addition to more than adequate padi land. Most of them own part or all of a *kolek* and contribute their nets to the boat group. Among these individuals, the imam and his father-in-law were mainly responsible both financially and because of the weight of their opinion in the community for acquiring the first village motorboat. In fact, this boat is so closely associated with the imam that it is referred to by the villagers as *mutu imam* (imam's motorboat).

There was a certain amount of criticism of the imam during the time that his boat was having repeated engine trouble. One man, the owner and steerer of one of the less successful *kolek* on the beach, summed up this segment of village feeling: "Religious leaders should have nothing to do with commercial enterprises such as this, in which other people and their money are involved. No leader should. The imam has already made mistakes with regard to the motorboat and is now taking sides in the question of what to do about the new engine. Because of this and because he is in open disagreement with a section of the village, the villagers do not listen to him or his advice, particularly regarding the coming election, as much as they did before. If he has money to spend, let him risk it on a venture that affects himself only. Another haji in the village has consistently acted properly as a leader, by not putting up shares in any of the motorboats and by refusing offers to help finance his pilgrimage to Mecca. This man will not even accept a share of the *zakat* to which he is entitled. He has enough and is not selfish."

CHAPTER X

Belief in Spirits

NOT far below his formal adherence to Islam and Islamic concepts of law and theology, the Malay possesses a deep substratum of beliefs and practices concerning a large population of spirits as well as rules for influencing their behavior toward men, either for good or for evil. Although belief in such spirits is against the teachings of the Koran and the practice of employing methods to control them is strictly interdicted, a large segment of the population of Rusembilan, knowing from experience the important role spirits play in various pursuits, continues to act in defiance to Islamic law in these matters. Even the imam of Rusembilan, on the whole a stanch opponent of the belief in spirits, sometimes joins with the *bomo* in public ceremonies held for their propitiation.[1]

The rationale whereby the belief in spirits, both *hantu* (indigenous Malay spirits) and *jin Islam* (Islamic spirits), can be reconciled with Islamic religion is provided by the story of

[1] See Robert Redfield, "The Social Organization of Tradition," *Far Eastern Quarterly*, 15:13–21, 1956, and also his *Peasant Society and Culture*, pp. 67–104.

creation. Men in Rusembilan relate that, with the creation of Adam and Eve, God granted a request of *Azazil* (Satan) for immortality and fertility until the end of the world. When *Azazil* deceived Adam and Eve, causing them to excrete bodily wastes, he was expelled from heaven along with them. God was furious and smashed all the palaces that *Azazil* had built in heaven, but granted Adam's request for forgiveness and appointed him the king of the world. *Azazil*, who after his fall became known as *Shaitan*, also begged forgiveness and was granted a limited degree of immortality, as well as his fertility, and the privilege of deceiving all those who forgot the Law of God. Because of his unlimited fertility, *Shaitan*, both before and after his fall, has produced a prodigious number of offspring to assist him in his deceptions. These offspring or *jin* are like man in that they are granted the power to choose between good and evil, but are unlike man in that they will continue to live until the end of the world. Although the Malays draw a distinction between the *hantu* and the *jin Islam*, and even recognize historically a difference in their origin, both classes are conceived to be the descendants of *Shaitan*.[2]

In Rusembilan, the distinction between *hantu* and *jin* is more firmly drawn than in other Malay communities. All spirits which are by nature malevolent are classed as *hantu*. These are the major concern of the *bomo*, as they are responsible for a large majority of illnesses. The spirits which may be either benevolent or malevolent, depending on their whim or how they are treated, are classed as *jin Islam*. The villagers are aware that several of the spirits they place in this latter category are not historically of Islamic origin, but their behavior logically places them in the category of true jinn. *Shaitan*, though he is the progenitor of both classes of spirits, remains outside of this classification. The villagers say, "*Shaitan* is within man; the spirits are external."

[2] Richard O. Winstedt, *The Malay Magician, Being Shaman, Saiva, and Sufi*, pp. 99 f.

Trees, locations, and various unusual objects occasionally have spirits. These are either classified with the *jin*, as in the case of the large group of sea spirits, or put in a separate category of *kerabat* (literally, of close relationship). The fate of people who are not given adequate funerals is a matter of some confusion in Rusembilan. Some say that they become malevolent ghosts or *hantu;* others claim that they become *kerabat* of a particular tree or spot; still others say that they are just dead and do not linger on earth at all. The second view is probably the most general, for it is commonly believed in Rusembilan that if a man has been murdered, his "ghost" will remain in the vicinity of the spot where the murder occurred.

This chapter will not attempt to deal with the enumeration and characteristics of the *hantu* and *jin* of Rusembilan, but rather with the way in which the beliefs and practices concerning them are integrated into the structure of the society. The descriptions of Malay spirits contained in other works [3] are detailed and complete, and although not all the *jin Islam* of Rusembilan are to be found there, most of them as well as all the *hantu* known to dwell in the Pattani area are included.

The concept of a soul or vital force (*semangat*) within all things is one which is difficult for the Malay villager to explain, but which is of considerable importance in his magical practices and even in certain types of religious ritual. Scholars differ in their opinion of what exactly is meant by *semangat*. Winstedt states:

For the primitive Malay looking below the outer aspect of men and beast and plant and stone found in all of them an energizing power that permeated them like electricity. . . . There is no "rank, condition or degree" to distinguish the vital force in man from the vital force in rice or the vital force in an animal. Nor is the idea of immortality associated with it. But certain objects like stones

[3] See Winstedt, *The Malay Magician;* J. N. McHugh, *Hantu Hantu: Ghost Beliefs in Modern Malaya;* Walter W. Skeat, *Malay Magic.*

and tough plants and certain parts of the body like the teeth and hair are prized as having it to an abnormal degree.[4]

Wilkinson writes that *semangat* is the

spirit of life, vitality, "soul" (in the old Indonesian sense). . . . The Indonesian "soul" is a bird of life, timorous and easily scared; its flight . . . is synonymous with weak vitality. . . . It leaves the body in sleep . . . and when absent from the body may be seduced or captured by other persons; magic is used sometimes to attract and so win a girl's *semangat*.[5]

The villagers of Rusembilan define it as a life force, *élan*, or soul of things, although not like the soul of a man. It manifests itself in a man as a sense of strength, or love of country, or a feeling of helpfulness or good. Without it, a man is selfish and has no feeling at all. To lose *semangat* is like the sensation that comes with fear. It dies with the man or object that possesses it. In various ceremonies *semangat* is gained by contact with certain objects and by eating ceremonial rice (*nasi semangat*), which is believed to contain large quantities of it.

Disease and Curing

As the imam is central to the religious organization of a Malay community, the *bomo* or shaman is central to that area of the culture concerned with spirits and magic and the body of beliefs and techniques associated with the curing of disease. To the villager, two well-defined and frequently antagonistic areas of supernatural affairs are as easy to accept as two major areas of economic pursuits or two schools which the village children must attend. Although Allah is omnipotent and is the ultimate cause of any event and should be worshiped as such, the spirits which the *bomo* can control are of great practical and immediate value and should not be ignored.

[4] Winstedt, *The Malay Magician*, pp. 16 f.
[5] R. J. Wilkinson, *A Malay-English Dictionary*, II, 419.

To become a *bomo* a man requires special knowledge (*ilmu*) which in present times may be acquired through reading. But first he must know "something" about being a *bomo*. This "something" commonly comes from being associated with a father or grandfather who is a *bomo* or from inheriting the proper predisposition. As with the special skills required of steerers of *kolek*, the *ilmu* of the *bomo* commonly passes from grandfather to grandson rather than from father to son. This is probably because of the closer and more informal relationship between the grandfather and the grandson and the willingness and patience of the former to help satisfy the curiosity of the latter. Legend explains that the first *bomo* learned their *ilmu* about spirits and ritual directly from *Shaitan*. When they died, their *angin* (literally, wind; spirit, soul) passed the *ilmu* to their grandchildren. The grandchild can then say, "If I have a powerful ancestor, come!" and the *angin* of the grandfather will come to teach the grandson and "help" him.

Curing of disease generally requires both contact between the *bomo* and the spirit causing the disease and the use of herbal decoctions prepared in accordance with proper ritual. Although all disease is not caused by malevolence of spirits, the *bomo* usually goes into a trance, *lupa* (forget [one's self]), to ascertain the cause of the disease, and if possible he effects a cure by establishing contact with the spirits in this manner. One of the two *bomo* at Rusembilan states that he disagrees with most *bomo* and considers that disease is not caused by spirits, but he uses the trance for diagnosis and cure as much as any other *bomo*. In spite of this, he is sure that the only successful cures are obtained by the use of herbal medicines, though he is not able to ascribe a cause to any disease.

The trance used for private curing is in all essentials the same as the *peterana* or more public séance performed to fulfill an obligation to, or amuse, the spirits or *angin*. All of the following spirits must be called in order to make the trance effective:

Sulong Mak Bonda, understood as the original human maternal
ancestor descended from Satan; *Sulong Ayoh,* a corresponding
paternal ancestor; *Setan Tengah* and *Setan Bahsu,* the middle
and the younger Satan; the four guardian archangels of each
individual—*Mikael, Israfil, Jibrael,* and *Israel*—who are called
first by their names, a second time by the characteristic features
of each, and finally by disrespectful, comical appellations.[6] The
bomo may call upon other spirits, such as the *angin* of the patient's ancestors, to direct him further in his search for the cause
and cure of the disease; or he may seek this information from the
eight he has originally called. If the actual spirit causing the
disease is detected, the *bomo* will enter into conversation with
it. Sometimes this spirit speaks through the patient's mouth,
whereas at other times it uses the mouth of the *bomo.* After the
bomo has learned the origins of the spirit and the reason it is
inhabiting the patient, he will attempt to exorcise it by reading
mystical or, occasionally, Koranic passages to it over a specially
prepared and censed bowl of water and tempting it with *pulot*
rice.

Often in his trance the *bomo* will learn that the disease is not
caused by a spirit residing in the patient. In one such case at
Rusembilan, the *bomo* was called in to treat a girl who was badly
constipated. He learned in his trance that while the girl's mother
had been pregnant her father had chased a monitor lizard into a
hole in the trunk of a tree and had sealed the hole to prevent the
lizard's escape. The hole was unsealed, and the girl recovered.

Specific remedies for diseases not caused by spirits are almost
as numerous as the diseases they purport to cure. Perhaps the

[6] It was extremely difficult to obtain information as to the alternate
names of the archangels. One set possibly is as follows: Mikael, *Awe Jide*
(young fellow pole star, star of Moses); Israfil, *Awe Maha* (young fellow magnificent); Jibrael, *Sidi Ali* (tiger of God); Israel, *Budak Mama
jang Payaraja* (young uncle who is king of the guardians). Compare
Jeanne Cuisinier (in *Danses Magiques de Kelantan,* pp. 18–19), who finds
terms in nine categories for each of the archangels.

simplest remedy is that for fever. The *bomo* puts water in a jar, chants a short passage over it, and drinks a small portion of it himself. He then adds *hati abu* (heart of the ashes) from a fire and gives this to the patient to drink. Sometimes the incantations, which are the real source of the cure, are from the Koran; more frequently they are traditional spells with or without later Islamic accretions.[7] Roots and bark from various local and exotic trees are usually added to the medicines; areca nut is usually chewed with lime and betel leaf by the *bomo*, and this may be applied to the patient during the course of treatment.

Malaria, because it is absent from Rusembilan and the villagers have therefore not built up a resistance to it, is a disease dreaded by the men who go into the jungle to work on rubber estates. Of the three methods employed by the villagers to try to control the symptoms of malaria, perhaps aspirin is the most effective. Sometimes the *bomo* attempts to effect a cure by giving the patient a decoction of fried honey and chili and by massaging the left side of the patient's abdomen, often swollen by an enlargement of the spleen, a characteristic of malaria. The third cure is preferred by many of the older residents of Rusembilan. This consists of leaving one's house just before the daily attack of fever and telling one's footsteps to inform the fever (in the form of small beetles) that the patient has gone to the north; the patient will then go to the west and avoid the fever. An alternative to this is to tell the fever that one is turning off the path for a moment and will be back soon to collect it. After leaving the fever waiting, the patient goes on by another route. In spite of the fact that the concept of disease as a beetle or other small material object exists at Rusembilan, there is no evidence that the *bomo* ever deals with this in his trances. The trance is for control of spirits only, and in order to remove a disease object from a patient, the *bomo* can only request, or force, a spirit or *angin* to do it for him.

[7] See Winstedt, *The Malay Magician*, pp. 147–150, *et passim*.

A few people at Rusembilan, particularly learned men, are known to keep familiar spirits (*pelesit*). These spirits are maintained for the protection of one's house and property. Thus, when a thief enters the house with the intent to steal, the *pelesit* causes him to believe that he is surrounded by water, and he is unable to escape until such time as the owner of the house has dealt with him. If these spirits are not properly "taken care of" and fed regularly, however, they will cause trouble and disease, usually to other people; and unless the owner's children take care of the *pelesit* upon his death, here again they will cause trouble. The disease caused by the pelesit is a fever accompanied by stomach-ache. The *bomo*, on diagnosing the type of disease agent, puts the patient into a trance and presses ground hot peppers on his thumb nail to lock the spirit in. The *pelesit* begins shrieking and shaking and in order to be let out tells the *bomo* who its father (i.e., owner) is and "all about itself." With this information, the *bomo* is able to effect a cure by demanding proper treatment of the *pelesit* by its owner or by holding a ceremony to send the spirit back to its original home.

A part of the practice of a *bomo* is concerned with the diagnosis and cure of mental diseases. There are five individuals in Rusembilan whom the villagers consider to be mad. One of these is said to be hopeless and sits in a state of catatonia all day; his children have stopped calling in *bomo* for him and are simply waiting for him to die. Two other individuals exhibit their symptoms only during the first week of the new moon. Although quite rational at other times, these individuals, one woman and one man, carry on confused monologues about presumed persecutors in these periods. Even, however, during one of their "fits," they are able to answer rationally any question that is put to them. Because they are not considered really sick, neither of these persons has had the *bomo* try to attempt a cure. The son of the former imam of Rusembilan, mentioned in the preceding chapter, also exhibits the same cyclical character in his symptoms.

When the moon is new, this person is in his "bad mood." Formerly, in this state, he would become violent; but at the time of this study, he lay in a stupor chained to the floor of his mother's house, occasionally rousing himself and reciting verses from the Koran. When he is in one of his "good moods" (which were becoming increasingly rare in 1956), he is a tireless worker for himself and for others and is reputed to be one of the wisest men in the area on the subject of religion. In an effort to cure him, his mother has enlisted the services of fifty-five different *bomo*. One woman in the village is said to be *latah*[8] and exhibits all the classical symptoms of this condition, such as paroxysms provoked by some unexpected incident, use of obscene language during a seizure, and both echolalia and echopraxia to a marked degree.[9] As she had had this disease from an early age and as it was of no serious consequence in her daily life, she had not been treated by a *bomo*. Many individuals in the village considered it a harmless amusement to tease these individuals, particularly the *latah* woman, whose mimetic actions provide a source of laughter in the coffee shops for days afterward.

A large area of Malay medical beliefs does not come under the direct purview of the *bomo*, but is the province of the *bidan* or *tok bidan* (midwife, grandmother midwife). Although the midwife has no actual control over spirits and must call the *bomo* in severe cases of illness connected with childbirth, she exercises during pregnancy and for forty days after the birth of the child a considerable amount of spiritual prophylaxis. Much of the practice of the midwife is, however, concerned with purely physical aspects of pregnancy and childbirth. This will be dealt with in Chapter XI in relation to its place in the

[8] Otto Klineberg, *Social Psychology*, p. 516.
[9] See David Aberle, "Arctic Hysteria and Latah in Mongolia," in New York Academy of Science, *Transactions*, 2d ser., 14:291–297, 1952.

individual's life cycle. The most important ritual duty of the midwife is in connection with a woman's first child. During the seventh month of pregnancy, the midwife performs over the expectant mother a small ritual called *melangan*. This consists of feeding the woman *nasi semangat* to strengthen her for her coming ordeal. The midwife then places her hands on the sides of the mother's abdomen to "place the child properly" and finally "breaks" a green coconut above the abdomen. This ritual is never repeated for subsequent children; it is considered that the mother will not be as weakened by later pregnancies and that she will "know" how to carry the embryo.[10]

Immediately after childbirth, it is not uncommon for the womb to be entered by *Hantu Niyam*. This spirit enters the woman and begins crying and scrambling about "like a madman," causing great discomfort to the woman and occasionally even causing harm to the newly born child. The *bomo* must be called immediately if this *hantu* is suspected, as the midwife is not able to deal with it. One of the *bomo* at Rusembilan is a specialist in the exorcism of this spirit, and by simply reciting several incantations and blowing on the afflicted woman, he is able to effect the cure. For the first forty days of a child's life, a string is kept tied around his waist to protect him from worms and from various spirits that might otherwise afflict him. Another string is tied so that it passes loosely over one shoulder and under the other; this will cause the child to "remember its great-grandfather," and the soul of the ancestor will help protect the child from illness and the malevolence of spirits. This string must never be cut, but is allowed to wear off, sometimes remaining for two or three years.

[10] In the Melanau community studied by H. S. Morris (*Report on a Melanau Sago Producing Community in Sarawak*, p. 120), a ritual is held in the seventh month of pregnancy in which a coconut is broken by a couple who already have children and its milk is washed over the woman expecting her first.

Magic and Divination

Villagers at Rusembilan state that today magic is not practiced to the extent that it used to be in the village, but that it is nonetheless just as effective. Much magic that is purely protective in nature the villagers do not include in this category. Thus, the strings adorning babies and young children, the amulets of older children, and the gold rings set with colored stones or teeth which every man wears are not magic, but operate in a slightly different chain of cause and effect, that is, in relationships directly between man and the spiritual world. To the Malay, a magical practice is that by which one human being produces an effect upon another through a spiritual or other preternatural agent.

In recent times, most of this type of magic practiced at Rusembilan has been "love" magic. Love potions are made by taking oil from the skin of a recent corpse and with this on the finger touching the object of affection. This oil is extremely powerful, and if even a small quantity of it is kept in a house with a sick child, the child will become seriously ill and may even die. Much magic is the result of jealousy between women, such as the case in which a man's second wife may be jealous of his divorced wife and her share of his property. To harm her opponent, the first woman must procure a photograph of the second. After needles are stuck in some or all of the joints of the image, the photograph is thrown into the well from which the victim gets her drinking water. Upon drinking this water, the victim will develop severe pains in the corresponding joints. When filings from the metal rice bowls carried by begging Buddhist priests are thrown under a house, they are very effective in inflicting severe illness on the occupant. Perhaps the most common and most dreaded practice at the disposal of a jealous woman is one which produces its effect on a philandering husband rather than on his wife's rival. The wife prepares a large pot of rice, and while it is still steaming, she sits over it so that her sweat is mixed with the grain. When her husband eats this preparation, he becomes totally impotent toward his paramour and is generally dull and "oxlike."

Another area of magic practiced occasionally at Rusembilan has to do with strength and invulnerability in battle. Even the strongest bully can be made to retreat before a man who has been given the correct potions to drink and the proper incantations to say.[11] If a villager can strike his opponent with a stick of *rotan semambu* (Malacca cane, *Calamus scipionum*),[12] the adversary will become "dull and foolish" for life. To bring about the death of an opponent, a man must bury under one of his opponent's footprints strips cut from seven different kinds of animal skins and pound the spot with any heavy object. Within seven days, the victim will develop severe pains in his heart and die. Battle magic is a favorite topic of conversation in the coffee shops of Rusembilan, and one of the most frequent subjects mentioned is the use of *belukar samah*. This is a tactic in use by Malays engaged in jungle fighting in Malaya, whereby the Malay will scribble quotations from the Koran on scraps of paper. As he travels through the jungle, he will from time to time drop one of these scraps, and his enemy, coming upon the scraps, will be afflicted with insects, disease, and general misfortune.

The cure for magical afflictions is the same as for any other disease. The *bomo* is called in to diagnose the complaint. It is not usually difficult to ascertain when a person is a victim of magic, as he will generally suffer from a fever that will not leave him. Frequently, in cases when magic is suspected, the *bomo*

[11] The invulnerable man occasionally draws around him a band of followers who go about pillaging and robbing the countryside. Such bands have sometimes operated against the Thai authorities in Pattani province. They are reported as taking part in nationalistic struggles and other outbreaks throughout Southeast Asia by Justus M. van der Kroef in "Southeast Asia: Some Anthropological Aspects," *Human Organization*, 10 (no. 1):9–10, 1951.

[12] Wilkinson, *op. cit.*, II, 349.

will employ an assistant who asks the *bomo* pertinent questions during the latter's trance. In the trance, the *bomo* must find out the exact nature of the disease, by what means it was caused, and by whom. Countermagic is rarely employed in these cases. Instead, the object directly causing the illness will be sought and removed or destroyed. The person responsible for the magic will be persuaded to give it up, or if the illness is caused by a spirit under the control of the magician, it will be dealt with as any other spirit. If the magician refuses to give up his magical practices when he is detected or if he denies having performed them, he is in danger of being seriously hurt or even killed.

Divination plays a relatively small part in the life of Rusembilan. Its most extensive use is in connection with choosing a marriage partner for one's child, particularly the son. In this connection, a system called *raksi* is employed. The complete form of this system is described by Wilkinson:

The cabalistic values of the letters in the names of an engaged couple are taken, added up and then divided by nine; the balance left over is the fateful number. . . . If the balance is inauspicious the pair are said to be *tiada saraksi* (not affinities). . . . The engagement should then be broken off.[13]

The cabalistic alphabet referred to in the foregoing passage is the *abjab*, in which each letter in the *Jawi* alphabet is assigned a number.[14] Divisors other than nine are used for obtaining different interpretations of the match and for different types of divination.[15] In Rusembilan, however, unless a professional diviner is called in, the *raksi* is somewhat simplified. The combination of the names is added up with matchsticks, units being represented in one pile, tens in another, and hundreds and

[13] Wilkinson, *op. cit.*, II, 304.
[14] The *abjad*, in most common use is found in *Kitab taj al-muluk*, p. 64.
[15] Wilkinson, *op. cit.*, I, 2.

thousands in two other piles. These piles are then divided in such a way that there may be three alternatives. These alternatives always refer to the lot of the man if he enters into the particular marriage. He will be either *penghulu*, a leader of men (*selawat, khatib, nebe*, or better if he is educated), or *hamba*, a slave, a man who works hard but is never able to save money, or *orang baik*, a good man, liked and respected.

Although divination is actually prohibited, since all events occur according to the will of Allah and cannot be foretold, no villager will undertake any important venture without first consulting this *kitab*. Here he can find which days are most auspicious for a given activity and how various dates in his own personal history will react with these days. He can find what signs portend failure or misfortune for a project, as well as those that will ensure success. No one will ever embark upon any undertaking on the day of the week on which his umbilical cord was cut or on any day that a monitor lizard or a snake crosses his path; but if a certain kind of bird is seen on that particular day or if the right nostril is "stronger" than the left i.e., if the left nostril is slightly stopped up, it is probably a good time to start. Although the information contained in the *Kitab taj al-muluk* is considered completely reliable, it does not affect the affairs of those who are not aware of it. Thus, the business transaction of a man who failed to see a monitor lizard cross his path or who was unaware of the meaning of this omen would not be foredoomed to failure, as it would be in the case of a man who chose to ignore the omen.

Amusements

An event looked forward to by a large segment of Rusembilan is the performance of a *peterana* (literally, patient's dais at exorcism ritual) or public séance held by the *bomo*. The purpose of these performances is to amuse the *angin* (spirits of the dead) and other spirits by letting them "play" a part through the medium of the entranced performers. Thus, the *peterana* is often referred to simply as *main* (play). The performances are almost always put on as a consequence of a successful cure by the *bomo*. In his trance to diagnose and cure a patient's disease, the *bomo* will frequently learn that the *angin* or other spirits are molesting the patient, usually one of their descendants, because they feel that they have been neglected. In return for their quitting the patient, the *bomo* and patient promise the spirits that a *peterana* will be held for them at some auspicious time in the near future. Depending upon the importance of the spirits, the seriousness of the disease, and the financial resources of the patient, the *peterana* will be scheduled to run for one, three, five, or seven nights. Three nights is the most common number, and once the number has been set, it can be changed only under the most exceptional circumstances and then usually only for the convenience of the spirits, not the performers. One case is all that can be recalled by the villagers of Rusembilan of the shortening of a *peterana* because of a performer. This was a young woman patient who was pregnant and was unable to lose herself completely in the trance; therefore after one and one-half nights it was decided to postpone the performance until sometime subsequent to the delivery of her child.

According to the situation as seen by the *bomo*, the *peterana* may be held either under a shelter erected out of doors, in the patient's house, or in the house of the *bomo*. Before the time the performance is scheduled, women and children begin arriving and settling themselves around the stage or area set off for the musicians and players. The music is started perhaps a half an hour before the *bomo* begins the main performance. The orchestra consists of a three-stringed violin, two double-ended drums, a two-toned hanging gong, and a large enameled tray which is beaten with chopsticks. On all these instruments, on the posts of the house, and on the decorations for the performance, small candles are affixed which are allowed to burn themselves out. Food, rice flour, and flower blossoms are brought in, and the *bomo* fans incense over them as well as his own body.

When preparations have been completed, the patient is led onto the stage and seated facing the "father" of the *peterana*. At Rusembilan, the "father" is the violinist and not the *bomo*. The father, to a large extent, directs the course of the *peterana*, asking questions of the spirits and influencing the tenor of the conversations and actions by the tempo of his music. The *bomo* places the food and incense in front of the patient, who is to be the medium during the first part of the performance, and brushes him with water containing the rice flour and blossoms. The music then begins, slowly at first, but with increasing tempo as the patient goes into a trance. During the early stages of the performance, or for the whole of the first night if the *peterana* is to last five or seven nights, the patient, in a sitting position, will do nothing more during his trances than twitch the muscles of his arms, legs, and back, jerk his body, and sway from side to side. Each trance lasts for about ten or fifteen minutes, during which time the "father" speaks to whatever spirit wishes to converse through the medium. In a typical *peterana* at Rusembilan, the following spirits talked to the "father" in the trances of the first night: a midwife ancestor of the patient, the great-grandfather of the patient and the elder and younger brothers of the great-grandfather, two of the guardian archangels, and the king of the *bomo*, who is the mythical originator of the curing art. The conversations, in keeping with the purpose of the performance as amusement, are generally of a humorous and occasionally obscene nature and are accompanied by laughter and unsubdued talking among the audience.

Later in the first night's performance and/or on succeeding nights, the spirits become more active in the trances of the medium, and through him they dance and act out whatever "play" is in their mind. Ordinarily, the *bomo* at Rusembilan joins in these "plays," so that two spirits may be acting together.

It is common for the spirit of the king of the *bomo* to enter the body of the medium, while that of an old man acting as a court jester enters the body of the *bomo*. The stage for the *peterana* is always decorated to represent the palace of the king of the *bomo*, with a white awning spread overhead and hanging with flowers, bananas, and palm-leaf crosses. After the spirits have made known by their conversations that they are ready to start acting, the medium is given a new sarong and a new turban in which he is dressed by the *bomo* to represent the finery of the *bomo* king. This stage of the performance goes on for as long as the spirits desire to play, sometimes lasting until ten in the morning. On the last night of the *peterana*, a small model house (*balai*) is constructed. After the playing is over, this house is taken to a remote spot in the mangrove thickets to the west of Rusembilan and set up on stilts about four feet off the ground. It is filled with various cooked sweets and with rice having candles burning on it. Sweet cakes are hung from the roof of the *balai*, and in the center of the structure is a coconut shell containing a palm-leaf cross and scented water. This is to inform the spirits that all the food is for them. It is assumed that after putting on the *peterana* for their benefit and offering them good food the spirits will be satisfied and will not molest the villagers again. Next to the *balai*, a small uncovered tray is erected which contains a coconut shell, a small dissected chicken, a ray, some shrimp, colored rice, and a bowl of scented water. This tray is called *pachayung eban* and is considered a part of the offering to the spirits, but, more important, it serves as a warning to anyone but the spirits that the food in the *balai* is for the spirits only.

Sometimes, after a *peterana* has been held, village children who attended the performance will act out various roles from it in their playing. Occasionally, one of the children will actually fall into a trance and "run around the village saying things." The adults of Rusembilan do not approve of this type of play, and any child found in a trance will be brought out of it as quickly as possible by any adult on hand. There seems to be no tendency for children who fall easily into trances to become *bomo* later in life.

In Rusembilan, somewhat infrequently, a *silat* or mock battle dance is put on for the entertainment of the spirits and the villagers. To please the spirits, food, rice flour, and blossoms must be prepared with incense, and each of the dancers are incensed. The *silat* is the traditional "Malay boxing" and consists of five or six separate acts in each of which two different men spar, with stylized positioning of the hands, feet, and body. In the last act, the best pair returns, and each tries to throw down the other, using the same type of movements as during the earlier dances. Villagers in Rusembilan say that this form of entertainment is rapidly dying out and that there are almost no teachers left in the area. An aspiring *silat* performer must take lessons in dancing from one teacher and in fighting from another. Old people in the village say that the *silat* came originally from the Minangkabau in Sumatra.

During August 1956, one man, the steerer of a co-operative *kolek*, awakened from a dream to find his house shaking. When he looked outside, he saw an amorphous white form; and the next morning, he found tigerlike claws where the form had been. The *bomo* told him that this meant the weretiger *hantu* wished to have a *silat* performed for him. The *silat* was performed before the *bomo* discovered that he had been mistaken and that the spirit had desired to participate in a *peterana*. Because the steerer had been having trouble with the spirits of his ancestors, he called together all of his close relatives for the *peterana* so that they all could petition the spirits not to make a nuisance of themselves again. It was suspected by the village that one of these ancestral spirits had a "bad character" and that he alone was responsible for the demands for the *silat* and the *peterana*, the other spirits just coming along to enjoy the performances. The villagers say that if a person always remembers to think about his ancestral spirits and feeds them regularly they will not come and bother the village.

The performance of other forms of entertainment for the spirits and large village audiences no longer, or only very rarely, takes place at Rusembilan. But previously, and still in the more remote inland villages, it was common to see Malay dances based on stories from the *Ramayana* and performed by women, as well as the *wayang kulit* or shadow play, also enacting sequences from the *Ramayana*. Villagers from Rusembilan eagerly take part in the *dike-ulu* (from *dikir*, chant) whenever one is being held in the vicinity of the village. This also is an entertainment for the spirits, in which two men from different villages, or two village teams, make up derogatory songs about the opposing man or team. The side whom the audience or judge considers to have made up the most derogatory and humorous songs over the course of the whole performance, sometimes running eight or ten hours, is the winner.[16]

Importance of Spirits to Economic Pursuits

As fishing is the most important and most uncertain area of economic enterprise at Rusembilan, it is here that the greatest emphasis upon the behavior of spirits and their propitiation is placed. Unlike inland villages in southern Thailand and Malaya, where each step in the agricultural cycle is attended by elaborate ritual for the benefit of the spirits of the rice,[17] practically no attention is paid at Rusembilan to agricultural ritual. Only when the rice seedlings are transplanted does the Rusembilan padi farmer occasionally set a bowl of colored rice in the corner of his field to please the spirits of the crop. The villager of Rusem-

---

[16] Rosemary Firth (in *Housekeeping among Malay Peasants*, p. 119) reports that on the east coast of Malaya *orang berdikir* are popular at entertainments. These men or groups of men chant verses from the Koran (*berdikir*) back and forth at each other.

[17] Winstedt, *The Malay Magician*, pp. 39–55, *et passim*.

bilan is aware that there are a great number of spirits which have some form of influence over the rice crop, but he is aware also of innumerable spirits and *jin* that might affect any other area of his life, and he must put his faith, therefore, in the efficiency of the guardian spirit of Rusembilan to cope competently with any supernatural situation that may arise.

Sea spirits, on the other hand, are outside the purview of the village guardian and must be dealt with directly by the fishermen themselves. The villagers recognize a large number of related sea spirits, all known by name, degree of relationship to one another, and physical form. Some of the fishermen maintain that each species of fish important to the village economy also has one or more spirits of its own. Little attention is paid to these fish spirits, however, as they are controlled by the more powerful sea spirits. In order to keep them from causing illness to the fishermen or causing the fish to escape from the village nets and the sharks to come into the nets, the sea spirits must be "taken care of." As was pointed out in Chapter IV, at the beginning of the fishing season each year, a small feast is taken out to sea by each *kolek* in order to "remember" the sea spirits; and each time the *kolek* are launched after the full moon, they are washed with lime juice and powdered water and decorated with flowers and cloth streamers to please the spirits.

At Rusembilan, the propitiation of all spirits except the village guardian spirit (see the next section) is on an individual or small-group level. Formerly, an annual ceremony was held at the end of the fishing season, rather than at the beginning, at which the whole village made sacrifice to the sea spirits. Now, at the large villages along the sandy beaches of the South China Sea, from Pattani as far as Trengganu, this ceremony is still held, and villagers from Rusembilan will sometimes travel to these villages to take part in the ceremonies and attendant festivities. These ceremonies last for three days. A white buffalo is procured, and during the first two days the *bomo* in charge of the ceremony will prepare half of the buffalo and other food for sacrifice. The other half of the buffalo will be used in the feasting held throughout the occasion. These first two days will be devoted mainly to group activities such as boat racing, kite fighting, and any of the entertainments already mentioned. On the last day of the celebration, the half of the buffalo and the other food that the *bomo* has been preparing for sacrifice are placed on a bamboo raft and pushed out as far as the men and boys crowded around it can go. At this point, one or more *kolek*, each with a minimum crew, take over and tow the raft far out to sea. It is generally considered that this offering is for the *hantu laut* or evil sea spirits, whereas the only spirits that Rusembilan is concerned with are the *jin laut* which are not by nature evil.[18]

Occasionally a spirit may be kept as a familiar by one individual. A very successful steerer or a diver may keep one of the sea spirits and feed him daily. In return for being kept, the spirit will grant his keeper amazing success in fishing, such as being able to lure fish out of another's net into his own or change the fish in the nets of a rival to leaves. The villagers tell of divers who keep such spirits and are able to anchor their boats in rough seas with only a fish-hook and piece of twine and can even change the course of steamships. Aside from the daily propitiation, a kept spirit must be provided with an annual feast of forty eggs and with special foods at the time of any feast or crisis rite. However successful the steerer or diver may have been with his personal spirit, when advancing age comes the spirit apparently leaves him, and he suffers hard times. A typical diver, who before the war was able to amass three or four times as much money as comparable fishermen without familiars, seemed with the passage of time to be unable to keep his money and now in old age is penniless and living off the charity of others.

[18] Raymond Firth, *Malay Fishermen: Their Peasant Economy*, p. 122.

Antagonism and Co-operation between Imam and Bomo

Both *bomo* in Rusembilan are highly respected men in the community. One of them is renowned throughout the Pattani area for his successful cures and is frequently called to villages far away from Rusembilan. In spite of antipathy between the institutions of religion and shamanism, both the *bomo* are as punctilious in their religious duties as the majority of the villagers. In their practice as *bomo*, they are filling a role as old as any in present-day Malay society. They are *bomo* because there is need for *bomo* in the community and because this role fulfills the need satisfactorily. Even those who most detest the practice of the *bomo* admit that the spirits are in and around the village; the *bomo*, being specially endowed, simply controls these spirits for the benefit of individuals and for the community as a whole.

Religious leaders of the community, however, take a firm stand against any kind of shamanistic practice. The imam stated the case as follows: "Religious leaders have to be opposed to this sort of thing, as it is against the Law, against the teachings of the Koran. Disease is sent by God, and only God can actually cure it. Medicine may be helpful in easing pain and relieving symptoms; but the invocation of spirits is against God's Will." Some of the more religious villagers maintain that it is wrong even to believe in the existence of spirits, but the imam points out that Mohammed preached to the jinn in the desert. He continues, "It is wrong to believe that the spirits are able to harm or to do good to humans, and to believe so is to follow the deceptions of *Shaitan* rather than the Will of God."

Unfortunately, however, the religious leaders occasionally become seriously ill. Until very recently, they had no alternative in such cases other than to call in the *bomo*. Whether the cure was successful or not, their objections to shamanism were strengthened. If the treatment failed, it was proof that such practice was not effective or that it was actually harmful. If the cure was successful, the religious leader was burdened with a certain amount of shame for having not trusted in God alone and would turn this shame against the *bomo*. Among the religious leaders, there are some individuals who can reconcile within themselves the antipathetic natures of Islam and shamanism. There is one *bomo* in a village near Rusembilan who is not only a haji, but a respected *guru*. The widow of the former imam of Rusembilan, herself a haji, as pointed out above, has called in fifty-five *bomo* to try to effect a cure for her mentally unbalanced son and has not given up her faith in their efficacy. So ingrained are the traditions connected with the profession of the *bomo* that, if ancestral spirits ask for the presence of a religious leader at a *peterana*, no matter how opposed he may be to the performance of these séances the religious leader will be there to take part as requested.[19] One very religious man building a house during the summer of 1956 was tying strips of black cloth to all the house posts before erecting them. He explained that superstitious villagers believed that these would keep evil spirits away—he himself did not believe in the malevolence of spirits, but the black cloth could do no harm.

Once a year, a ceremony is held in honor of the guardian spirit of Rusembilan. This spirit, *Jin Gite*, is also a specific protector from cholera. The first part of the ceremony takes place at a special shrine to the spirit located in the mangrove thicket to the west of the village. Here the *bomo* prepares *pulot* (glutenous) rice, eggs, a chicken half of which is cooked and half uncooked, and shark and crab meat. He lights a candle and calls the spirit by name. When the spirit comes, it obliterates the candle flame, and after taking what it wants of the "spirit of the

[19] In Charles Wagley's Amazon Town (*Amazon Town: A Study of Man in the Tropics*, pp. 232–233), there is no conflict between the areas of curing and of religion except by the Catholic priest on his periodic visits to the community. The shamans function in curing illness, and the saints in maintaining community welfare.

food," it leaves, and the flame is once more allowed to burn.

After the *bomo* has made the offering to the spirit, the whole village is supposed collectively to remember their guardian and themselves offer it food. This part of the ceremony is held at the time of the afternoon prayer. In 1956, it was held in the courtyard of the house of the *bomo*. All villagers were supposed to attend and contribute rice or money; those particularly adept at saying prayers were requested to pray individually during the ceremony. Four people made prayers for the continued well-being of the village. Three of these men, including the imam and the *khatib*, belonged to the group of religious leaders antagonistic to contact with spirits. Before they spoke, the *bomo* offered a form of prayer remembering the past "great" men of the village. Bowls of water were then brought and placed at the supplicants' feet and were to be blessed during the prayers. After the prayers had been said, red and yellow *nasi semangat,* prepared by the family of the *bomo* from the villagers' contributions, was served. Although they could take no active part in the ceremonies, women and children helped to consume the food, as it is an insult to the guardian spirit to leave any food at this time. Finally, the imam led the group in the afternoon *sembayang hajat;* and the people went home taking with them the blessed water, to be used for washing their babies.

This is the only time in Rusembilan that there is active co-operation between the religious organization and the practices of the *bomo*. The religious leaders explain that this co-operation is necessary because the purpose of the ceremony is to keep evil, sickness, and ghosts away from the village; thus the *bomo* must be in charge of the ceremony. But as it involves prayers to God, it is a religious function as well. Although the ritual is oriented on the level of propitiation of spirits, the religious elements of the community feel that by limiting their participation to seeking God's aid they have not committed themselves to a belief in the benefit or even efficacy of contact with spirits.

CHAPTER XI

The Life Cycle

BEFORE attempting to analyze the community as a dynamic system continuously readjusting in response to changing tensions, the interrelation of the sociocultural system and of the individual passing through it will be examined. The life of an individual represents a temporal continuum within the sociocultural framework, each stage of life being characterized by different structures and values or status roles. An examination of the individual life cycle will therefore help to illustrate the integration in diachronic terms of the several facets of Rusembilan which were described synchronically in the preceding chapters.

It is only the individual, as the basic unit of society, who accepts his culture from others, gives it existence, modifies it, and passes it on to other individuals. At different points in his life, he comes in contact with different aspects of his culture and with changing points of view. The following sections break the life of the individual into six stages and examine the representative types of sociocultural participation characteristic of each.

Pregnancy and Birth

Almost without exception, families in Rusembilan desire children, and pregnancy is considered a happy and fortunate event. There is no preference as to the sex of the child, unless one sex is overwhelmingly represented in the family already. On the rare occasions when family economic pressures make the arrival of a child undesirable, the villagers practice a method of birth control which they say usually proves effective. This method involves the use of a certain root, a decoction of which must be taken with rice morning and evening for two months following the birth of a child in order to prevent becoming pregnant again. How long this treatment remains effective is not certain. Its effect would appear to be only temporary, however, as it is again prescribed when the woman becomes pregnant. At this stage in the treatment, the decoction is taken until abortion occurs. After induced abortion, as well as spontaneous abortion, the midwife is called in and prescribes another kind of herbal medicine. No special treatments or precautions are indicated if the woman is prone to abort. In June 1956, one woman called in the midwife because she was losing her child after five months of pregnancy. The midwife and the *bomo* went to her home, where the latter prepared herbs, water, areca nut, and betel leaves for the woman. The midwife massaged the woman's sides to induce delivery of the fetus. After the delivery, the stillborn child was washed, wrapped in white cloth, and buried near the house. The afterbirth was also wrapped and buried nearby. After this abortion, the woman was given no further medicine, but was "cooled" by pouring water over her head while heat was being applied to her abdomen.

During a normal pregnancy, the midwife is summoned in the seventh month "to place the child correctly" and feed the mother *nasi semangat* if it is her first pregnancy (see the preceding chapter). The midwife is also called at any time that a pregnant woman is in pain. The only special precaution taken during pregnancy is the prohibition against eating "hot" foods (*makanan panas*). This concept of heat is not based upon temperature or seasoning, but upon a condition of the type of food itself. Thus, all meat and certain fruits such as durian, rambutan, and certain root preparations are considered "hot" and are banned during pregnancy. "Cold" foods (*makanan dingin*), including most of the vegetable products eaten in the community, must not be eaten with "hot" foods, although, ordinarily, meat may be eaten with "hot" or "cold" foods. "Hot" foods are also prohibited when an individual is suffering from fever or is showing blood in any form. But during convalescence from fever and after childbirth, the "cold" foods are banned.

The midwife is again called after labor has started. At this time, she rubs oil on the mother's abdomen, but does nothing to ease the pains. In the case of an obstruction, labor may continue for six or seven days before the woman is taken to the Thai doctor in Pattani. Because almost all deliveries after this length of time result in the death of the mother and/or the child, the villagers consider that both the doctor and the hospital are dangerous. Only when all other methods fail will they accept medical care. After a normal delivery of the child, a cord is bound tightly around the abdomen to prevent the placenta from slipping upward and causing complications. The mother is given cool drinks to speed its expulsion. Extreme care is taken with both the placenta and the umbilical cord so that the mother will not hemorrhage. If the placenta is not expelled within a reasonable amount of time, the *bomo* is called to prepare medicines to force it out. If the woman hemorrhages, she is given water to drink, and cool water is poured over her head until the bleeding stops or until she dies. The afterbirth is washed and wrapped with salt in a clean cloth. In some families, this is kept by the mother for forty days before it is buried; in others, it is buried immediately. Whatever the case, it is usually buried under the house or in a clean sandy place near the house where it will not be disturbed. For her services, the midwife is paid four quarts of rice.

Ordinarily, the midwife will on the day of birth cut off half of the umbilical cord and wash the infant. The half of the umbilical cord remaining on the child is allowed to shrivel and drop off of its own accord, although the process is somewhat speeded by wrapping it in a cloth kept warm and dry with hot stones. The day of the week on which the cord falls off is considered as inauspicious throughout the life of the individual, whereas the day of the week on which he was born is considered lucky.

The actual birth of the child is not treated with great ceremony. Close friends of the family, however, usually just women, will come to visit the mother and child, bringing with them gifts of bananas and occasionally other food or gifts of money. The father and some of the more respected men in the community will visit the child and whisper the call to prayer (*bang*) in its ear, the right if it is a boy, the left if it is a girl.[1]

For forty days after the birth of the child, the mother is kept resting in a special room or curtained area of the house, and a fire is kept burning next to her.[2] Except at the time of the *bang* or in case the *bomo* is required, no men are allowed in this area. During this period, after it is certain that the child will live, a string is tied around the child's waist to protect him from worms, illness, and evil spirits. Also at this time, a string is tied across

---

[1] Allahu akbar/ ashahadun la-illa-'llah/ ashahadun Muhammad al Rasul Allah/ hei 'Ali al-saleh/ hei 'Ali al-faleh/ Allahu akbar/ la-ilaha-illa-'llah. (Each line is repeated.)

[2] *Post partum* "roasting" is commonly reported throughout Southeast Asia, for example by Charles S. Brant, *Tadagale, a Burmese Village in 1950*, p. 18, among the Burmese and Thai, and by H. S. Morris, *Report on a Melanau Sago Producing Community in Sarawak*, p. 120.

the chest of the child so that he may "remember his great-grandfather" and be protected by him.[3]

In theory, on the seventh day of the child's life the *akikah* ceremony is held for him. Actually, this ceremony is more usually held when the child is about three months old. Although this ceremony is *sunat* (religiously commendable but not obligatory), it is usually given for a child. This ceremony is never the occasion for a general *makan pulot,* but is held only for close friends and relatives of the family and for the respected men and religious leaders of the community. The first part of the *akikah* is the brief naming ritual. The name has previously been chosen by the parents from the twenty-five Moslem *nabis* or prophets. The imam or a respected relative repeats the chosen name, together with any title either parent may have, into the ear of the child several times. This is followed by the *belah mulut* (literally, splitting mouth) or mouth-opening ceremony. For this part of the *akikah,* four containers are prepared: one, containing salt and water; the second, rice; the third, gold, usually a ring, in water; and the fourth, silver, also a ring, in water. The silver and gold are alternately passed over the child's lips by the namer, then dipped in the salt water and passed over the lips again. This operation is repeated rhythmically several times. The namer then puts his thumb into the child's mouth and exerts pressure upward and forward. Finally, rice is put in the child's mouth, and its name is repeated by the original namer and other men attending the ceremony.

Following the *belah mulut,* all present rise to sing of the character of Mohammed, "so that the child may be like him." During the singing, the imam places the child on a tray for the *chukur* or haircutting. The imam and each of the respected men present are expected to cut off a small lock of the child's hair.[4]

[3] Walter W. Skeat, *Malay Magic,* pp. 332–352.

[4] Brant, *op. cit.,* p. 20, reports a ritual hair washing in connection with the naming ceremony in Burma. In Cambodia, the head is shaved

After this has been done, the imam places the child in its decorated cradle and allows it to sleep. The feast that goes with the *akikah* is one of the two occasions (the other being *Hari Raya Haji*) when the food prepared can be eaten only by Moslems. It is usually mutton and curry.

Infancy and Childhood

For the first forty days of life, during his mother's seclusion, a child is fed his mother's milk and small quantities of mashed cooked bananas. After the forty-day period, this diet is supplemented by rice and/or oatmeal. After one year, the child eats much the same food as adults. Complete weaning usually does not take place until the child is two years old or even older.[5] A few infants are given bottles containing tinned milk either because their mothers are unable to feed them or more usually because the mothers spend every day in the market. At the end of the first forty days, every child in Rusembilan is given one or more silver bracelets to wear. A child must wear jewelry in order not to look poor. These bracelets are either passed down from older siblings or purchased new for the child. Girls are frequently given a silver chain-link apron which hangs from a waist chain. Its only purpose is "for the sake of decency." Not until they are about four do children wear clothes, and even then the sarong is more apt to be carried in the hand or hanging around the child's neck than suspended properly from the waist. During a girl's first years, her hair is shaved on the front of her head so that it will grow in thicker. Occasionally, the back of the head is shaved for the same reason, though it is never shaved both front and back on the same individual. Boys' heads

---

except for a topknot (Human Relations Area Files, Inc., *Cambodia*, Subcontractors' Monographs, pp. 325–326).

[5] In spite of a Thai government order prohibiting nursing in public, it is common to see Malay mothers nursing two- and even three-year-old children in public places.

are frequently shaved, as are men's, so that they will be more comfortable.[6]

Like weaning, toilet training is put off until the child can be made to understand the need for it and his co-operation can be enlisted. Since the infants wear no clothing, there is little concern over their excretions, which can simply be covered with sand on the beach or washed through the cracks in the floor boards indoors. To begin toilet training, the child is merely told to relieve himself outside of the house. He soon learns from example and from older children the principles of modesty.

Until a child is five or six, he is always in the company of an adult or a responsible elder sibling. Several parents in Rusembilan, because they had children only after a long childless period, kept their children with them constantly. One man gave up fishing in order to be with his son all the time. Children are universally liked and are to be found helping in or merely watching any adult occupation, except fishing, at any time of day or night. Almost the only duty that all children are expected to perform is bathing three times daily. This routine is enforced by the mother sometimes through persuasion, occasionally through force. Children are expected to obey commands of adults, particularly their parents. Frequently, however, nothing is done about it if the commands are ignored. "Old-fashioned" parents occasionally cane their children when the latter have been disobedient, and the child will often seek refuge with his grandparents. If a child uses bad language (e.g., the words "pig" and "dog"), he will be severely scolded or his cheeks pinched. The young child is generally felt to "belong" more to its mother than to its father, but only because more time is spent with the mother and because she is responsible for most of the child's discipline. After eight or nine years of age,

[6] See Richard O. Winstedt, *The Malay Magician, Being Shaman, Saiva, and Sufi*, p. 108.

sons spend most of their time in the company of their fathers and other men and are thought of as "the son of so-and-so."

From the age of five or six until a child is eight or nine, he is almost constantly in the company of other children, in more or less organized gangs. In the earlier years, these gangs contain about the same number of boys and girls, but as the group becomes older, it tends to be limited to the members of one sex. Within the groups, some children are leaders, being able to direct the activities of the other children and think up new amusements. Bullies, however, are not liked in the community and likewise are not tolerated in the children's gangs. Moreover, the gang never teases an individual who may be left out of it for some reason and is always ready to exert pressure if one of its own members is detected in this act. If members of the gang have younger siblings of whom they are in charge, the small children are brought along by the elder ones, no matter what the gang may be doing.

At this same age, some boys in Rusembilan run away from home for several days. Usually, it is because they do not wish to read the Koran or go to school. In general, the runaway will remain in Rusembilan, staying out of sight during the daytime and sleeping underneath some house other than his parents' at night. He may, however, go to another village and stay with a relative there. Ordinarily, the child is allowed to come home whenever he wishes, in two or three days, that is, but sometimes he is followed or met by a friend and brought home.

After he is eight or nine, the child spends less and less time with his gang and more and more time helping adults with their daily tasks. It is at this time that the girls are taken by their female relatives into the house and kitchen to learn the routines of cooking and housekeeping. In effect, this is the beginning of the girl's seclusion until after she is married. By the time she is nine, a girl has usually finished with her instruction in the

Koran, and there is no enforcement of the laws requiring children to attend school until they are fourteen or fifteen. A few girls of ten or eleven can be seen around the community, but as soon as they start developing into womanhood, they are kept carefully sheltered and chaperoned. The boys begin helping their fathers by running errands, carrying water, leading cows to pasture, and learning how to repair nets. Boys are not taken out in the fishing boats until the time when they are able to do almost a man's share of the work. A boy remains totally ignorant of cooking and housework. Unless he attends the religious schools later, where he must do his own cooking and housework, these activities will remain outside his sphere of knowledge throughout his life. Girls, on the other hand, are taught by their mothers much about the agricultural activities of the community and the activities carried on ashore connected with fishing. The formal education received by the children of Rusembilan was discussed in Chapter VII. Several families who disapprove of the Thai educational system keep their children at home and personally instruct them in matters which the community considers more worth while than those taught in the school. Two men send their children into Pattani, where they are given private instruction in the English language.[7]

During childhood, a child begins to assume religious responsibilities. Aside from receiving his instruction in the Koran, he is expected to learn to say the five daily prayers and to treat Friday as a day of prayer and rest although he will not attend service in the mosque until he becomes an adult. He must contribute the *zakat pitrah* of four quarts of rice at the end of the fasting month and is urged to contribute to beggars in the Pattani market. He is also encouraged to observe the Ramadan

[7] Mohammed Abdul Kadir, interpreter for the author, held classes once a week for about forty Malays in the area. The knowledge of English was considered by the Malays as one way of exhibiting superiority to the Thais.

fast even though he is not required to do so until after puberty. At the end of his Koran studies, the *khatam Kuran* feast is held in his honor, conferring on him membership, albeit limited, in the religious organization of the community.

Puberty and Youth

Probably the most important event in the life of a man at Rusembilan is his *masuk Jawi* (entering Malay-hood) ceremony. Admittedly, this ceremony is supposed to be held at puberty, but actually it is held when most convenient for the family of the boy or when there is a group of boys more or less the same age ready to participate in it jointly. The average age is fourteen or fifteen, but boys of twelve are frequently given the ceremony, and occasionally they may be as young as eight. Although this ceremony includes the universal Moslem custom of circumcision and there is evidence that it was practiced among the Malays before the advent of Islam in the area,[8] it is considered by the villagers of Rusembilan as *sunat* rather than a religious obligation.[9] Actually, no case could be recalled of a boy in the village who was not circumcised. There is no corresponding ceremony for girls, though the villagers point out that defloration at birth can be considered as a parallel.[10] In terms of ceremonial roles, however, there is a closer relationship between the sponsor of the boy in the *masuk Jawi* and the sponsor who feeds the girl *nasi semangat* at her wedding.

The *masuk Jawi* involves two feasts. The first is held for the imam and the hajis, *guru*, and respected men of the community and surrounding communities. After this, a general *makan pulot* is held for the villagers and outsiders. During the first feast, long passages are read from the Koran, and prayers are said by

[8] Skeat, *op. cit.*, p. 360; Winstedt, *The Malay Magician*, p. 112.
[9] Winstedt, however, says of circumcision, "Today it is regarded as a Muslim obligation" (*loc. cit.*).
[10] Winstedt, *The Malay Magician*, p. 114.

all for the well-being and health of the young man in his new status. At the *makan pulot,* the family of the boy is presented with gifts of money from all the guests, more or less in proportion to the degree of closeness between the parties.

The ceremony preceding the actual circumcision is the most elaborate held at Rusembilan.[11] It commences with a parade. If the family of the boy is wealthy enough, an elephant is procured to carry the boy; otherwise he is carried on the shoulders of men. He is taken to a specially prepared and decorated chair where his fingers are stained with henna, and he is fed *pulot kuning* (yellow glutenous rice) and *nasi semangat* by his sponsor. The boy is then led away from the onlookers by his sponsor, and the actual circumcision is performed by a specialist (*tok buding*). The wound is covered with hot rags to keep it from contact with the rest of his body. While the healing process continues, the rags must be left in place, and the boy is forbidden to eat "hot" foods. The sponsor, frequently, though not always, a relative, is chosen by the parents of the boy on the basis of long and close association with the boy. The sponsorship, although requiring no type of formal reciprocal obligations, is always remembered by the boy, and he will "love his sponsor more because of this relationship." In effect, the sponsor is brought into the boy's kinship frame of reference, sometimes even superseding the father in terms of respect, mutual helpfulness, and advice.

The period of youth does not correspond exactly for girls and for boys in Rusembilan. The girl's youth may be said to begin with the period of her apprenticeship to her mother in housekeeping duties at eight or nine when she leaves the childhood gangs and to end at the time she marries at fifteen or sixteen. For the boy, this period frequently does not begin until the

---

[11] Winstedt (*ibid.,* pp. 111–114) describes this elaborite rite. He reports that in Pattani the boy is carried on a model of Vishnu's Garuda rather than on an elephant (p. 112).

masuk Jawi ceremony, though he may have been helping with men's jobs for some time. Correspondingly, it is later before a boy enters full manhood. The *masuk Jawi* theoretically marks this transition, but actually the youth does not assume full adult responsibilities until he becomes a member of a boat crew and is married, at about the age of twenty. During the period of youth, both boys and girls are fully supported by their parents.

Formerly, at Rusembilan, there were gangs of "troublemakers" at this age level, but the villagers state that now the adolescents are too serious-minded, too interested in religion to cause trouble. As pointed out in Chapter IX, many of the youths of Rusembilan are sent to religious schools. When these boys return to the village for holidays, they give evidence that they take their studies seriously. They are always willing and eager to take part in any religious affair, leading in the singing and praying if they are allowed. They enjoy talking about religion to anyone they can find who is interested. The youths who are not attending a religious school, or have finished their training there, and who have not yet married do have a tendency to form groups. Much of the time, these groups are not at Rusembilan, but are generally moving from one *makan pulot* to another or going in pursuit of any carnival or other form of entertainment, including the cinema, which may be in the area.

Although military conscription did not reach Pattani province until 1954 and only two youths from Rusembilan had been drafted by the time this study was completed, every eighteen-year-old boy was required to register. Drafting is held once a year, and those who became twenty-one in that year are called for physical examinations and selection. If the family of a boy is wealthy, the boy's name can be kept off the register through the payment of about one thousand baht ($50). Even though so few have actually been drafted, most youths of Rusembilan approaching twenty-one feel threatened by military service. Primarily, they dislike the thought of being placed in a training camp among Thais and away from their homes and their own people. They are usually unable to speak the Thai language, and much of the Thai food is forbidden them by the Koran. It has been suggested by government officials that they buy their own food, but their wage is only four baht (20 cents) per day plus a clothing and maintenance allowance of sixty baht ($3) per month. Military service or its threat has one further effect in the community. Because it is possible that any youth may be away from the village during his twenty-first and twenty-second year and thus be unable to support a family, some parents are tending to put off the marriage of their sons until after they pass draft age. This requires that the youth be supported by his family for one or more years after he ordinarily would start supporting himself and a family. If he does marry and is subsequently drafted, his wife and whatever children he may have must be supported by either his or his wife's parents.

Marriage and Divorce

Except in cases of extreme physical or mental disability, everyone in Rusembilan is expected to marry. Marriage, coming at the age of fifteen or sixteen for girls and from nineteen up to twenty-two for boys, marks the transition from the stage of youth characterized by few responsibilities to full adult status, which involves religious, social, and economic obligation to the family and the community. For the young men of Rusembilan, the transition is minimized by the fact that they usually settle in the village with their brides, thereby retaining close contact with their families and groups of friends. For the bride the transition is severe. Often she must go to live in the village of her husband where she has few, if any, close friends. Furthermore, for at least four years before her marriage she has been secluded in the house of her family, with little or no opportunity to associate with boys or even young women of her own age; and upon her marriage, she is thrown into an entirely new role, often in a different environment, and is expected to respond quickly and competently as her husband's mate and as co-manager of the new family.

Marriage choices and arrangements are universally made by the parents of the couple rather than the couple themselves. These proceedings are initiated by the boy's father, who for some years prior to the time his son is ready to be married has been making mental inventory of acceptable girls in neighboring villages. The villagers consider that a good wife must possess at least one of the following characteristics: beauty, a good family background, wealth, or education and religious training. Each of these characteristics is considered of equal importance, and the more a woman possesses the more desirable she is, but as the villagers say, "One can't expect a perfect woman." Naturally, the more desirable a woman's characteristics are, the higher *isikawin* or monetary settlement her father will demand for her. At Rusembilan, where women must take part in the economics of the fishing industry, diligence is also considered a virtue in women. When the time comes for settling on the marriage, the father usually calls in an intermediary, often from another village. This man arranges with the parents of a suitable girl for her to be at a certain spot at a given time on some plausible pretext. He and the father of the boy will be concealed nearby at that time in order to observe the girl. The father of the boy is also expected to learn all that he can of the character of the girl through reports of people who know or have met her. If the girl is considered to be satisfactory, the intermediary will enter into further negotiations with her parents. When the arrangements have been accepted by both sets of parents, those of the girl will tell her that she is to be married within a month or two, and she is expected to begin making her clothes for the wedding and for her trousseau.

If the wedding is the first for both parties, two ceremonies are held, usually from two to four weeks apart. The first of these is the "marriage in religion," and it is the only ceremony held for remarriages. In the case of first marriage, the union may not be consummated until after the second ceremony. The "marriage in religion" consists of the religious sanction for the marriage and a formalized bargaining over the arrangements which have previously been settled; it is accompanied by a small feast for members and friends of the immediate families. The bride is not present at this ceremony, her part being taken by a male representative of her family. After the feasting and prayers led by the imam of the girl's village, witnesses must attest to the single status of both parties. In the case of a remarriage, oral testimony is *wajib* or obligatory, but legal certification of divorce is *sunat*. After these preliminaries, the bargaining is begun between the male representative of the bride's family and the groom or his representative. "I give you in marriage this woman, daughter of Che Ali, in return for four thousand baht ($200) *isikawin*." "I accept marriage of this woman, daughter of Che Ali, for two thousand baht ($100) *isikawin*." Bargaining continues in this way until the previously arranged amount is reached by both parties. The *isikawin* or monetary settlement paid by the groom for the bride is then given to the bride's representative. For a first marriage, the *isikawin* is usually between two and four thousand baht ($100-$200); it is generally a thousand ($50) or less for a remarriage. The ceremony is concluded by the *khotebah* (formalized sermon) and prayers.

The second marriage ceremony is always the occasion for a large *makan pulot*. This *makan pulot* is outranked only by that held on the occasion of a boy's *masuk Jawi* ceremony. Both sets of parents invite their own circle of friends and neighbors. The feast itself is prepared by the bride's family. On the day of the ceremony, the bride stays in the house while she is prepared for the wedding. These preparations are under the direction of the girl's "sponsor" (cf. boy's sponsor in *masuk Jawi* ceremony, above.) Included are the filing of the girl's teeth, shaving her facial hair, combing and elaborately arranging her hair, and dressing her in the style agreed upon previously. Two styles of dress are favored for Rusembilan marriages, the Malay dress consisting of a white coat and trousers and the haji dress of a long white robe and a headdress.

After the house has been cleared of those who were invited just for the *makan pulot*, the party of the groom begins to advance toward the house, singing the praises of the Prophet. At the foot of the house ladder, the groom is met by a woman from the bride's family and is led by her into the house, where he is seated next to the bride on a marriage seat decorated with flowers and Islamic designs. This is ordinarily the first time that the bride and groom have seen each other. While seated, the couple is fanned by two girls who are relatives of the bride. The bride's sponsor touches *sireh*, a ritual preparation of betel leaf and areca nut, to the heads of the pair and feeds the couple red and yellow *nasi semangat*. Feeding the couple *nasi semangat* completes the actual ceremony of the marriage. After this, all the villagers present for the ceremony rise and pass before the couple, at the same time depositing from ten to one hundred baht (50 cents to $5) in a tray before them. This is the *menggenal* ("to see the bride"). In large town weddings, only the guests from the groom's side contribute at this time, donations from the bride's side being reserved for a reception held later at the groom's village "to see the groom." In village weddings, however, because the contributions tend to be smaller than in the towns, it is common for everyone present at the marriage ceremony to contribute both times. This money is taken care of by the bride's sponsor and is either invested in gold jewelry for the bride or given to the couple to provide capital for their new family. At this time, the family of the bride presents the groom with *kain bersaling* (a change of clothes). This is usually a new Malay suit or a new sarong and shirt. In large and elaborate ceremonies, the *kain bersaling* may approach the proportions of a complete new wardrobe.

Ordinarily, after the ceremony the groom goes to his own village with his wedding party, returning to his bride after two or three days. Occasionally, however, in village weddings, he may stay with the bride for several days and then return with her to his village. Whatever arrangement is followed, the couple alternately resides in each of the villages for periods ranging from two days to a week, until they decide to settle in one of the villages, either in the home of the parents or in their own home. On the occasion of the first arrival of the couple in the groom's village, a reception and feast are held by the groom's parents for the villagers accompanying the bride. It is at this reception that the *menggenal*, "to see the groom," is collected by his family. In some cases, even this *menggenal* may be collected by the bride's sponsor, as it is the mutual property of the couple. During the period of the bride's initial residence in the village of the groom, she is accompanied by her sponsor, whose duty is to see that she is treated well by her in-laws.

Because of the abruptness of the transition for the girl from secluded youth to married woman, tradition prohibits consummation of the marriage for at least three nights. The first night, three pillows are placed in the middle of the sleeping mat with a bowl of water on top. The second night, one pillow and the bowl of water are removed, and each succeeding night another pillow is removed, until there is no physical barrier left between the couple. Neither the bride nor the groom receive any form of premarital instruction, although the groom is often informed to some extent by the conversations of other boys and men.

Not infrequently, at Rusembilan, a couple may not speak to each other for as long as two to three weeks. This is considered normal shyness on the part of the girl, but if it lasts for more than two weeks, certain steps are taken by the bride's father and the groom. The bride's father may put cigarettes on the couple's sleeping mat, but no matches. In this case, when the couple retires, the groom is forced to ask his wife, "Where are the matches?" and her reply breaks the barrier of silence. Or the father may place money on the sleeping mat, with instruction to his daughter that if the money is there she is required to answer any question her husband may ask her. Once the bride has spoken, further efforts are entirely up to the groom, and he is considered as much at fault as the bride if their relationship fails to improve.

Before a marriage is consummated, separation is simply a matter of the return of one of the partners to his or her parents' home and the arranging for repayment of the *isikawin*. In these cases, and when the marriage has been consummated but the partners are still in a stage of readjustment, the imam is usually called in to advise the couple and seek a reconciliation (see the last section of Chapter IX). After the marriage has been established, divorce is left entirely to the couple's judgment. To effect a divorce, all that is required of a man is to say three times before witnesses, "I divorce you." If the wife is pregnant, divorce must usually be put off until after the child is born. For a woman, divorce requires that she show cause, usually non-support, to the imam. In the case of divorce of an established couple, there is no repayment of either the *isikawin* or any of the *menggenal;* the husband is bound, however, to divide evenly with his wife all capital accumulated during the period of marriage. Thus, one man in Rusembilan who came from a wealthy family is now almost penniless, as he has had eleven wives in the process of seeking one who would produce an heir. For each divorce he must share his accumulated property, and for each marriage he has had to pay the *isikawin*.[12] Old residents of Rusembilan say that there is a great deal of divorce in the village

[12] It seems probable that the property distributed represents more than simply what was accumulated during the course of the marriage.

now, whereas there was little before. Actually, if annulments and
divorce of couples married less than a year are discounted, marriages in Rusembilan appear to be extremely stable.

Although polygyny is permitted by Islamic law, there is almost none in the Pattani area, and when it exists, it is limited to
hajis and *guru*. Polygyny is against the Thai law, but enforcement has not been strict. Probably the chief reason that it is not
more common is economic. Unless a man is very wealthy, he is
unable to support more than one adult woman in his family. The
last man to have two wives in Rusembilan died in 1954. In one
case, there was a suspicion that a man was marrying a second
wife, but it was found later that he had divorced his first one.
Some men in Rusembilan joke with their wives about taking a
second wife. Lest the husband become serious, the wife will
immediately become indignant. Rarely, a man may keep a second wife, usually a widow, in another village. In these cases,
only the imam and a few trusted friends are told of the arrangement. The villagers say that it is very hard to keep two wives in
the same house—"even the Prophet had trouble with his wives"
—and one must resort to charms given by the *bomo* to keep
peace. All marriages of either party subsequent to the first are
celebrated only with the "marriage in religion" and the payment
of the *isikawin*.

Adult Status

After a man and wife have been married long enough to be
established, usually six months, they are considered to be fully
adult members of the community. Until this time, they have
been supported by their parents, and usually whatever money
the man made was kept by him to help establish his new family.
Even after a couple has been established, however, the parents
are expected to help out if necessary in any social or financial
crises. In the case of a widow, she is expected to return to her

parents if they are living and be supported by them just as if she were an unmarried girl.

There is little occupational specialization among members of the same sex at Rusembilan, and in many areas of life both sexes participate to the same degree. Women are always responsible for the care of the children and looking after the house and preparing the meals. They also do most of the marketing, both buying and selling, help with the agricultural work, and contribute to the fishing operations on the beach. Occasionally, a widow with no parents to go to will set up a small shop on the beach and by preparing breakfasts for other villagers is able to support herself; or she may agree to labor in another's padi field on a share-crop basis. The economic role of women in the fishing activities of Rusembilan has already been discussed in Chapter IV.

Men participate in fishing, either individually or as members of boat groups, and in agricultural work which, except for the plowing, they generally share with the female members of their families. Any building or construction in the village is always performed by men, and only men are called out on co-operative work projects. Malay villagers are always appalled when they occasionally see a Thai woman working at heavy labor along with men, for instance, on highway construction projects. There is more opportunity, though it is limited, for specialization and variety of occupation among men than women. Such occupations as running coffee shops, driving buses, and operating trishaws in Pattani are open to men who prefer not to make a living by fishing or agriculture alone. One or two men in the village are able to maintain themselves and their families by being carpenters. The role of a religious leader or a *guru* is always open to men. With the introduction of motorboats to Rusembilan, there is the beginning of an occupational specialty in mechanics.

The greatest nonoccupational distinction between the sexes is made in religious affairs. Although some women come to be considered religious leaders in the community, no woman may hold formal religious office, nor may she be a *guru* or a teacher other than in her role of instructing village girls in the Koran. Friday prayers are not compulsory for women, and when a woman chooses to pray at the Friday service, she is separated from the men by a curtain. This same distinction obtains at *makan pulot*, whether these are connected with a religious occasion or not; the women, after serving the men in the main room, eat in the kitchen or other back room. There is no tradition of purdah among Malay Moslems, however. Villagers say that "men don't expect much from women; and they never say hard things or strong words in front of them." It is very difficult for a man to refuse the request of a woman. Consequently, when a man desires something from a friend, he will frequently have his wife make the request in order to ensure compliance.

Almost all adults of Rusembilan regulate their behavior so that it coincides remarkably closely with the accepted norms. All men try to live up to the criteria of respected men (see Chapter VIII) and ordinarily work diligently to support their families. Women always attempt to be good wives to their husbands, to keep a neat and hospitable house, and to raise a large family. Occasionally, however, a dispute arises, usually over land or property settlement, which cannot be settled to the satisfaction of all parties. Violence on these occasions is not uncommon. During the course of this study, two women attacked each other with soda bottles as a result of a land dispute. Two men also came to blows over the same dispute. When such incidents occur in Rusembilan or in other villages, they provide topics of conversation in the coffee shops for weeks afterward.

Aside from the cases of mental disease discussed in Chapter X, there are one or two instances in Rusembilan of individuals who exhibit atypical characters. None of these people is maladjusted enough to be unable to lead an adequate life in the community, but each is different enough so that he is not well liked or included in many community activities. One of these men is employed by a Thai merchant in Pattani to keep his fighting bulls. This man is away from the village all day, usually until about nine in the evening, taking care of "business about the bulls." He does not participate in religious services in the mosque and during Ramadan refused to fast. Villagers say that in his youth he was a "gangster" and served a jail sentence for killing a man. Another man, a respected carpenter, is considered deviant in the opposite direction. This man is *betul* (literally, straight), wants no trouble, and will do no harm to anyone. Frequently, his possessions are stolen, but the man will do nothing to apprehend the thief, who might be hurt by such actions, nor does he take precautions against future thievery. This man, although he is respected as a carpenter and his behavior is approved of in theory, is not well liked, because he is considered too unrealistic.

Old Age and Death

In Rusembilan, there is no firm line of demarcation between the time when full participation as an adult ceases and old age begins. Men in the village speak of the situation in larger fishing villages along the east coast and farther north in Thailand in which a man is unable to get a position in a boat group when he is only a little past middle age. The fishing activities of those villages are highly organized commercially, and the fishermen are aware that as a man begins to age his productivity starts to drop off. In Rusembilan, however, there are usually enough boat groups so that older men are needed to fill them all. Here, even though an older man may not be able to do quite as much work or do it as fast as a younger man, he is welcomed on the boat groups because of his knowledge and long fishing experience. It is not uncommon to find men of sixty-five or even older going out in boat groups every night during the *kembong* fishing sea-

son. Many of the steerers are men of about this age, having
acquired enough capital during their lives to invest in a *kolek*
of their own.

When a man begins to stop engaging in strenuous occupations
is entirely a matter of his own judgment and preference. The
society places no maximum limits based on age alone for any
activity. If a man is wealthy enough when he desires to retire
from *kembong* fishing, he usually will devote some of his time
to cultivation of padi and perhaps to garden crops and will spend
much of his time sitting and talking in the coffee shops. If he is
less well off, he may have to supplement his agricultural income
by some form of fishing. Commonly, this is limited to netting
crabs during the night and a small amount of work netting small
shrimps in the daytime with the *jala* and the *pukat sinyoh*. The
strenuous occupation of *kembong* fishing seems to be the only
activity in Rusembilan in which age and failing strength ever
force a man to retire completely. As long as a man remains
healthy, he may continue to be active in any other occupation
or trade in the village. During the period of this study, there
were three men in Rusembilan whose ages were given by the
government census as ninety-five.[13] One of these men was blind
and had to be supported by his son. The other two, however,
managed to support themselves and their families adequately,
one by crabbing and cultivation of a small field of padi, the other
by agriculture alone. The latter individual during this period
was preparing an extensive fenced-in area for the cultivation of
salable garden crops. Because of a dispute with his children and
grandchildren over land boundaries, he received no help on this

[13] Government of Thailand, *Census BE 2499* (1956). The accuracy of
these figures is not certain, as Malays do not bother to keep exact count
of their own or their children's ages, usually reckoning from some important event, for example, "My child was born near the time when the
Japanese were here." Compare Raymond Firth, *Malay Fishermen: Their
Peasant Economy*, p. 72.

project. By himself he dug trenches, some six feet deep, and set five- or six-foot coconut logs into the ground as fence posts.

If a man becomes enfeebled by age or is otherwise unable to work to support himself, his children or occasionally other relatives are expected to look after him and support him. This task usually devolves upon the youngest child, as he or she frequently falls heir to the parents' house after all other children have married and started families of their own. Whenever the aged are able to live alone, however, they prefer to do so rather than impose on their children. It is not uncommon to find an aged couple who are living in hardly more than a shack on the beach after having given their house to their youngest child.

Women, although younger than their husbands, do not ordinarily outlive their mates. If a wife remains healthy, her occupations throughout life parallel those of her husband. As long as she is able, she maintains the house and cooks for her husband. While her husband is working with a boat group, she is occupied with the marketing and distribution of his shares of the catch. When he retires to crabbing and netting small shrimp, she assumes the responsibility for the marketing of these, either alone or in co-operation with other women in a similar situation. She continues to help in the padi field and to perform whatever other occupational duties she shared with her husband in earlier life. Thus, although both men and women keep as busy as they can during their old age, there is a parallel diminution in their activities since they tend to work as a team throughout life, either complementing each other's activities as in fishing or supplementing them as in agriculture.

When a person dies, the drums at the mosque and the *balaisa* are beaten to notify the village. At this time, all activities are supposed to stop until after the burial. Work in the fields ceases, fishing boats may not go out, and many villagers, especially friends and acquaintances of the family of the deceased, gather near the house where the death occurred. The women will visit (*melawat*) the house to pay their condolences and leave a small sum of money. Meanwhile, the men set to work building the coffin. This usually requires a trip to Pattani to procure the lumber, although every effort is made to bury the body as soon after death as possible. White cloth for the funeral clothes must also be purchased in Pattani and given to a village seamstress to cut and sew into the funeral garments.

As soon as the funeral clothes and the coffin are ready, the imam enters the house to prepare the body for burial. Water for washing is made ready by swirling a cloth containing bark, herbs, and mud through a bowl of water. The imam covers his hand with a glove made of the funeral cloth and pats sand on the body which is held facing Mecca by a relative. The washing water is poured over the body, and the imam bathes it completely, using commercial or locally made herbal soap. The body is then rinsed and dried with cotton, and all orifaces of the body are cleaned and stopped up with cotton. After the washing of the body, the relative who has been holding it must be massaged, as he feels "pained and weak" from his contact with the corpse. The imam then dresses the corpse in a blouse and sarong made of the funeral cloth, bundles it in three, five, or seven wrappings of the same cloth, and ties the wrappings at either end of the body. It is placed face down on a pillow in the coffin and covered with colored cloth. The imam must then cleanse his own head, face, hands, and feet before leading a series of prayers for the deceased. A large procession escorts the four coffin bearers to the burial ground southeast of the village, where a simple grave is dug and the coffin is placed facing Mecca. Women are excluded from the actual burial, as they are apt to weep, and it is considered bad to weep or show "weakness" over death.

Prayers will be said at least seven times a day in the house of the deceased until the seventh day after death, when a small feast will be held for the imam and other religious leaders and very close male friends of the deceased. The feasting is preceded by the *menatip*, consisting of general prayers, prayers committing the deceased to the mercy of God, and prayers for forgiveness of sins of both the living and the dead. Another similar feast is held on the fortieth day after the death of the individual, and smaller feasts are held on each anniversary of his death for three years.

There is no general rule of inheritance followed in Rusembilan. Usually, an old man will distribute his property to his heirs before he dies, often little by little as his activities diminish. The drafting of wills is becoming increasingly common. Property will ordinarily go to an individual's surviving spouse rather than to his children, and it is common for male children, when they do inherit the property, to receive slightly larger shares than daughters. If a man dies intestate or if his will is contested, the matter is referred to the Moslem Religious Board for adjudication. In these cases, decisions are almost always based on Islamic law.

CHAPTER XII

Patterns of a Changing Community

THE present chapter analyzes the data set forth in the preceding chapters and outlines a system of social and cultural patterns. The abstraction and isolation of such patterns from the day-by-day routine of the members of a society constitute a task essentially foreign to the people themselves, and perhaps none but the most sophisticated of them would be able to recognize his specific activities reflected in such generalized patterns.[1] Careful abstraction and generalization are, however, valid tools of social science. Even though such processes involve distortions like those found in perspective drawing,[2] abstraction and generalization are the only means of condensing a mass of data to proportions that make the facts suitable for comparative purposes and for formulating the "laws" and theories about human behavior.

[1] The people of Manus, however, in choosing and working for social and technological change have created conceptual models or abstract constructs of existing as well as desired sociocultural patterns. See Margaret Mead, *New Lives for Old*, and Anthony Wallace, "Revitalization Movements," *American Anthropologist*, 58:264–281, 1956.

[2] Ralph Linton, *The Study of Man*, p. 443.

The first sections of the chapter deal with the orientations of the culture. These orientations are conceived to be the largest consistent units that can be derived from the culture. Each is made up of several series of smaller units, the smallest of which is the individual "culture trait." [3] Thus, the orientations take into account not only what the people of Rusembilan do but also their system of values and the major goals that the culture holds to be important. Individualistic and communal orientations are considered, and then the polarity between them and how it operates in the culture. The final section is devoted to a brief analysis of the social structure of the community in terms of three "dimensions" of social interaction.

Cultural Orientations

Individualistic orientations. In relation to the major patterns of activity and governing set of values, the most important cultural orientation of Rusembilan and other coastal villages in the area is in the economic sphere. Because these villages have taken part in the market relationships of Pattani for many years, their economic orientations have come to differ widely from the co-operative, communal, and kinship-based orientations of the inland agricultural communities. This economic orientation can be summed up as stressing individualism, competition within limits, and acquisition and utilization of capital goods. Individualism, as a value is persistently expressed by the villagers of Rusembilan. Emphasis is placed upon diligence and productive enterprise by the individual rather than upon group activity. In agriculture, each man endeavors to do as much of the preparation of the field, planting, and harvesting as he and his immediate family can manage. When he is required to call upon the services of others, it is on a strictly reciprocal basis. Most of the land in Rusembilan is individually owned, and although the ties of

[3] Compare John Gillen, "Cultural Adjustment," *American Anthropologist*, 46:429–437, 1944.

an individual to his land may not be as strongly enforced by tradition as they are in agricultural communities, the landowner feels compelled to make his land produce its maximum crop. Economic motives predominate, but some of the values associated with the padi field and its cultivation place it a little beyond the purely economic sphere. Rice is the traditional form of payment of the *zakat*, thus associating the crop more closely than other products with religion. Money is never invested by the villagers in padi land, and ownership of it, unlike rubber and coconut land, is considered almost as much a prestige factor as an economic asset.

Although the important cash fish, *kembong*, requires group effort for efficient netting, the avowed orientation of the fisherman is individualistic. The steerers of most of the *kolek*, through their own knowledge, initiative, and hard work, are individually responsible for the continued success of the boat. Crew members are taken on and remain with the crew on the basis of the amount of personal effort they put forth in the fishing operations and not, except in the case of the less successful and less popular *perahu serikat*, on the basis of more communal criteria such as kinship or common ownership. Some few individuals prefer to pursue the less profitable forms of fishing that can be done alone rather than minimize the effect of their individual effort to the extent of joining a boat group.

Distribution and marketing of the *kembong*, unlike the catching of the fish, require little group organization and are carried on in a highly individualistic manner. The allotment of shares is made on the basis of the fisherman's role in the boat group, a meticulous count being made and deficiencies in shares being tallied against the next night's catch. The share immediately becomes the property of the fisherman and his family, and the marketing of it devolves upon the fisherman's wife or, rarely, upon his mother. Each woman is responsible for selling her share of the fish as profitably as she can in one of the several buyer-seller relationships, without regard to, or in conscious competition with, the transactions of the other women.

As in our own culture, the operation of individualistic and competitive values in the economic culture of Rusembilan is supported and complemented by an orientation toward investment in capital goods and the accumulation of money as a goal in itself without direct reference to its use as a medium of exchange. Land, excluding padi land discussed above, has always been a major form of capital investment at Rusembilan. Until recently, capital investment in land was limited to coconut plantations, but with the rubber boom after World War II, the villagers quickly began investing in land suitable for rubber production in spite of the fact that each rubber tree requires almost twice as long as a coconut tree to begin making any returns on the initial investment. Since its introduction into Rusembilan more than a quarter of a century ago, the *kolek* has been a favorite object for investment and speculation among the wealthier villagers. Sometimes a good boat may pass from one owner to the next six or eight times during its life of ten or twelve years. The introduction of motorboats in 1956 illustrated the positive value attached to investment in capital goods. Rather than wait for one boat to prove or disprove its worth to the fishing economy, the villagers acquired four boats within three weeks and with each one explored independently the different possibilities of use and different ways of organizing the *kolek* in the tow group. Although by the following season it was found that the use of separate outboard motors on each *kolek* was more efficient in terms of fishing operations and cheaper to operate, three of the four original motorboats were still being used in the village, presumably for their value as tangible symbols of invested wealth.

Beyond the economic sphere of the culture, the individualistic orientations extend over into the area of those institutions functioning to regulate behavior within the community. In this area, they sometimes come into conflict with orientations of a different sort. These orientations and the type of conflict that occurs will be considered in following sections of this chapter. The basic regulatory institution in Rusembilan is the nuclear family, consisting of father, mother, children, and, occasionally, grandparents or grandchildren. Within the family group, strong stress is laid upon individualism. Children are to a large extent encouraged to lead their own lives with a minimum of guidance and discipline. By about the age of six, they are given money for odd jobs and as presents on special occasions and are themselves responsible for safeguarding and spending it wisely. The individual within the family is respected, and although Rusembilan is a Moslem community, women are accorded equal rights with men in family matters and occasionally even in business.

Within the framework of the community itself, except for religious and external political institutions, the sole regulatory institution is the unformalized group of respected men. These men, on the basis of their wealth or their experience and authority in fishing, are looked to by the community both as examples of *orang baik*, "good men," and as arbiters in any conflicts and disputes that may arise in the village. They can be described as a group in relation to the social and cultural organization of the community, but they are not viewed as such by the villagers. Each man stands as an individual in relation to all those who may come to him for advice and in relation to the other *orang baik* of the community. The solution of conflicts and disputes, and even questions of punishment for some crimes under provincial jurisdiction, are suggested by these men individually and involve individual action on the part of the parties to the dispute rather than any form of community action.

It seemed logical to the Thai officials of the district and the province that these men would form the core of village councils and that they would take active part in village meetings with the district officer. But since whatever respect and authority they have in the eyes of the community is because of their typification of the individualistic orientations, they could not readily adapt to the communal and democratic ideals represented by these government institutions. Consequently, both the village meetings and the recent village council in no way reflect the true structure of authority within the community or approximate the villagers' system of values, but simply remain frameworks which are meaningless to the community or at best serve as focal points for negative attitudes directed at the Thai government.

Communal orientations. The communal orientations of the culture of Rusembilan are based upon those clusters of values associated with the kinship group beyond the nuclear family and with religious and ceremonial institutions. They stress, rather than individualism, values of community integration, wider family solidarity, and common participation in Malay culture beyond the confines of the community.

The religious organization of the community, and particularly the religious instruction given to children and youths, is the primary means of directing individuals in accordance with the communal orientations. Islamic values, in contrast to the individualistic values discussed above, stress more the subordination and superordination of parts within an organized whole. Religious obligations, the interpretation of doctrine in terms of culture, and the maintaining of correct relationships with God, the community, and the family are important values within this orientation.

In filling the roles of both *orang baik* and religious leader, a man is faced with the alternative of interpreting for the community either of two sets of values which are not in complete agreement with one another. Ordinarily, a person in this position limits his activities of leadership to the areas of the culture concerned with religion and not with economic matters. Religious participation, religious education, calendrical and passage celebrations, all tend to emphasize the unity of the community and minimize aspects of personal achievement. Although there are occasional conflicts between the religious and economic "compartments" of the culture, in general the villagers seek and receive leadership in the different areas from different men.

As mentioned above, the cultivation of rice is felt by the villagers to be set off slightly from other economic activities which are governed solely by individualistic orientations. The cooperative labor at the time of transplanting and harvesting the rice, though obligating reciprocation, is enlisted more on the basis of kinship and religious associations than in terms of ordinary boat-group coactivity. The point was made in Chapter VIII that the traditional kinship basis for group organization was almost completely lost in the maritime economy of Rusembilan and that even the kinship terms facilitating solidarity among a large group of kin had ceased to be used in the community. Rice cultivation, being the major traditional activity in inland villages, but relatively unimportant in the economy of Rusembilan, seems to have retained a measure of its communal orientation in the face of the economically predominant individualistic orientations of the culture.

Ceremonial occasions demand a co-operating group that could not well be organized in terms of individualistic orientations. Family solidarity is stressed by participation of the family and the larger kinship circle. In addition, passage rites affirm the family solidarity and consonance with the values of the culture when the individual passes from one stage of the culture to another as a member of his family group. More important, however, than the ceremony itself in terms of the communal orientations is the *makan pulot*, the attendant feast. Any large ceremony is limited to the members of the individual's family and close friends. But the accompanying *makan pulot* not only includes all or most of the community but people from communities throughout the area where the individual or his family have friends, relatives, or friends of friends.

As Spicer says in writing of the annual pueblo fiesta in the Yaqui community of Potam: "The fiesta orientation may be regarded as having three major meanings; first, that of fulfillment of obligations to fellow-villagers, second, that of public display of one's resources with accompanying prestige, and finally, that of social excitement and pleasure." [4] This formulation is as true a picture of Rusembilan as it is of Potam if the first point also includes obligations, usually unformalized, to members of the family and kin group and obligations to other Malay communities in the area.

Although conflicting in basic ideals and hypotheses, the religious institutions of Rusembilan and the body of spirit beliefs and shamanistic practices share the same goals and cultural orientations. This concurrence is most obvious in the annual ceremony to ensure the well-being of the community, in which both the imam and the *bomo* stress the value of personal and community integration and co-operation. The curing practices of the *bomo* as well as the religious services of the imam are directed toward the integration of the individual with the community. Public performances of the *peterana*, like the *makan pulot*, are oriented to stress the individual's obligations to his family, including his ancestors, and to his fellow villagers and are in addition a display of his resources and entertainment for the community. Individualism appears as a negative value in the religious institutions of the community and also in the area of spirit belief where it appears as magic. Both economic individualism and magic, stressing individual gain of one sort or another, are in conflict with the orientations emphasizing integration and communality.

Cultural Polarity

The foregoing discussion of the orientations of the culture of Rusembilan has made it clear that there exists a basic polarity between the orientations of the individualistic type and those of the communal type. The former stress values of individualism,

[4] Edward H. Spicer, *Potam, a Yaqui Village in Sonora*, p. 183.

competition, and the accumulation and use of personal capital, whereas the latter stress values of communal welfare, kinship and community co-operation, kindness, and generosity. In most ordinary situations in the lives of the villagers, there is little or no contradiction in terms of their orientations: individualism prevails in economic activities, and communality in religious and ceremonial activities.[5]

It is within the institutions which regulate behavior that the conflict between orientations is most noticeable to the villagers. This conflict is reflected in the definitions given for *orang baik*, the good men who act as leaders and exemplars of the community. Wealth, practical knowledge, and personal accomplishment are stressed in the definitions, but so are generosity, religious wisdom, and willingness to help those in need. Implicit in these definitions is the idea of a judicious balance between the conflicting values. The individuals discussed in Chapter XI who typify the polar extremes are not admired by the villagers. One of these individuals was completely oriented toward individualistic, commercial activities, not even bothering to feign fasting during the month of Ramadan; the other was *betul*, or leading an "ideal" life, in which he was unable even to protect his own property for fear of hurting others.

But beyond a balance between the two types of orientation, there must also be a relative emphasis upon one set or the other. Although a leader in secular affairs must be a good Moslem and is expected to participate fully in other communally oriented areas of the culture, his leadership does not extend into these areas. The religious leader is expected to follow the individualistic orientations to the extent of properly maintaining and marketing his economic assets, but he must keep in the background in economic or political matters. The severe criticism of and partial loss of faith in the imam was occasioned by the fact that he took a major role in the introduction of motorboats. The criticism

[5] Robert Redfield, *The Little Community*, pp. 132–148.

was based not on the fact that he might be incompetent in dealing with economic matters, but on the assumption that by attempting to use his authority in accordance with the individualistic orientations he would be less able to reinforce and interpret for the community the communal orientations of his own religious area of leadership.

As commercial and economic activities become increasingly important at Rusembilan and other coastal communities, the individualistic orientations tend to overshadow the communal orientations within the community as a whole. They also seem to be encroaching on areas which formerly were more communally oriented. An example of this is the series of rituals for the propitiation of the sea spirits at the seasonal and periodic launchings of each *kolek*. The elements of ritual have been taken out of their religious and ceremonial orientations and made to adapt to, or even reinforce, the economic individualistic orientations. Thus, the rituals appear to be directed not toward securing an abundant supply for the whole community, but rather toward increasing the efficiency and "luck" of a particular *kolek* and its crew in a competitive situation. The sacrifice of a white buffalo by the whole community to the sea spirits is no longer performed at Rusembilan, as it is a ceremony in the economic sphere which could not be adapted to the individualistic orientations.

Even in the *makan pulot*, serving both to mark a religious occasion and as a symbol of solidarity and integration of kinship, community, and wider groups, the individualistic orientations are playing an increasingly important part. The desire to make a *makan pulot* pay for itself or possibly show a profit, the feeling that one's *makan pulot* should be bigger and more elaborate than that of one's neighbor, and the calculations based on cost of transportation and loss of economic activity to determine the amount to be contributed by each participant—all point to encroaching individualistic orientations. The *makan pulot* for three thousand people mentioned in Chapter VIII is an extreme case, but the villagers feel that it represents a trend.

Norbeck found a similar shift from communal to individualistic emphasis in the Japanese fishing village he studied. The changes in the culture of Takashima, he writes,

may be summed up as the adoption of a money economy with attendant emphasis upon individuality and a decrease in communal activity; social status based largely on wealth; a decrease in the size and importance of the extended household; a tendency toward ever-larger community structure; the end of isolation and self-sufficiency for the *buraku* or small community; the adoption of a great many foreign inventions and ideas and a decline in religious faith.[6]

As long as contradictory orientations at Rusembilan can be kept relatively compartmentalized within the culture and the number of conflicts remain small, the cultural polarity need not be disintegrative and, in fact, may even function adaptively. Changes in economic activities of the community are taking place fairly rapidly. New technological forms are being introduced, and elements of the social structure are being adapted to deal with them. The individualistic orientations operating in the economic sphere tend to favor the technological innovations which come ultimately from the Western industrial cultures. If, however, the orientations in the economic and religious areas tended to correspond and if there were closer functional relationships between the two areas, adaptations to innovations in one sphere would imply parallel changes in the other sphere which would not necessarily be adaptive. With the cultural orientations of the community relatively independent, such nonadaptive changes do not occur, and each area of orientation remains relatively consistent within itself.[7]

[6] Edward Norbeck, *Takashima, A Japanese Fishing Community*, p. 214.
[7] Spicer (*op. cit.*, p. 208) points out a similar hypothesis for Yaqui culture.

A Concept of Social Dimensions

This section will attempt to draw together the data presented in the preceding chapters into a concise model of the social structure of Rusembilan. The accompanying diagram (Figure

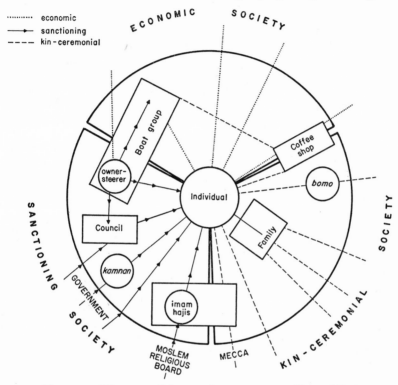

.... economic
———► sanctioning
– – – – kin-ceremonial

Figure 11. Diagram of interaction patterns at Rusembilan.

11) indicates the main patterns of social interaction which fall into the categories of this model. The diagram has the individual as its focal point and maps interaction patterns radiating from him to other individuals and groups within the community and beyond. The society of Rusembilan, is, of course, made up of the sum of the patterns of all the individuals interacting within the community and from it to the wider society beyond. The

term dimension will be used in analyzing the types of interactions rather than some more delimiting concept in order to suggest that these patterns extend through a wider society than Rusembilan itself. In this formulation, Rusembilan can be imagined both as an incomplete microcosm of the total society and as a particular cross section in the total stream of interactions of that society. The definition of this "total society" is admittedly vague, for it varies according to the types of interaction patterns that are being considered. In terms of the political structure, the "total society" is the nation of Thailand; in economic relationships, it is a segment of the international market; and in ceremonial relationships, it may include as little as southern Thailand and Malaya or as much as the whole Moslem world.

Within a relatively self-contained community, such as Rusembilan, the patterns of interaction will be most intense within the community itself, but there will also be a degree of intensity between the community and other communities in habitual relationship with it.[8] In the case of Rusembilan, practically all extracommunity relationships are with Pattani, except interactions of a ceremonial type which tend to be dispersed evenly among Malay villages of the area. Pattani serves not only as the market center for Rusembilan, but also as the center of government authority on the district and provincial level and as representative of the national power structure. Even extracommunity religious relationships tend to focus on Pattani as the seat of the provincial Moslem Religious Board.

In the present analysis, as in the diagram, the social structure of Rusembilan is thought of in three "dimensions" of interaction. The first comprises those types of interaction characteristic of the economic activities of the community. The second type is formed of relationships of power or authority which differ from the economic type in that they are essentially one-way relation-

[8] See Redfield, *The Little Community*, pp. 113–131, and *Peasant Society and Culture*, pp. 49 f.

ships, usually stemming from the larger society and acting on Rusembilan as a terminus. The final dimension consists of interactions, mostly in the sphere of kinship and ceremonial activities, that are characterized by a diffuseness and lack of specification of particular roles within the pattern of relationships. Basic to all three types of interaction is the nuclear family, within and from which institution each dimension of interaction operates.

The patterns of economic interaction at Rusembilan involve roles which are essentially equivalent in their origination of action.[9] There is little tendency in these relationships for decisions or authority to be concentrated in only one or the other of the interacting parties. These patterns can be thought of as straight-line segments of a longer and broader straight line. For example, the interactions between the collector and vendor of rattan inland and the purchasing fisherman at Rusembilan, and between the village woman selling her fish and the wholesaler in Pattani, and between the same woman and the vendor of vegetables in the Pattani market are all essentially similar patterns in the chain of two-way economic relationships throughout south Thailand and beyond.

The interaction patterns defined here as sanctioning are, unlike the economic patterns, characterized by inequality of the roles within the relationships. Action is almost always originated at the one end and terminated at the other. And in interactions extending beyond Rusembilan, the community is usually the terminus. Because of this characteristic, these interaction patterns do not form a broad, straight, reciprocating system as do the economic patterns. These can be thought of as chains of interaction with a marked direction of flow through a hierarchy from the top to the bottom. Patterns of both religious and political authority fall within this dimension. For example, the implementation of an order from the Prime Minister of Thailand involves

[9] See Eliot D. Chapple and Carleton S. Coon, *Principles of Anthropology*, pp. 277–462.

a series of one-way interactions: from the government in Bangkok to the governor of Pattani, from him to the district officer, again from this person to the *kamnan* at Rusembilan, and finally from the *kamnan* to the ultimate terminus, the villager.

Unlike the economic and sanctioning dimensions of interaction, the patterns of kin-ceremonial interaction do not tend to run in straight lines. They form rather what Barnes [10] has characterized as a network of interactions, a web with nodes representing individuals and with threads of relationship, from tight to open, which connect them with *many* other nodes. Like the economic and sanctioning interactions, these extend beyond the horizons of the community, but whereas the other two pass through or terminate in the community in a certain constant one- or two-way direction, the kin-ceremonial interaction patterns radiate from many different communities like so many circles with overlapping and intersecting segments. Individual relationships within the pattern tend to be equivalent and on the whole nondirectional and may persist in time without fulfilling any specific function that the villager can name. An example of this type of kin-ceremonial interaction can be found in the relationships involved in the *makan pulot* which were discussed in Chapter VIII.

[10] J. A. Barnes, "Class and Committee in a Norwegian Island Parish," *Human Relations*, 7 (no. 1):39–58, 1954.

CHAPTER XIII

Sociocultural Change

THE period of field work for the present study was too short to observe and analyze in detail the total range of sociocultural change that has taken place and is in the process of taking place in Rusembilan; but certain generalizations can be made about the factors at work that favor change in some areas of the socio-cultural system and not in others and about the dynamics of the process of change in the community. The following analysis will deal briefly with the different types of change that appear to be taking place at Rusembilan, first, in terms of patterns reported and reconstructed from the past and their relation to the present cultural orientations and social structure of the community and, secondly, in terms of acceptance of and resistance to innovations from the culture and society of the Thai nation. Further research will be needed to verify some of the assumptions made here and to fill in the total picture of the effects of Thai-Malay culture contact upon both Malay communities and the Thai culture of the peninsular south.

Ecological Factors

The first set of factors involved in sociocultural change at Rusembilan derives from the position of the community in relation to geographical and natural characteristics of the country and to the distribution of the population of the area. Although the changes considered in this section are attributed to ecological factors, it is necessary to remember that, even when an ecological factor is sufficient by itself to cause changes in the sociocultural system, the specific forms that the changes take are determined largely by the system. In short, the ecological factors can be thought of as factors predisposing or limiting changes which are actually brought about in response to disequilibriums in the social or cultural organizations of the community. The changes discussed in this section will be those in which environmental pressures on the society and culture seem to have been the strongest, but by no means exclusive, factors.

The most remarkable change in the history of Rusembilan is its transformation from a subsistence rice-farming community to one dependent upon commercial fishing. The changes involved in this process are dependent to a large extent on the location of the village near the sea. The original settlement of Rusembilan was about half a mile from the coast, and the village families relied chiefly upon rice cultivation for their living. Some fish were probably taken by trap or line from the shallow waters along the beach as well as from the flooded padi fields. As individuals moved from the original settlement and started putting their houses directly on the beach, reliance on fishing grew for two reasons. In the first place, the sea became part of the ecological scene of the new settlement, and harvesting its products came to be as natural to the villagers as harvesting the products of the land. In the second place, because it fronted on the sea, the village could no longer be surrounded by its rice fields, thereby effectively doubling the average distance from a man's house to his fields.

The early fishing activities of Rusembilan were carried on as individual enterprises. Each man, as he moved to the beach with his family, would take up fishing as much or as little as suited him. With a minimum of equipment, he could fish from the shore, or he could use a small boat with one or two drift nets for catching fish offshore. Because of the accessibility of the Pattani market, sale of fish for cash or commodities presented no problem, so that offshore fishing with its greater yield of marketable fish began to supersede fishing from the beach which satisfied little more than the needs of an individual family. A continued desire for more efficient exploitation of their maritime environment led to the introduction of *kolek* into the village by men still living in 1956. The *kolek* increased the yield of fish by providing a greater range of fishing areas because of their speed and by providing a larger netting area because of the number of crew they could carry. The effects of introducing *kolek* and, later, motorboats will be discussed in the following section.

Relative scarcity of rice-producing land continued to exert pressures throughout the history of Rusembilan. Aside from encouraging a shift toward a fishing economy, these pressures also had the effect of forcing the villagers to utilize land which was not suitable for rice production. Thus, the villagers began raising coconuts for commercial sale rather than for purely domestic uses. As the high sandy ground on which the coconuts grew was limited by village boundaries and by the sea and mangrove swamps in the same way that padi land was, the maximum number of plantations possible was reached by the resident and nonresident landowners in Rusembilan. With this situation and with the increased amount of capital available for investment which was being brought into the village through the commercial sale of fish and copra, the villagers turned to rubber planting as an alternative to both rice and coconut raising.

Ecological factors have played a decisive role in establishing the present settlement pattern of Rusembilan and other coastal villages. Inland villages depending on rice production for their

living tend to be formed in a circular pattern. There is generally
a nucleus consisting of ten or more houses, the mosque, and
coffee shops, if any. Surrounding this nucleus are the village
ricelands, and scattered throughout the fields, particularly on
sandy outcroppings or along natural watercourses, are the houses
of the other members of the community, sometimes a single
compound containing one house and its outbuildings, sometimes
several adjacent compounds or compounds containing more
than one house. In areas near population centers, it is common
for the outlying houses of one village to merge with the outlying houses of another, in these cases the only definition of
community membership being which village mosque the members of the outlying houses attend. This situation is changed by
the maritime orientation of the fishing villages. Not only does
the position of the nucleus on the beach preclude any expansion
in the direction of the sea, but it is no longer to the advantage
of a man to live away from this center. In the inland village, the
outlying villager established his home in relation to his occupation, rice cultivation, which was away from the center of the
village. In the fishing village, the occupational center of all or
most men is on the beach, thereby discouraging individual
settlement inland. Ordinarily, the original nucleus of such a
fishing village will grow in both directions along the beach,
expanding slightly in an inland direction. As the concentrated
population of a fishing village spreads along the beach, the
original nucleus will lose much of its meaning as the central
point geographically and socially of the community, either
shifting in relation to the houses of important fishermen or, more
usually, giving way to several small nuclei along the length of
the settlement.

In Rusembilan, the original nucleus was situated inland from
the beach, at Kampong Surau. A secondary center was established when the population first started moving to the beach,
and, in time, it came to overshadow the original nucleus, except

for religious activities which were centered in the mosque at Kampong Surau. With the spread of the village along the beach, four new nuclei were established, each containing a coffee shop, one containing the home of the imam as well as the *balaisa*, which in many ways has now assumed more importance than the mosque as the religious center of the village. In the expansion of the village, a limiting point was reached. In one direction, expansion was stopped by dense mangrove swamps extending from the water about half a mile inland. In the other direction, the land between the shore and the inland rice fields was owned by a Thai from Pattani, so that further expansion was precluded. Faced by continuing population growth, villagers were forced to resettle in the area of the original community nucleus, Kampong Surau, and eventually to settle in a new area among the rice fields, Kampong Baru. Because of the pattern established on the beach of a compact group of closely spaced houses and because of the continued maritime orientation, the two hamlets were settled in the same manner rather than in the more dispersed pattern of other communities away from the sea.

Sociocultural Factors

Although ecological factors and situations of culture contact may exert strong pressures toward certain types of change or act as catalysts in the process of change, it is the sociocultural patterns of the changing community that can be said to initiate and determine the course of transition from one state of equilibrium, or near equilibrium, to a new adjustment. Of course, as neither society nor culture has existence without human populations, social and cultural change requires human agents. As Hallowell [1] sees it, the process of change starts from a base of cultural (and social) adaptation. The first stage involves an individual re-adaptation and readjustment in terms of the element undergoing

[1] A. Irving Hallowell, "Sociopsychological Aspects of Acculturation," in Ralph Linton, ed., *The Science of Man in the World Crisis*, pp. 177 f.

change, and the process is complete only when the sum of individual readaptations and readjustments has resulted in a new cultural (and social) adaptation and adjustment.

Because of differential rates of cultural adaptation and social adjustment to a given innovation, an over-all disequilibrium in the sociocultural system may be the result of change. If this disequilibrium is too great, it may require further adaptations or adjustments within the culture or the social structure. These secondary modifications are less apt to operate on the innovation itself, as in the case of primary adaptations and adjustments, than on the areas of the society or culture most closely associated with the innovation.

Geertz writes in an article on social change:

In most societies, where change is a characteristic rather than an abnormal occurrence, we shall expect to find more or less radical discontinuities between the two [culture and social structure]. I would argue that it is in these very discontinuities that we shall find some of the primary driving forces in change.[2]

The discontinuities between the social and cultural systems, caused by adaptations in one or the other of them as a response to innovation, operate to cause secondary modifications or, in Geertz's formulation, exert pressures to further change.

In Rusembilan, there has been fairly rapid social and cultural change within the fishing industry over a relatively short span of years. The following attempt to analyze briefly these changes is based on the assumption that the process as a whole cannot be understood without taking into account the secondary adaptations and adjustments of the social structure and the orientations of the culture of the community.

With the settlement on the beach at Rusembilan, ecological factors, discussed above, favored the individual adoption of

[2] Clifford Geertz, "Ritual and Social Change: A Javanese Example," *American Anthropologist*, 59:33, 1957.

fishing. It is probable that the villager soon found that fishing was more satisfying to his economic needs than was agriculture or at least that it added significantly to their satisfaction. His social frame of reference had been until this time a large co-operating kinship group. Fishing was an individual occupation, and the individualistic nature of it was reinforced by the advantages of competitive commercial sale of the catch in the nearby Pattani market. Because of the decline in agricultural activity on which his previous social organization had been based and because of the new settlement pattern along the beach which allowed the villager greater independence from a tightly nucleated community unit, both the social organization and the cultural orientations tended to shift toward the pole of individualistic effort and values.

The *kolek* was introduced into Rusembilan by a small group of men because of the obvious economic advantages it had over smaller craft and probably also because of the prestige they felt the innovation would bring them. Along the coast of the South China Sea where the *kolek* had originated and was being used at that time, it was paddled by up to twenty-five men for the relatively short distances from the shore to the fishing grounds. Probably because of difficulties in recruiting large crews from the individual fishermen at Rusembilan, however, the *kolek* "complex" was modified by the addition of sail and rowing bars so that as few as eight men could handle the boat on the longer trips to the fishing grounds outside Pattani Cape. But in order to realize the greatest commercial profit, the *kolek* had to be operated by a tightly structured group. The readjustment of the social structure to this pressure did not follow the lines of the co-operating kinship groups characterizing padi field activities. Rather, it was based on the individualistic criteria of fishing skill, experience, and diligence. This fact gives further weight to the assumption that prior to the introduction of the *kolek* the orientations of individualism had been firmly entrenched in the economic sector of the culture of Rusembilan and, further, that reliance on rice cultivation had diminished sufficiently so that its traditionally associated social organization did not present itself as a serious alternative in the process of organizing the boat groups. It should be mentioned here again that in two of the *perahu kolek serikat* owned co-operatively by related members of the hamlets of Rusembilan a kin-based co-operative social organization is found which parallels the groups associated with rice cultivation in these two inland settlements.

In accord with Linton's outline of the process of change,[3] the acceptance of the *kolek* initially involved a small group of fishermen and was determined by economic advantage, probably increased prestige, and possibly the novelty of the innovation. Dissemination to others was partial at first and later was accepted almost universally, although ownership was limited to men of wealth. As the accepting individuals were respected men, there was no status or prestige limit to dissemination; and the innovation, because it proved its economic advantage, remained functional within the culture. Adjustive modifications operated to alter the form of the innovation slightly by the addition of sail and rowing bars; its meaning remained much the same, an economic tool and a prestige symbol. In the case of the *kolek*, however, the important adjustive modification was the adjustment (secondary) of the social system in response to organizational requirements for efficient utilization of the innovation.

For much the same reasons that the *kolek* were introduced into Rusembilan, a group of individuals introduced motor tow boats into the village. The prestige value of this innovation was of particular importance as older forms (i.e., *kolek*, coconut plantations, plank and tile houses) were losing their value as

[3] Ralph Linton, "Acculturation and the Processes of Culture Change," in Linton, ed., *Acculturation in Seven American Indian Tribes*, pp. 468–482.

symbols. Thus, before the economic advantages of the innovation had been proved, four motorboats were introduced almost simultaneously. This is not to imply that the factor of economic advantage was lacking in the innovation, for the villagers had observed the efficient use of motorboats in other areas of south Thailand. Although during 1956 the motorboats were used in a majority of the fishing operations, dissemination of the innovation did not occur as it was the innovating group only who were using the motorboats to tow *kolek* in which they had interest.[4] And by the following season, actual rejection of the innovation had begun.

The reasons for the lack of dissemination and for rejection of the motorboats are to be found in the process of adjustive modification and secondary adjustment and adaptation. Although many of the men at Rusembilan had seen motorized fishing operations elsewhere, the type of fishing operations in the Pattani area seemed to preclude their motorization according to such models. Thus, the innovation was adapted to conform with the existing fishing methods. Each *kolek* remained the basic fishing unit and with its boat group still formed the only clearly defined social grouping. With this group as a model, not for the actual fishing operations, but for the distribution of the fish, the total catch of each tow group was divided on a share system among the crew members of all the *kolek* in the group. While this organization functioned, almost the total fish production of Rusembilan was originating from four large tow groups, each distributing shares from its total catch and, in effect, in competition only with the other three groups. This situation represented a marked disequilibrium between the individualistic, competitively oriented economic culture and the social system as it was crystallizing in the tow group. Individual tensions under this disequilibrium reached such a point that heated quarrels broke out in the village over the distribution of shares equally

[4] See Chapter IV and Appendix A for details of motorboat ownership.

among "good" and "bad" *kolek;* tow groups were forced to stay ashore some nights because of the refusal of individual *kolek* to co-operate in certain situations; and even the position of religious leadership was attacked for attempting to maintain the organization. At this point, the group organization underwent a secondary adjustment to reduce the disequilibrium and individual tension. The organization for daytime fishing, requiring the co-operative use of the nets of several *kolek*, was dropped. The tow group itself gradually became restructured not as a co-operating, equally sharing group, but as two or three competing *kolek* which for a fixed price were towed to the fishing grounds by the same motorboat.

By the summer of 1957, this secondary adjustment away from a formally structured tow group had progressed so far that one of the village motorboats had been sold, and the *kolek* which had been in its tow group, as well as *kolek* from other tow groups, had individually invested in outboard motors. Although the outboard motor was not as satisfactory a prestige symbol as a motorboat, it embodied all of the economic advantages of the latter and yet stressed the individual fishing *kolek* as the basic producing unit of the economy. It seems probable that the motorboats remaining in Rusembilan will continue to operate for several more seasons, mainly because they are owned in large part by wealthy men who can afford to maintain economically inefficient prestige symbols. Individual *kolek* will undoubtedly continue to break away from tow groups; perhaps some of the less successful *kolek* will try joining or rejoining tow groups. It seems likely, however, that unless new, economically advantagous uses are found for the motorboats they will gradually be replaced by individual outboard motors on the Rusembilan *kolek.*[5]

[5] See Raymond Firth, *Malay Fishermen: Their Peasant Economy,* pp. 46, 114–120, as a contrast to the situation at Rusembilan.

Assimilation and Resistance to Change

"Although it is never fully realized, assimilation implies an essentially unilateral approximation of one culture in the direction of the other, albeit a changing or ongoing other." [6] Assimilation as defined by this statement, rather than the broader term acculturation, will be used to indicate the essentially one-way direction of cultural and social innovation in the south of Thailand. Assimilation here is far from fully realized; in fact, it is strictly channeled into certain areas of the culture such as economic technology while certain other areas such as religion are consolidated behind barriers of resistances. It is the purpose of this section to say something about the forms of assimilation (toward Thai culture) taking place in the Malay fishing villages of southern Thailand and to analyze the reasons for differential rates of acceptance in terms of the formulations presented in the preceding section.

In general, the cultural items introduced into the area of economics and technology stem originally from Western culture and pass through Thai culture only as an intermediary step to the Malays. The initial acceptance of such items as motorboats in the economic sphere is practically unrestricted in the fishing villages, both because of their obvious or presumed advantages in terms of the economic pursuits of the community and because of the individualistic and competitive values associated with this area of the culture. The institution of a bus line from Rusembilan to Pattani has been favored by the villagers, in spite of governmental disapproval, for a number of years and seemed in 1956 to be finally established. Inland villages, however, appear to be much slower in taking over economic or technological items of culture although they must place greater reliance on such

[6] Social Science Research Council Summer Seminar on Acculturation, 1953, "Acculturation: An Exploratory Formulation," *American Anthropologist*, 56:988, 1954.

items as buses and rice mills than the coastal villages. A partial explanation for this inland resistance to technological change lies in the generally poorer economic position there than in the coastal fishing villages. But it seems that the inability to purchase machinery is not the whole reason. There appears to be no desire on the part of the inland villagers to have buses or rice mills of their own; they are content to let other people mill their rice and provide their transportation to market. In terms of the analysis presented in the last section, this can be explained as the resistance of co-operative, kin-based social organization and associated cultural values in the economic activities of inland villages to cultural traits associated with individual enterprise.

At Rusembilan, in other, noneconomic areas of the culture, assimilative changes are much less obvious than in the economic sector, and they are frequently linked with reservations or partial resistances. Although many of the resistances are due to discontinuities between the transmittable items of Thai culture and the values of Malay culture or between the cultural values and the social organization, another, purely psychological, factor is important in hindering assimilation. In writing of group hostility, Parsons states:

The "out-group" should . . . be a group in relation to which one's own group can feel a comfortably self-righteous sense of superiority and at the same time a group which can be plausibly accused of arrogating to itself an illegitimate superiority of its own. Correspondingly it should be a group with strong claims to a position of high ethical standing of its own which, however, can plausibly be made out to be essentially specious and to conceal a subtle deception.[7]

The fact that the Malay "self-righteous sense of superiority" is not comfortable and the fact that "essential speciousness" and

[7] Talcott Parsons, "Certain Primary Sources and Patterns of Aggression in the Social Structure of the Western World," *Essays in Sociological Theory Pure and Applied*, p. 269.

"subtile deception" of the Thai position are not seriously plausible in Thailand tend to increase the in-group solidarity and conservatism of the Malays as a national minority, albeit a regional majority.

Linton describes how this type of attitude can act as a deterrent in the process of taking over cultural elements:

The attitudes of the receiving group toward the donor group will attach themselves, at least initially, to the elements of the culture which contact between the two groups makes available for borrowing . . . influencing the response to these elements and also to the innovators who are seeking to introduce them.[8]

An illustration of the operation of these principles is provided by the reaction of the villagers of Rusembilan to scientific medical practices. In Pattani, there is a well-equipped Thai government hospital with two doctors who speak the Malay language and several nurses. Almost none of the Rusembilan villagers would avail themselves of these medical facilities although they were offered free of charge if the patient could not afford to pay.[9] In Saiburi, thirty miles from the village, a British missionary and his wife had established a small dispensary. A fair number of people from Rusembilan went each week to the missionaries for "injections." Even though the Malays at Rusembilan found the religious teachings of the missionaries laughable, there was no unfavorable, "out-group" attitude attached to the missionaries, and, consequently, their medicine could be accepted more easily than that of the Thai hospital.

In the area of political institutions, several different factors appear to be operating to produce a picture ranging from com-

[8] Ralph Linton, "The Process of Culture Transfer," *Acculturation in Seven American Indian Tribes*, pp. 484–486.

[9] See p. 194, above. During the course of this study, one man was taking a regular series of vitamin injections to combat a nutritional deficiency. He did this only because of the urging, and the transportation provided, by the author's wife.

plete acceptance of certain forms all the way to complete rejection of others. In the case of the institutions established at the village level by the Thai government for the purpose of "democratizing" the villages, two factors are working strongly toward rejection. The most obvious is the hostility to the Thai "out-group" and the social forms imposed by it. Further, it is doubtful if such "democratizing" institutions would have been accepted by the culture in any other context. These institutions, the village council and village meetings, fall within the area of culture characterized above by individualistic orientations. This part of the community culture is dominated by the *orang baik* who individually advise a person on individual problems. Because of the respect and prestige accruing to these men for individualistic achievement, they will not consent to be formalized into a council or committee, particularly under the supervision of the district officer. On the other hand, the election of provincial representatives to the national assembly is accepted by the Malay population of the south more avidly, if anything, than by Thai villagers of other parts of Thailand.[10] Because the national assembly is a government institution far removed from village life, there is not the intense hostility toward it that is felt toward local institutions of government; and because of this situation, the Malays are able to look at it rationally. They seem to feel that by taking an active part in provincial elections they can assure for the Malay "in-group" a share of the prestige of the elected Malay representative and a measure of group superiority. Campaign promises are most often phrased as counter-

[10] Virginia Thompson (in *Thailand: The New Siam*, p. 83) and John E. deYoung (in *Village Life in Modern Thailand*, p. 149) report that the Thai participation in the first national election and the national election of 1952 was only 10 per cent and 39 per cent respectively. In the 1957 elections in Pattani province, a total of 126,725 votes was recorded out of a population which in 1947 numbered 203,155 (information from the Office of the Governor, Changwat Pattani, Pattani, Thailand, and personal communication, February 1957).

measures to announced local government policy and, though almost never fulfilled, serve to channel off otherwise unacceptable aggressive feeling toward the Thai group.

Secular education has been readily accepted at Rusembilan, although compulsory education in Thailand and the village school in Rusembilan not only represent government institutions in close proximity to the community, but also attempt to inculcate alien values in the village children. Education represents a strong value in Malay culture, both in relation to religious values of the culture, where its analogy is the religious education each child and most youths are given, and in relation to the individualistic orientations of other parts of the culture, in that it stresses the individual tools necessary for competitive enterprise. Because educational values partake of both major cultural orientations of the community, children from almost every family in the village are sent to the school for at least parts of each term. Acceptance of educational values and attendance at school do not, however, necessitate the acceptance of what is being taught. Among the villagers of Rusembilan, there is universal criticism of the school curriculum, many people saying that the children learn nothing at all in their four years of schooling. Although the Malay language is almost exclusively used in the Malay provinces of Thailand, school subjects are usually taught in Thai, and the little formal instruction in Thai given in the school rarely makes any impression on the children. The teaching of Buddhist morals is the most common basis for attack upon the curriculum; but it seems to be felt that, as long as Buddhism can be associated with Thai culture and as long as Islamic values and ideals can be reinforced in the children through daily religious instruction, the positive value of education outweighs the specific negative values of the curriculum.

In the same article cited above, Parsons, speaking of the insecurity introduced into traditionalized areas of a society by change, points out that "the result is to stimulate . . . a 'fundamentalist reaction,' a compulsively distorted exaggeration of traditional values and other related patterns." [11] This phenomenon is manifested in the area of traditional values in Rusembilan, although with a minimum of "compulsive distortion." According to older members of the community, there is a much greater emphasis now being placed upon religion than in the "old days." Larger numbers of people are observing *sunat* religious ritual, such as the six additional days of fast after Ramadan, and optional passage rites, and there seems to be a tendency away from the perfunctory observation of the major passage rites toward a reintensification of their meaning in terms of the traditional values of the culture. Because of the strengthening of religious values of the culture, there has been a corresponding weakening of those antagonistic values associated with the practices of the *bomo* and the belief in spirits. Only in the case of disease, where concomitant personal anxiety reinforces the traditional values and beliefs in this area, do beliefs in spirits and shamanistic practices persist vigorously in opposition to Islamic values.[12]

Perhaps the whole ethos of Rusembilan can be best summed up in the words of the old men of the village. "Rusembilan today is not the same as in the old days. We used to fish for one kind of fish only, and rest when that wasn't available. The young men today are diligent: when the prawns are gone, they go out for *kembong,* and during the rains they catch fish along the shore. Today, everyone has money all the time, not just when there are *kembong.* The young men today are better than we were—they like to talk about religion and to go to *makan pulot.* They know that religion is good, especially in hard times."

[11] Parsons, *op. cit.,* p. 268.

[12] Raymond Firth (in "The Peasantry of South East Asia," *International Affairs,* 26:503–514, 1950) points out that the Islam of the Malays, being part of a world religion, is a more progressive part of the culture than the traditional, conservative area of adat and the *bomo,* thus explaining why rapid technological change may be accompanied by an increase in religious faith. Compare the statement about Takashima, p. 228, above.

Chronological Outline of the Introduction of Motorboats at Rusembilan

The following account summarizes discussions and roles of the principal village boatowners and steerers deliberating the advantages and disadvantages of investing in one or more motorboats to tow the Rusembilan *kolek*.

Until the middle of April 1956, there had been general talk in Rusembilan about the desirability of having one or more motorboats, but apparently little or no consideration of the advantages or disadvantages of various types or of the expenditure involved. On April 25, there was an informal discussion on the beach, the principals of which were the imam (owning a half share in a *kolek* with his father-in-law, Paw Ming), Paw Ming (owning one *kolek* and half of one with the imam), and Paw Sa (owning one *kolek* and a half share in another which he steers). The imam maintained that a twenty-horsepower engine costing forty to fifty thousand baht ($2,000–$2,500) would be required to tow three *kolek*, but that a neighboring village purchased for half the price a smaller boat which could tow two *kolek*. This village was able to catch *kembong* in the daytime each day of the month and was able to command a higher price at the market as it got the fish to the beach sooner. Paw Ming stated that he had had sufficient capital to buy a motorboat; he had first wanted to purchase a bus to run between Rusembilan and Pattani, but was discouraged by the difficulties that it would involve and so invested part of his money in a coconut plantation. People were now telling him to invest in the motorboat, but he wondered about the difficulties of operating and maintaining it, as well as the problems of pulling it through the mud to the beach and permanently beaching it during the monsoon season. Paw Sa had just returned from looking at and pricing motorboats in the area and had decided that there were too many (unspecified) factors against them. A crew member from the "imam's" *kolek* suggested that an engine could be bought from Bangkok and a hull built in Taluban. Some discussion followed, but most people drifted away. Ma, owner of the nearby coffee shop, also a member of the "imam's" crew, reported that it was always difficult to get the villagers started on a new project, but that, once initiated and proved, many others would also take it up: "If one man buys a bus, three or four others will get buses also."

On May 13, the *kolek* of Latih (steerer and owner) was becalmed and towed to the beach for fifty baht ($2.50). He said that because his boat was able to reach shore early the three thousand fish caught would bring a high price in the market. (In addition, the previous day had been a holiday and no fish were brought to market.) Each crew member (excluding Latih) had contributed four baht (20 cents) for the tow.

On May 15, Paw Sa and Uma (son of Paw Sa and steerer of his *kolek*) were discussing the financing of a motorboat. Paw

Sa wanted to mortgage his coconut plantation to raise the major part of the price, with the crew of his two boats sharing the rest. He thought that it would be desirable if the propeller could be detached so that the boat could be beached. Pachu Ma (Latih's brother, steerer of "imam's" *kolek*, who later bought his own *kolek* which Suf steered) reported the unpredictable behavior of motorboats from other villages, which cut through the net circles of other boats and tore the nets. Ma and Pachu Ma argued about three types of motorboat: A boat costing sixty thousand baht ($3,000) could tow all the village *kolek* (twelve at that time); that would mean, however, that all *kolek* would return from fishing at the same time regardless of when they had finished netting and that the market would be glutted, thus lowering the price. Pachu Ma favored a secondhand boat for about eighteen thousand baht ($900) that could tow three *kolek* or, as a compromise, one for forty to forty-five thousand baht ($2,000–$2,500) that could tow six.

On May 17, Waw Se (steerer of a co-operative *kolek*) said that his crew was thinking of getting a ten-horsepower outboard motor for six thousand baht ($300), so that the *kolek* would be independent of others and could return to shore and market in time to get a high price for the fish.

On May 19, at the conclusion of a feast served in the *balaisa* to celebrate *Hari Raya Enam*, most of the *kolek* owners and steerers remained to discuss the motorboat situation more formally. The foregoing discussions had been between only two or three of the interested parties, but those present knew very well the points of view of all the others. Pachu Ma and Paw Sa (and their ideas) dominated the gathering. Waw Se added, in favor of outboard motors, that the beaching and monsoon-protection problems would not arise if the *kolek* were motorized and that, although the total cost for three *kolek* would be about the same, the outboard motors would represent smaller units of capital.

On May 20, Paw Sa reported that he could raise twenty thousand baht ($1,000) by mortgaging his coconut plantation and his house.

On May 21, it was decided by the imam, Paw Ming, Pachu Ma, and Latih that Pachu Ma would go to Songkhla, Nakorn Sritamarat, and other ports the following day to find and buy a motorboat. Each crew member of the "imam's" and of Latih's *kolek* would be asked to contribute one thousand baht ($50) toward the motorboat. (Paw Ming was not wholly in favor of getting a motorboat without further investigations and thus did not commit the crew members of the *kolek* that he owned exclusively. See June 3.) Other *kolek* wishing to be towed by the motorboat would have to contribute two shares of their catch. Pachu Ma summed up by saying: "We will have to work extra hard to justify the boat. Each man will have to have four nets [instead of two]. We must fish during the daytime as well as at night; the motorboat will take the fish to market and bring food back to the *kolek* [which will presumably remain at sea from Friday night until the following Thursday]. When *kembong* is not running, we must fish far offshore for *kerisi*."

On May 22, Pachu Ma, Latih, and the imam left for Songkhla.

On May 24, Waw Se stated that seven of the thirteen men on his crew had agreed to contribute to buying an outboard motor. The remaining crewmen "lived far away" and could not be contacted until fishing resumed after the full moon.

On June 2, Pachu Ma, Latih, and the imam returned with a motorboat which had broken down on the way from Songkhla. The engine, a twenty-horsepower Petters mill engine, had started making a "different noise" while running full throttle from Songkhla to Rusembilan, but the engineer (formerly a bus driver in Nakorn Sritamarat) had not been awakened until oil had started spurting from the crankcase. Total cost had been about forty thousand baht ($2,000) including spare parts and registration fee.

On June 3, Paw Ming said that he considered the purchase of the motorboat a very foolish thing. There had been "bad signs" connected with the boat: he, Paw Ming, had come down with fever while the party was off investigating the motorboat; six hundred baht ($300) of the purchase price had been lost prior to setting off to buy the boat (this was later found); and the imam neglected to follow specific advice and common sense by agreeing to buy the boat without stripping and inspecting the engine. Paw Ming also maintained that the boat was constructed for river work and was not suitable for use at sea.

On June 4, a Malay repairman from Pattani talked to the imam for about an hour on board the motorboat and said that he would repair the engine for twelve hundred baht ($60). Twice the imam consulted Pachu Ma, who was lying on the beach near the boat; finally, the conference was moved from the boat to the beach, where, in a crowd of onlookers, Pachu Ma became the center of the discussion.

On the same day, Paw Sa reported that he was having friends in Nakorn investigate a motorboat in which he was interested.

On June 5, Paw Sa reported having bought a boat in Nakorn for seventeen thousand baht ($850). This boat, with a ten-horsepower engine, would only be able to tow his two *kolek.*

On June 6, Paw Te Se went to Nakorn to investigate buying a motorboat to tow his *kolek* (steered by his son), the *bomo*'s *kolek* (steered by the *bomo*'s son-in-law), and the co-operatively owned *kolek* steered by Ma No. (Paw Te Se owns one *kolek* and a half interest in another with Paw Sa. He is one of the few wealthy men in Rusembilan who is not considered an informal leader of the village, as he tends too much to "go along with the *kamnan.*" He is a member of the newly elected village council; see Chapter VII.)

On June 11, the engineer of the first motorboat (imam-Pachu Ma-Latih) started reassembling the engine before the repairman had arrived in the village. When the repairman arrived, he found that the parts had been put together wrong. Both the repairman and the imam were extremely angry with the engineer for his mistake. Pachu Ma was angry with the imam: "We should probably have no more to do with this boat; if we are angry with the boy [engineer], he will go back to Nakorn, and who will run the boat?" Pachu Ma felt no shame about the breaking down of the boat, as he "knows nothing about motors"; if he had bought a defective net he would be ashamed, as he knows about them. Both the engineer and the repairman claimed that the other was irresponsible, and each had a small faction behind him.

On June 16, the *bomo* said that he was considering buying an almost new motorboat at nearby Tujong for fifty thousand baht ($2,500). Each crew member of his, Paw Te Se's, and Ma No's *kolek* would have to contribute more than one thousand baht ($50) toward it.

On June 20, Paw Sa said that he would like to sell his motorboat if he could make a small profit on it. He claimed that it was too slow and that it was guaranteed for only three months.

On June 26, Paw Sa started tearing down and rebuilding the cabin on his motorboat. The work was done voluntarily by crew members of the two towed *kolek*. Paw Sa was unconcerned that some crew members did not appear so long as there were enough there to get the work done.

On the same day, the *bomo* and Paw Te Se arranged to have a motorboat from a neighboring village tow their *kolek* each night on a share-hire basis.

On July 1, the *bomo* and Paw Te Se, together with most of the crew of their *kolek*, bought a two-thirds interest in the motorboat mentioned in the preceding paragraph, the remaining third being retained by the original owner who was to be responsible for all repairs during the following three months. The boat had an eighteen-horsepower mill-type engine, and the

two-thirds interest cost thirty thousand baht ($1,500). Ma No
had planned to have his co-operative *kolek* included in this tow
group, but he became angry at the *bomo*'s son-in-law for com-
plaining that he (Ma No) was too slow about making up his
mind on the arrangements. Paw Ming agreed that his *kolek*
(steered by the *selawat*, Paw Sa's brother) should join the tow
group on a share-hire basis.

On July 9, a new crack developed in the crankcase of the first
motorboat (imam-Pachu Ma-Latih). The imam stated that he
would like to forfeit his interest in this boat and sell his coconut
plantation in order to buy a new motorboat on his own. Mesung
(the imam's mother-in-law, Paw Ming's wife) said that she was
interested in furnishing the money to buy a new motor for the
first motorboat and then using the old one to run a village rice
mill, so that it would be unnecessary to send rice to the mill at
Pakhago. Paw Ming was trying to locate a new boat.

On July 15, Che Te (the imam's brother, a religious student
with no interest in the motorboat situation except that of keeping harmony within the village) was discussing with Pachu Ma,
at times heatedly, a dispute which had become manifest on July
7. On that date, the wives of the crew members of the "imam's"
kolek and Latih's *kolek* decided that the fish would no longer be
shared among the whole tow group, but would be split only
among the members of the *kolek* netting them. This was largely
because the women of the "imam's" *kolek* felt that the superior
skill of the steerer (Pachu Ma) produced more fish than Latih
could (this was essentially correct) and that it was thus unfair
to average the unequal catches. Later, it was reported that some
of Latih's crewmen felt they could not afford to pay part of the
costs of the diesel fuel for the motorboat. Pachu Ma reputedly
was irritated at this and "said bad things" about his brother's
crew. Latih, in turn, became angry and refused to take part in
the tow group. Che Te, in talking to Pachu Ma, was trying to

reconcile the two brothers, and he was finally successful. Pachu Ma claimed that this was the first he had heard of Latih's decision not to be towed. He said that he was annoyed at crewmen in both boats for not paying for the oil, but that he felt that Latih should come to him sometimes to discuss problems and make suggestions, instead of his having always to go to Latih.

On July 31, after being repaired for a second time, the crankcase on the first motorboat (imam-Pachu Ma-Latih) cracked again. Paw Ming went to Haad Yai and Nakorn to try to locate a new crankcase.

On August 4, Paw Ming returned saying that he had had a crankcase ordered in Nakorn, but before he had gone to pick it up, another man had bought it. After this, he would be interested only in stock on hand.

On August 11, the crankcase cracked for the fourth time. A Thai arriving in the village said that he would repair and guarantee for six months the old engine or send it to Bangkok in exchange for a new one. He claimed that he had had experience in dealing with European firms. Pachu Ma, one of the few men in the village able to speak Thai, acted as interpreter and did most of the talking for the village side as well. Ma, owner of the coffee shop where the discussion was taking place, said that before any final decision could be made all the crewmen who had contributed toward the motorboat should be consulted. Pachu Ma asserted that all the crewmen had decided to send Paw Ming to Nakorn with five thousand baht ($250) to get a new crankcase and that he had returned with nothing—"We are sitting and doing nothing; we should at least get the engine repaired so that the boat can be used."

On August 14, having heard nothing from the original repairman or the Thai that offered to repair the engine, the imam and Paw Ming decided to buy a new engine from a firm in Pattani. Pachu Ma and other interested persons reluctantly agreed.

On August 15, the new engine, also a Petters mill engine, was delivered, and installation was started by representatives of the firm. The total price was twenty-two thousand baht ($1,100). Seven thousand baht ($350) was to be allowed for the old engine; Paw Ming put up eight thousand baht ($400), and the remaining seven thousand baht ($350) was to be paid out of the profits of the motorboat over a period of five months without interest.

On July 31, Waw Se, Ma No, and Ma Li, all steerers of co-operative *kolek*, acquired a motorboat from Nakorn on a trial basis. During this trial period, the owner was to receive from each boat on each trip the proceeds of four large shares of fish, or forty baht ($2) if no fish were caught.

On August 13, Waw Se decided to buy an interest in the boat for six thousand baht ($300). He wanted to find someone else to take another share in the boat, or to borrow money, as the crew was unable to pay; if the original owner retained the largest interest in the boat (thirty thousand baht, or $1,500) he could take it back to Nakorn whenever he wished, "and we will be left without our means of livlihood."

On August 14, the final day for making arrangements, Waw Se persuaded Daut (unrelated and not on a *kolek* crew) to con-tribute four thousand baht ($200); and he found a boy from a neighboring village, a schoolmate of Paw Sa's son at one of the religious schools, with friends in Nakorn who would put ten thousand baht ($500) into the motorboat. Thus, the boat was no longer controlled by the original owner, who had a ten thou-sand baht ($500) share remaining.

By the end of the *kembong* season of 1957, one year after the field work for this study was completed, three of the motorboats were still being used by the fishermen of Rusembilan. Four of the *kolek* that previously belonged to tow groups had acquired outboard motors, and apparently the village felt that the latter system was preferable in all respects. The following is part of a communication from the author's interpreter written in September 1957:

> Villagers still use motorboats to tow the *kolek*. Some are using new outboard motors. But the engines are not real outboard engines. They bought other kinds of engines and converted [them] by adding the necessary parts. They found [them] much faster than towing with motorboats. The 7 h.p. [engines sell] at 3,700 bahts [$185]. . . . They have no more quarrels now since they [have] separated and [are] using outboard motors; each boat has its own engine, and also no quarreling about distributing the fish.

Paw Sa sold his motorboat, and both he and Uma were using outboard motors. The *kolek* of Pachu Ma, the imam, and Latih continued to be towed by the original motorboat. One *kolek* left each of the other two tow groups and was being used with an outboard motor, that is, Waw Se's *kolek* from Ma No and Ma Li's group and Paw Ming's *kolek* from the *bomo* and Paw Te Se's group.

The imam and one of the crewmen from his *kolek* took over the maintenance and running of their motorboat, allowing the "engineer" to leave the village. In order to devote his time to this job, the imam gave to his wife the job of instructing the village children in reading the Koran.

The Language of
Rusembilan

Phonology

1. Voiceless stops, except /ʔ/, occur aspirated initially and medially following a vowel. Unaspirated /p/ and /ʔ/ occur in final position following a vowel.

2. Voiced stops occur slightly aspirated initially and following a vowel medially. They occur in final position only in loan words.

3. Affricates occur initially or medially following a vowel or /n/. Medially following /s/ or finally they occur only in loan words.

4. Fricatives occur initially and medially following a vowel. /h/ occurs in final position following a vowel.

5. Nasals occur initially and in medial position following a vowel. In final position they occur following any vowel except /a/.

6. Voiced lateral occurs initially and in other positions following a vowel. Trilled uvular vibrant, approaching, in some individuals' speech, a back velar fricative, occurs initially and medially following a vowel.

Chart 1. Consonants. Phonetic positions represented by consonant symbols are used throughout this section. Numbers refer to paragraphs describing distribution of consonants. Parentheses indicate that the enclosed symbol occurs only in loan words, usually Arabic, and is usually pronounced as the variant given.

Type		Bilabial	Alveolar	Alveo-palatal	Velar	Uvular	Glottal	No.
Stops	vl:	p	t		k		ʔ	1
	vd:	b	d		g			2
Affricates	vl:			ch				3
	vd:			j				3
Fricatives	vl:	(f) ~ p	s	(sh) ~ s	(kh) ~ k		h	4
	vd:		(z) ~ j					4
Nasals	vd:	m	n		ng			5
Trill	vd:					r		6
Lateral	vd:		l					6

7. /y/, voiced high close front unrounded nonsyllabic vocoid, occurs initially, medially following a vowel or /n/, and finally following a vowel. /w/, voiced high close back rounded nonsyllabic vocoid, occurs initially and in other positions following a vowel.

8. High and mid close vowels, except central, occur initially and in other positions only in open syllables.

9. High and mid open vowels occur in medial position in closed syllables only. In Standard Malay, the open vowels are allophones of the close vowels and are treated as such in this paragraph. Because of certain sound changes, however, to be discussed below, they have become phonemic in some instances in the Pattani dialect.

>   Standard Malay   /haji/ > /ji/   "haji"
>   Standard Malay   /jɪn/ > /jɪ/   "Moslem spirit"

10. Low open front unrounded vowel /a/ occurs initially, medially, and in final position only in words which have lost the final Standard Malay consonant /t/, /s/, or /r/ or when the corresponding Standard Malay word ends in the diphthongs /ai/ or /au/.

>   Standard Malay   /panas/ > /pana/   "hot"
>   Standard Malay   /kədai/ > /kəda/   "market"

11. Low close back rounded vowel /ɔ/ occurs as an allophone of /a/ in final syllables closed by /h/ or /ʔ/ and in final position in words which in Standard Malay end in /a/.

Standard Malay	/rumah/	> /rumɔh/	"house"
Standard Malay	/muka/	> /mukɔ/	"face, front"

12. Mid close central unrounded vowel /ə/ occurs only medially. It is never stressed, and in many instances in the Pattani dialect is not pronounced at all.

Standard Malay	/pərahu/	> /prahu/	"boat"

Chart 2. Vowels. Phonetic positions represented by vowel symbols are used throughout this section. Numbers in parentheses refer to paragraphs describing distribution of vowels.

		Front unrounded	Central unrounded	Back rounded
High	Close (8)	i y (7)		u w (7)
	Open (9)	ɪ		ʊ
Mid	Close (8)	e	ə (12)	o
	Open (9)	ɛ		ø
Low	Close			ɔ (11)
	Open	a (10)		

13. Diphthongs /ai/ and /au/ occur initially and medially.

Phonological Changes from Standard Malay

1. Consonant clusters, nasal and stop:

mp > p	/kampong/	> /kapong/	"village"
nt > t	/pintu/	> /pitu/	"door"
ngk > k	/bangkok/	> /bakoʔ/	"Bangkok"
mb > m	/jambu/	> /jamu/	"a fruit"
nd > n	/pandai/	> /pana/	"cleaver"
ngg > ng	/pinggan/	> /pinge/	"dish"

A few exceptions occur among the voiced clusters:

| mb > mb | /kəmbong/ > /kəmbong/ | "mackerel" |
| ngg > g | /tənggəlam/ > /təgəle/ | "to sink" |

It is possible that these represent more recent additions to the language and that the first example, although now very important in the culture, has not yet undergone any change, whereas the second was changed by analogy to the more common voiceless forms.

2. Final stops:

final p > p	/hidup/ > /hidup/	"alive"
final t > zero	/təmpat/ > /təpa/	"place"
final k > ?	/kolek/ > /kole?/	"a boat"

3. Final alveolar consonants:

final t > zero	/sangat/ > /sanga/	"very"
final s > zero	/panas/ > /pana/	"hot"
final n > zero	/turun/ > /turu/	"fall"
final r > zero	/dəngar/ > /dənga/	"hear"

Frequently, final /n/ is not lost.

| final n > n | /angin/ > /angin/ | "wind" |

4. Final nasals following /a/:

final am > e	/hitam/ > /hite/	"black"
final an > e	/makan/ > /make/	"eat"
final ang > e	/pisang/ > /pise/	"banana"

5. Final diphthongs:

| final ai > a | /pantai/ > /pata/ | "beach" |
| final au > a | /surau/ > /sura/ | "mosque, chapel" |

6. Final /a/, /ak/, and /ah/:

final a > ɔ	/mata/ > /matɔ/	"eye"
final ak > a? > ɔ?	/anak/ > /ana?/ > /anɔ?/	"child"
final ah > ɔh	/sudah/ > /sudɔh/	"already"

Morphology and Syntax

1. In the Pattani dialect, each word is usually composed of one morpheme. There are isolated instances in which the syntactical morphemes of Standard Malay appear in the Pattani dialect; in these cases, however, the speakers of the dialect consider the total utterance as a root unit.

/mə/ "action prefix" plus /lawat/ "visit" > / məlawa/ "visit"
/mə/ "action prefix" plus /pukat/ "net" > /muka/ "to net"
zero (noun form) plus /pukat/ "net" > /puka/ "net"

2. One Standard Malay enclitic was found to be in use in the Pattani dialect. This will be considered as a word, as it is sometimes used as a complete utterance.

/lah/ "emphatic assent, encouragement"
/mari lah/ "Come on!"

3. Reduplication is employed to express adverbial relationship.

/lamɔ/ "length of time"
/keche lamɔ-lamɔ/ "Speak slowly."
/masi/ "while"
/masi-masi adɔ anɔʔ/ "Each has a child."

4. Reduplication may rarely be employed to express continuity or collectivity.

/duʔ keche-keche/ "They were (sat) talking."
/keche-keche tu banyɔʔ ama/ "He speaks too much (his words are too many)."

5. Stress falls upon the final syllable of the word. Heavier stress is placed upon the final syllable of a sentence or utterance.

/aˈdɔ aˈnɔʔ braˈpɔ orˈʹe/ "How many children are there?"
/t aˈdɔ s orʹe aˈʹʹbu/ "There is no one at all."

6. All objects for enumeration are classified by coefficients into groups according to characteristics.

/eko/	"tail"	for animals and fish
/ore/	"man"	for people
/buɔh/	"fruit"	for large objects

7. Personal pronouns of Standard Malay are known and occasionally used in formal speech. Two prounouns are employed when necessary for clarity.

| /ning/ | "this" (I, you, it, this person) |
| /nung/ or /itu/ | "that" (you, he, it, that person) |

8. Plurality is not expressed except by the use of numbers or numerical words to amplify the word which is plural.

/batu ata pata/	"There are rocks on the beach."
/tengɔ batu limɔ buɔh/	"I saw five rocks."
/adɔ banyɔʔ batu/	"There are many rocks."

9. Sentences are composed in the following order: agent, action, object of action. Each element may be amplified by words usually placed after it or may be zero.

/gi kəda/	"I went to market."
/anɔʔ ning mani lau/	"This child swims (bathes sea)."
/make pulo/	"We ate glutinous rice."

10. Time of action is usually not expressed. When necessary, it is expressed by an action amplifier. There are only two common amplifiers indicating time of action.

| /nɔʔ/ "wish" | /nɔʔ nyanyi/ | "I will sing." |
| /dɔh/ "already" | /ore sie mari dɔh/ | "The Thais had come." |

Bibliography

Aberle, David F. "Arctic Hysteria and Latah in Mongolia," in New York Academy of Science, *Transactions*, 2d ser. 14:291–297, 1952.

Adams, Inez. "Rice Cultivation in Asia," *American Anthropologist*, 50:256–282, 1948.

Andrews, James M. *Siam: Second Rural Economic Survey, 1934–35.* Bangkok: Bangkok Times Press, 1935.

Aziz, Ungku Abdul. *Some Aspects of the Malayan Rural Economy Related to Measures for Mobilizing Rural Savings.* (Document E|CN-11|T&T|WP1|L18.) New York: United Nations, 1954.

Barnes, J. A. "Class and Committee in a Norwegian Island Parish," *Human Relations*, 7 (no. 1):39–58, 1954.

Bauer, P. T. *Report on a Visit to Rubber Growing Smallholdings of Malaya.* London: His Majesty's Stationery Office, 1948.

Benedict, Ruth F. *Thai Culture and Behavior: An Unpublished Wartime Study, Dated September 1943.* (Cornell University, Southeast Asia Program, Data Paper no. 4.) Ithaca, N.Y., 1952.

Brant, Charles. *Tadagale, a Burmese Village in 1950.* (Cornell University, Southeast Asia Program, Data Paper no. 13.) Ithaca, N.Y., 1954.

Briggs, Lawrence P. "The Khmer Empire and the Malay Peninsula," *Far Eastern Quarterly*, 9:256–305, 1950.

Brown, C. C. *Kelantan Malay*. (Papers on Malay Subjects, 2d ser.) Singapore, 1927.

Chapple, Eliot D., and Carleton S. Coon. *Principles of Anthropology*. New York: Henry Holt and Co., 1942.

Cortesao, Armando, trans. *The Suma Oriental of Tomé Pires and the Book of Francisco Rodrigues*. 2 vols. London: Hakluyt Society, 1944.

Cuisinier, Jeanne. *Danses Magiques de Kelantan*. (Université de Paris, Travaux et Memoirs de l'Institut d'Ethnologie, vol. XXII.) Paris: Institut d'Ethnologie, 1936.

Dale, W. L. "Wind and Drift Currents in the South China Sea," *Malayan Journal of Tropical Geography*, 8:1–31, 1956.

deYoung, John E. "San Pong, a Village of North Thailand." Unpublished manuscript, 1954.

——. *Village Life in Modern Thailand*. Berkeley: University of California Press, 1955.

Firth, Raymond. *Malay Fishermen: Their Peasant Economy*. London: Kegan Paul, Trench, Trubner and Co., 1946.

——. "The Peasantry of South East Asia," *International Affairs*, 26:503–514, 1950.

——. *Report on Social Science Research in Malaya*. Singapore: Government Printing Office, 1948.

Firth, Rosemary. *Housekeeping among Malay Peasants*. (London School of Economics, Monographs on Social Anthropology no. 7.) London, 1943.

Geertz, Clifford. "Ritual and Social Change: A Javanese Example," *American Anthropologist*, 59:32–54, 1957.

Gillin, John. "Cultural Adjustment," *American Anthropologist*, 46:429–437, 1944.

Ginsburg, Norton, and Chester F. Roberts, Jr. *Malaya*. (American Ethnological Society.) Seattle: University of Washington Press, 1958.

Goldsen, Rose K., and Max Ralis. *Factors Related to Acceptance of Innovations in Bang Chan, Thailand*. (Cornell University, Southeast Asia Program, Data Paper no. 25.) Ithaca, N.Y., 1957.

Graham, W. A. *Siam*. 3d ed., 2 vols. London: Alexander Moring, 1924.

Hall, D. G. E. *A History of South-East Asia.* New York: St. Martin's Press, 1955.

Hallowell, A. Irving. "Sociopsychological Aspects of Acculturation," in Ralph Linton, ed., *The Science of Man in the World Crisis.* New York: Columbia University Press, 1945. Pages 171–200.

Hanks, Lucien M. "A Note on Psycho-social Tensions in a Thai Village after the Advent of Occidental Technology," *Economic Development and Cultural Change,* 1:394–396, 1953.

Harrison, Brian. *South-East Asia: A Short Cultural History.* London: Macmillan and Co., 1954.

Hartley, C. W. S. "Establishment of New Rice Areas in Malaya," *World Crops,* 3:171–175, 1951.

Hauck, Hazel M. *et al. Aspects of Health, Sanitation, and Nutritional Status in a Siamese Rice Village: Studies in Bang Chan, 1952–1954.* (Cornell University, Southeast Asia Program, Data Paper no. 22.) Ithaca, N.Y., 1956.

Hooton, Earnest A. *Up from the Ape.* New York: Macmillan Co., 1946.

Human Relations Area Files, Inc. *Cambodia.* (Subcontractors' Monograph, HRAF 21-Chi 14.) New Haven, 1955.

——. *Thailand* (Subcontractors' Monograph, HRAF-42 Cornell-4) New Haven, 1956.

Ingram, James C. *Economic Change in Thailand since 1850.* Stanford: Stanford University Press, 1955.

Janlekha, Kamol. "A Preliminary Study of the Economic Conditions of Rice Farmers in Bang Chan, Thailand." Unpublished M.S. dissertation, Cornell University, 1951.

——. *A Study of the Economy of a Rice Growing Village in Central Thailand.* Ph.D. dissertation, Cornell University, 1955. Ann Arbor: University Microfilms.

Jay, Robert. "Local Government in Rural Central Java," *Far Eastern Quarterly,* 15:215–227, 1956.

Kattenburg, Paul M. *A Central Javanese Village in 1950.* (Cornell University, Southeast Asia Program, Data Paper no. 2.) Ithaca, N.Y., 1952.

Kaufman, Howard K. *Bangkhuad: A Community Study in Thailand.*

Ph.D. dissertation, University of Indiana, 1955. Ann Arbor: University Microfilms.

Klineberg, Otto. *Social Psychology.* New York: Henry Holt and Co., 1940.

Kroef, Justus M. van der. "Southeast Asia: Some Anthropological Aspects," *Human Organization,* 10 (no. 1):5–15, 1951.

Lewis, M. S. *Teach Yourself Malay.* New York: David McKay Co., for English Universities Press, n.d.

Linton, Ralph. *Acculturation in Seven American Indian Tribes.* New York: D. Appleton–Century, 1940.

——. *The Study of Man: An Introduction.* New York: D. Appleton–Century, 1936.

McHugh, J. N. *Hantu Hantu: Ghost Belief in Modern Malaya.* Singapore: Donald Moore, 1955.

Malaya, Federation of. *Annual Report,* for various years. London: Her Majesty's Stationery Office.

Mead, Margaret. *New Lives for Old: Cultural Transformation— Manus, 1928–1953.* New York: William Morrow and Co., 1956.

Moreland, W. H., ed. *Peter Floris: His Voyage to the East Indies in the Globe, 1611–1615.* (Hakluyt Society, 2d ser., vol. 74.) London: Hakluyt Society, 1934.

Morris, H. S. *Report on a Melanau Sago Producing Community in Sarawak.* (Colonial Research Studies no. 9.) London: Her Majesty's Stationery Office, 1953.

Norbeck, Edward. *Takashima, a Japanese Fishing Community.* Salt Lake City: University of Utah Press, 1954.

Parsons, Talcott. "Certain Primary Sources and Patterns of Aggression in the Social Structure of the Western World," *Essays in Sociological Theory Pure and Applied.* Glencoe: Free Press, 1949. Pages 251–274.

Pickthall, Mohammed Marmaduke, trans. *The Meaning of the Glorious Koran.* (Mentor Books.) New York: New American Library, 1953.

Purcell, Victor. *The Chinese in Southeast Asia.* Oxford: Oxford University Press, 1951.

Purchas, Samuel. *Hakluytus Posthumus; or, Purchas His Pilgrimes.* 22 vols. Glasgow: Herdruk, 1905–1907. Vols. I–V, X, XI.

Redfield, Robert. *The Little Community: Viewpoints for the Study of a Human Whole.* Chicago: University of Chicago Press, 1955.

——. *Peasant Society and Culture.* Chicago: University of Chicago Press, 1956.

——. "The Social Organization of Tradition," *Far Eastern Quarterly,* 15:13–21, 1956.

Roberts, Chester F., Jr., ed. *Area Handbook on Malaya.* Preliminary ed., Human Relations Area Files, Inc. Chicago, University of Chicago Press, 1955.

Royal Asiatic Society. *Journal, Straits Branch,* 1887–1923; *Malayan Branch,* 1923–1958. Singapore.

Sarasas, Phra. *My Country Thailand.* Bangkok: Chatra Press, 1954.

Sastri, K. A. Nilakanta. *South Indian Influences in the Far East.* Bombay: Hind Kitabs, Ltd., 1949.

Sharp, Lauriston, Hazel M. Hauck, Kamol Janlekha, and Robert B. Textor. *Siamese Rice Village: A Preliminary Study of Bang Chan, 1948–1949.* Bangkok: Cornell Research Center, 1953.

Skeat, Walter W. *Malay Magic.* London: Macmillan and Co., 1900.

Skinner, G. William. "Chinese in Thailand," *Journal of Asian Studies,* 16:237–250, 1957.

——. *Chinese Society in Thailand.* Ithaca, N.Y.: Cornell University Press, 1957.

——. *Report on the Chinese in Southeast Asia, December 1950.* (Cornell University, Southeast Asia Program, Data Paper no. 1.) Ithaca, N.Y., 1951.

——. *A Study of Chinese Community Leadership in Bangkok Together with a Historical Survey of Chinese Society in Thailand.* Ph.D. dissertation, Cornell University, 1954. Ann Arbor: University Microfilms.

——. *Thailand: Population Density* (map). Bangkok: Cornell Research Center, n.d. [1954].

Social Science Research Council Summer Seminar on Acculturation, 1953. "Acculturation: An Exploratory Formulation," *American Anthropologist,* 56:973–1002, 1954.

Spencer, Joseph E. *Asia East by South.* New York: John Wiley and Sons, 1954.

Spicer, Edward H. *Potam, a Yaqui Village in Sonora*. (American Anthropological Association, Memoir no. 77.) 1954.

Steiger, G. N. *A History of the Far East*. Boston: Ginn and Co., 1936.

Steward, Julian. *Area Research: Theory and Practice*. (Social Science Research Council, Bulletin no. 63.) New York, 1950.

Taj al-muluk, Kitab (in Malay). Penang: Kitab Islam, n.d.

Taylor, E. N. "Malay Family Law," *Journal of the Royal Asiatic Society, Malayan Branch*, 15 (pt. 1):1–78, 1937.

Terpstra, H. *De Factorij der Oostindische Compagnie te Patani*. (Verhandelingens van het Koninklijk Instituut voor de Taal-, Land- en Volkenkunde van Nederlandsch-indië, deel 1.) 's-Gravenhage: Martinus Nijhoff, 1938.

Thailand, Government of. *Census BE 2490* (1947).

——. *Census BE 2499* (1956).

——. *Thailand, Nature and Industry: Physical Features, Geology, Climate*. Bangkok: Ministry of Commerce, Department of Commercial Intelligence, 1951.

Thompson, Virginia. *Thailand: The New Siam*. New York: Macmillan Co., 1941.

——, and Richard Adloff. *Minority Problems in Southeast Asia*. Stanford: Stanford University Press, 1955.

Wagley, Charles. *Amazon Town: A Study of Man in the Tropics*. New York: Macmillan Co., 1953.

Wallace, Anthony. "Revitalization Movements," *American Anthropologist*, 58:264–281, 1956.

Whittingham, Barbara. "Patani Appeals to UNO," *Eastern World*, 2 (no. 4):4–5, 1948.

——. "The Singapore Conspiracy," *Eastern World*, 4 (no. 2):25–27, 1950.

Wilkinson, R. J. *A Malay-English Dictionary* (Romanized). Reprinted in Tokyo: Daito Syuppan Kabusiki Kaiaya, n.d. 2 vols in 1.

Winstedt, Richard O. *The Malay Magician, Being Shaman, Saiva, and Sufi*. London: Routledge and Kegan Paul, 1951.

——. *The Malays: A Cultural History*. London: Routledge and Kegan Paul, 1953.

Wood, W. A. R. *A History of Siam*. Bangkok: Siam Barnakich Press, 1933.

Zainal-'Abidin bin Ahmad, "Malay Festivals and Some Aspects of Malay Religious Life," *Journal of the Royal Asiatic Society, Malayan Branch*, 22 (pt. 1):94–106, 1949.

Zimmerman, Carle C. *Siam: Rural Economic Survey*, 1930–31. Bangkok: Bangkok Times Press, 1931.

Index